DANGER AND
OPPORTUNITY

AN AMBASSADOR'S
JOURNEY THROUGH THE MIDDLE EAST

Edward P. Djerejian
with
William Martin

Threshold Editions
New York London Toronto Sydney

Threshold Editions
A Division of Simon & Schuster, Inc.
1230 Avenue of the Americas
New York, NY 10020

Copyright © 2008 by Edward Djerejian

All rights reserved, including the right to reproduce this book
or portions thereof in any form whatsoever. For information
address Threshold Editions Subsidiary Rights Department,
1230 Avenue of the Americas, New York, NY 10020.

First Threshold Editions trade paperback edition August 2009

THRESHOLD EDITIONS and colophon are trademarks
of Simon & Schuster, Inc.

For information about special discounts for bulk purchases,
please contact Simon & Schuster Special Sales at
1-866-506-1949 or business@simonandschuster.com.

The Simon & Schuster Speakers Bureau can bring authors
to your live event. For more information or to book an event
contact the Simon & Schuster Speakers Bureau at
1-866-248-3049 or visit our website at www.smonspeakers.com.

Designed by Carla Jayne Little
Map designed by Paul Pugliese

Manufactured in the United States of America

10   9   8   7   6   5   4   3   2   1

Library of Congress Cataloging-in-Publication Data is available.

ISBN 978-1-4391-1412-4 (pbk)
ISBN 978-1-4165-8025-6 (ebook)

To the memory of my Father
Peter Minas Djerejian

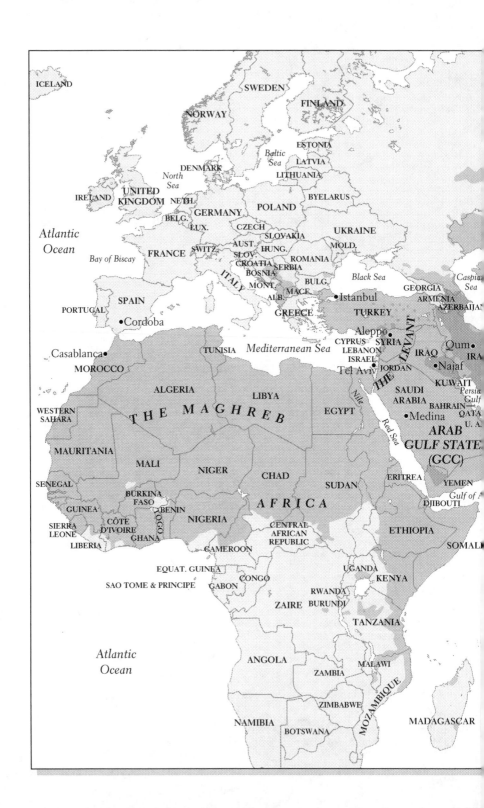

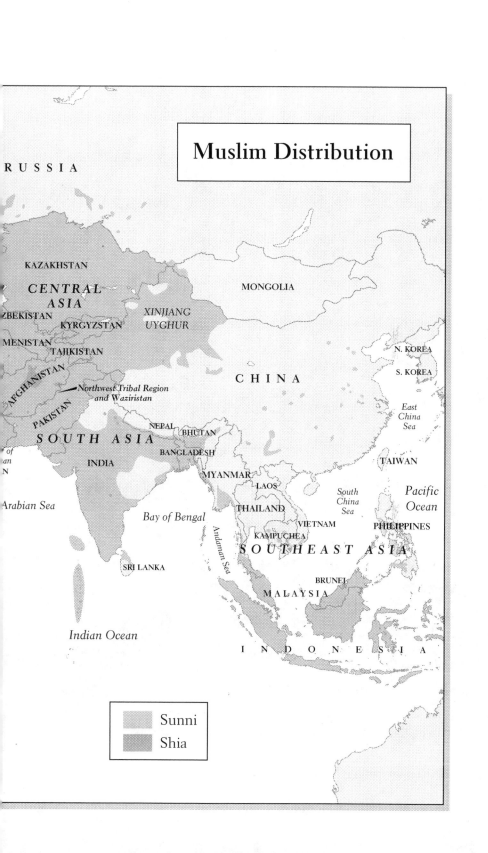

Muslim Distribution

RUSSIA

KAZAKHSTAN

*CENTRAL
ASIA*

ZBEKISTAN

KYRGYZSTAN

MENISTAN

TAJIKISTAN

AFGHANISTAN

Northwest Tribal Region
and Waziristan

PAKISTAN

SOUTH ASIA

NEPAL

BHUTAN

BANGLADESH

INDIA

*of
an
N*

Arabian Sea

MYANMAR

LAOS

THAILAND

Bay of Bengal

Andaman Sea

SRI LANKA

KAMPUCHEA

VIETNAM

SOUTHEAST ASIA

Indian Ocean

*XINJIANG
UYGHUR*

MONGOLIA

C H I N A

N. KOREA

S. KOREA

*East
China
Sea*

TAIWAN

*South
China
Sea*

*Pacific
Ocean*

PHILIPPINES

BRUNEI

MALAYSIA

I N D O N E S I A

Sunni

Shia

Contents

FOREWORD TO THE
PAPERBACK EDITION

W hen I started to write this book in early 2007 on my personal and professional insights concerning U.S. policy toward the broader Middle East, I had in mind as one of the key audiences the next president and administration of the United States. This is exemplified in the book by the opening "A Letter to the Incoming President." My book was published on the eve of the elections in September 2008, and at the time it was unknown who the new president would be.

I am truly gratified that many of the assessments and recommendations contained in this book are being considered and adopted by President Barack Obama and his administration, namely:

- Early engagement on the Arab-Israel negotiating front
- Conflict resolution instead of conflict management

- The focus on Afghanistan and Pakistan in the struggle against Islamic radicalism and terrorism
- The need to engage our adversaries such as Syria and Iran in a comprehensive and tough-minded dialogue
- President Obama's direct and effective engagement in public diplomacy and outreach to the Muslim world with a view of marginalizing the extremists and strengthening the moderates
- The urgent need to build our professional cadres of civilian, military, and intelligence personnel to be proficient in the languages and culture of the Muslim world
- Complementing the courageous role of our military personnel by promoting national service in civilian government operations and institutions in lieu of military service
- And pursuing our national-security interests by using the broad range of instruments, both soft and hard, available to us in our diplomacy.

As I conclude in the letter to the president, "We must learn from the successes and failures of the past and have the humility and courage to recognize where we have gone wrong in order not only to not perpetuate failed polices, but to restore the power and standing of the United States of America in the world as a unique experiment in democracy, liberty, and freedom. The stakes are simply too high to do otherwise."

PREFACE

This book is the story of an American diplomat who has served both Democratic and Republican presidents under eight administrations from John F. Kennedy to William Jefferson Clinton. A career's worth of experience and my active involvement at home and abroad and at different levels of government moved me to write this book. I offer you the narratives and anecdotes of my life as a diplomat, as well as the insights I have gained into the forces at play in the Arab and Muslim world, my perspective on the inadequacies of current policies, and some forward-looking strategies necessary to respond effectively to the critical historic challenge posed by the struggle of ideas in the Muslim world.

In the heady days at the end of the Cold War, marked by the fall of communism in the Soviet Union, some argued that the era of ideological struggles had ended and that we were approaching the "end of history." In the 1990s, the United States mistakenly began to dismantle the instruments of persuasion that helped bring down the Iron Curtain and gave moderate forces in the communist world tools to help them change their governments. Professional diplomats and policymakers knew this was a mistake, but their concerns about the Islamic world and their advice to political leaders were not listened to and therefore did not lead to informed and effective policies geared to dealing with the gathering storm.

More than three decades of government service gave me a deep personal and professional understanding of the culture and politics of the Middle East and the Muslim world and afforded extensive contact with the people in the region. Given the misinformation and propaganda that surround much of the public discourse on these issues, accurate treatment and understanding of this subject requires an intimate insider's view of policy formulation from the perspective of both regional leaders and the Washington political establishment.

I began my diplomatic career during the Kennedy administration, as special assistant to Undersecretary of State George W. Ball, and later as executive assistant to Undersecretary of State Joseph Sisco when Henry Kissinger was secretary of state. My first foreign assignment was in the political section of the U.S. Embassy in Beirut, Lebanon, where I served from 1965 to 1969. My meeting there with a charismatic Shiite religious leader, the Imam Musa al Sadr, who had a major impact on the political evolution of the Shiites in Lebanon, convinced me of the need for our diplomats to engage with important religious and Islamist leaders in the region.

A decade later, after various assignments to Morocco, Washington, D.C., France, and Germany, I served in Moscow for three years (1979–81) as political counselor in charge of the political section of the U.S. Embassy during the critical years of the Soviet invasion of Afghanistan. This experience gave me important insights into the Soviet Union's role in shaping the modern Middle East. From Moscow I was assigned to Jordan where I was the deputy chief of mission at the U.S. Embassy in Amman. In addition to my State Department service, I gained expertise in public diplomacy as White House special assistant to President

Ronald Reagan and deputy press secretary for foreign affairs between 1985 and 1986.

In 1988, I was appointed U.S. ambassador to Syria, where I served until 1991. My extensive dealings with the late Syrian president Hafez al-Asad underscored the importance of the United States' engaging and dealing effectively with our adversaries.

I served as the assistant secretary of state for Near Eastern Affairs (the top-ranking State Department official for the region) in both the Bush 41 and Clinton administrations. I was the only regional assistant secretary kept on in the first Clinton administration in order to preserve the momentum of the Middle East peace process and bring the Madrid Peace Conference framework forward from a Republican to a Democratic administration.

In that capacity, between 1991 and 1993, I argued privately and publicly that the fall of communism was not the end of radical political ideology, that extremism and terrorism, wearing either a secular or a religious cloak, would continue to threaten national security and world peace. In a major address I authored and delivered at Meridian House in Washington in 1992 (Chapter One), I articulated official U.S. policy toward the Arab and Muslim world and outlined the direction it should take in the future. The strategic thrust of that policy is to promote political and economic stability and progress in the Middle East and to undermine the attempts of Islamic radicals to exploit these issues to achieve their own political ends.

Efforts to foster peace in the Middle East are intrinsically difficult and the need to assure all parties that we are honest brokers between Arabs and Israelis in any negotiations or agreements is therefore critical. This was brought home to me pointedly in September 1993, when Yasir Arafat came to Washington to sign the Oslo Accords and Declaration of Principles between the Israelis and Palestinians. The White House decided that, as the assistant secretary of state for Near Eastern Affairs, I was the most appropriate senior United States official to greet Arafat at his arrival.

This was a delicate matter. Before this historic ceremony, the

Palestine Liberation Organization, led by Arafat, had been designated a terrorist organization. In fact, it had been my responsibility to sign official letters of waiver to allow PLO officials to come to the United States to attend meetings at the United Nations. When I received word that I was to go to Andrews Air Force Base to officially greet the chairman of the PLO, I knew that I had to avoid being embraced by Arafat in the traditional Arab manner, with kisses on both cheeks. Given the political sensitivities involved, that first photo had to be a professional handshake, not an embrace. So, the day before the ceremony, I called my trusted and able deputy assistant secretary of state, Daniel Kurtzer, to my office. I said, "Dan, I have to greet Yasir Arafat at Andrews Air Force Base tomorrow. So I want you to try to hug me." Dan looked at me in bewilderment, obviously thinking I had lost it. When I explained my predicament, he quickly understood and we rehearsed a virtual ballet maneuver whereby I would raise my left arm to catch Arafat by the shoulder to stop any hug and kissing on the cheeks, while my right hand was extended to grab his and execute a handshake.

The next day, as I later learned, when officials accompanying Arafat on his airplane saw me at the head of the reception line, they said, "It's Djerejian. We are finally legitimate!" Fortunately, the maneuver Dan and I had practiced worked beautifully. I said, "Mr. Chairman, on behalf of the United States government, I welcome you to the United States on this historic occasion, which we hope will lead to peace throughout the Middle East." Arafat replied, "I thank you and I, too, am hopeful that this will lead to peace."

I was pleased at the occasion, pleased at a favorable story in the *New York Times*, and especially pleased that no one seemed to have noticed my deft greeting of Chairman Arafat. The next day, the *Washington Post*'s "Reliable Source" column published a photo of the handshake, under the headline, "Avoiding a Hug for History." There are no secrets in Washington.

In 1994, I was appointed ambassador to Israel, where I served for a year. One of the most meaningful moments of my career came when Israeli prime minister Yitzhak Rabin raised his glass to toast my farewell at his Jerusalem residence at the end of my tenure in Israel. Rabin said, "The people of Israel thank you for all you have done to educate us about our Arab neighbors." After all those years of service in the Middle East, the words of the late prime minister and Nobel-winning peacemaker truly gave me a sense of having done my modest part in helping to bridge the Arab-Israeli divide.

In a career that involved numerous diplomatic assignments, some highlights for me were my active participation in the Geneva Summit between President Reagan and President Gorbachev in 1985, the 1991 Geneva Summit meeting between President George H. W. Bush and Syrian President Asad, the Madrid Peace Conference in 1991, and the White House ceremony for the signing of the Oslo Accords in 1993.

Chapters Three to Seven draw on these years of my direct involvement in the Middle East.

Since retiring from the Foreign Service in 1994, I have been the founding director of the James A. Baker III Institute for Public Policy at Rice University, where I continue to be closely involved in both foreign and domestic policy issues and in advising both Democratic and Republican administrations. One of the more important missions I have undertaken since leaving the Foreign Service was to chair—at the request of Secretary of State Colin Powell—a bipartisan congressionally mandated advisory group on United States public diplomacy in the Arab and Muslim world. In blunt terms, Congress wanted an answer to the question "Why do they hate us?" The report we published in October 2003, *Changing Minds, Winning Peace*, is now recognized as a template for public diplomacy strategy regarding how the United States can help win the struggle of ideas with extremists in the Arab and Muslim world.

As a result of this work, Secretary of State Condoleezza Rice asked me to prepare a strategic game plan for the State Department's strategy on public diplomacy toward the Muslim world. I advised the top policymakers on these issues and, while much more progress needs to be made on how we convey the "Voice of America" abroad, especially in the Muslim world, many of our recommendations for reforming the instruments of public diplomacy were adopted, thereby providing the next administration with a better base to build on. Chapter Ten, "Public Diplomacy—The Voice of America," deals with these issues.

I was also senior policy advisor to the congressionally mandated "Baker-Hamilton" Iraq Study Group (ISG), which produced in December 2006 a major bipartisan, independent, "fresh eyes" assessment of the then current and prospective situation on the ground in Iraq, its impact on the surrounding region, and consequences for U.S. interests. Chapter Eight, "Baghdad," deals extensively with this issue.

In the fourteen years since I left government service, I have watched as Democratic and Republican administrations have paid lip service to viable policies, but have consistently failed to follow through with a coherent strategy that reflects not only our values and interests but also the culture and realities of the broader Middle East region. It took the traumatic events of 9/11 for the United States government to move from talking the talk to walking the walk in its efforts to engage these problems seriously. We finally realized that internal instability in the countries of the Middle East, left unresolved, could affect the security of our own homeland, but our response has been mixed, with some policies clearly wrongheaded, while others offer more promising ways to assist and strengthen the forces of moderation in the region in addressing some of the region's structural problems.

As the world's preeminent power, America's leadership is essential in helping shape the international community's response to extremism and terrorism. We must act on the basis of both our values and our interests. We must lead with an understanding that it cannot be "our way or the highway." We must rebuild solid alliances and instruments of international cooperation to succeed. The political, economic, commercial, cultural, and military stakes are high, as evidenced by the continuing Arab-Israeli conflict, the wars in Afghanistan and Iraq, and the dangerous situation in Pakistan and in the region as a whole emanating from deficits in political participation, the economy, education, and human rights. That the Middle East and Southeast Asia are major oil- and gas-producing regions adds a critical geopolitical dimension to this struggle. I address this issue in Chapter Nine, "The Geopolitics of Energy."

I have avoided detailed excursions into the long and complex history of the region's conflicts and religion, since those subjects have been well covered by historians and other scholars and by regional and policy experts. I have chosen instead to concentrate on relatively recent events about which I have intimate knowledge.

I will share, for the first time publicly, my interaction with the secular and religious leaders of the region. I also share my experience of working with officials and political leaders in Washington—of both Democratic and Republican administrations. These personal narratives will, I hope, bring key political and policy issues to life and provide readers with a broad overview of the Arab, Israeli, and Muslim world—a region that will engage United States administrations for years to come.

To close this brief preface, let me recall two small, but memorable, incidents.

In the buildup to Desert Storm to reverse Saddam Hussein's invasion of Kuwait, I consulted with a number of ambassadors in Damascus, including the ambassador from the People's Republic of China. We discussed the current crisis, and he commented that the Chinese word for *crisis*, *weiji*, contains characters that connote both danger and opportunity. He said we should keep this in mind as we faced the imminence of war and the risks and opportunities that might follow in its aftermath, in Iraq itself and in the region as a whole. A few days later he sent me a framed calligraphy of that Chinese word for *crisis*. It hangs in my office to this day and inspired the title of this book, which I hope will help the reader appreciate both of these critical aspects of U.S. engagement with the Arab and Muslim world.

On the eve of our departure for Damascus in 1994, when my wife, Françoise, and I paid our farewell call on Secretary of State George Shultz in his office on the seventh floor of the State Department, he recounted having asked every new American ambassador to step over to a large globe of the world and point to his country. All of them would point to their country of assignment, except for Senator Mike Mansfield, who was going out as ambassador to Japan. Mansfield put his hand over the United States and said, "This, Mr. Secretary, is my country." Shultz smiled at us and said no more. It was an invaluable lesson that I never forgot.

My years of exposure to cultures quite different from that of the United States, as well as my association with people whose outlook and interests sometimes conflict with those of our country, have, I believe, broadened my outlook and enabled me to see things from a variety of viewpoints. As this book will make clear, I have been and continue to be critical of some major aspects of American foreign policy, particularly with regard to the Middle East, but I am convinced that we, as a great nation, can craft the policies that will serve both our values and our interests in a more intelligent and effective manner. I hope this book will serve to further that purpose.

A LETTER TO
THE INCOMING PRESIDENT

Dear Mr. President:

I have had the privilege of serving eight United States presidents, from John F. Kennedy to William Jefferson Clinton, in times of peace and war, in both the United States military and the Foreign Service. One of the positions I held at the White House and the National Security Council was special assistant to President Ronald Reagan and deputy press secretary for foreign affairs. There I caught firsthand a glimpse of the power and heavy responsibility of the presidency and, also, of the loneliness of the occupant of the Oval Office at times of critical decision-making.

During President Ronald Reagan's second term, tensions in South Asia over Afghanistan and between India and Pakistan over nuclear weapons were on the rise. We scheduled an interview for the president with a prominent journalist of the *Times* of India, to give the president an opportunity to underscore United

States policy goals in the region. There were some key points the president's advisors thought he should make, and I was assigned the task of ensuring that this was done. Whenever I entered the Oval Office, I would always have a sense of awe at the power and responsibility the incumbent held. This time was no different. As I proceeded to brief the president just before the interview, I stood dutifully in front of his desk, referred to the talking points we had prepared for him, and reiterated the key statements he should make.

I wasn't sure the president had focused on them, so I did something I should not have done. I walked behind the desk and, leaning over the president's shoulder, pointed to the key phrases. I thought we were alone in the Oval Office, but a White House photographer was in the room and caught the scene. Several weeks later I found on my desk a signed photo of this moment, with the following annotation, "To Ed Djerejian. Who says we don't take our work seriously? Very best wishes and regards, Ronald Reagan."

"The Gipper" had seen right through my excess of zeal and made his point in a most gracious manner. So it is with this sense of humility that I, as an American diplomat who has pursued our nation's interests in this part of the world for over thirty years and who has served on both sides of the Arab-Israeli divide as United States ambassador to Syria and Israel, would like to share with you, the next president of the United States, some thoughts on the key challenges in the broader Middle East and the Muslim world at this time of danger and opportunity.

In a speech at Meridian House in Washington, D.C., in 1992, when I was assistant secretary of state for Near Eastern Affairs, I said, "The United States government does not view Islam as the next 'ism' confronting the West or threatening world peace. . . . Americans recognize Islam as one of the world's great faiths. . . . Our quarrel is with extremism, and the violence, denial, coercion, and terror which too often accompany it." It was clear to me then, some nine years before 9/11, that with the end of the Cold War and the defeat of communism the next "ism" the United States and the international community would confront would be extremism and terrorism. The critical struggle of ideas between the forces of extremism and moderation in the Muslim world is a generational challenge, one the United States can influence but not decide. That task is in the hands of the Muslim people themselves.

It is important to avoid politically rhetorical flourishes that cannot produce the anticipated results. As with the "War on Drugs" and the "War on Poverty," the misnamed "War on Terror" will not end with a dramatic raising of the flag in a clear moment of victory. These are worthy causes, but they are long-term struggles that need to be addressed boldly and intelligently; sloganeering should not distort good public policy. Terrorism is a lethal subset of the larger struggle of ideas between the forces of extremism and moderation, and we must combat it with all the means available to us. The option of military action is always available to you and the Congress when the national security of the United States is threatened, but guns alone cannot achieve success in the overall campaign against terrorism. That task requires a more broad-based and comprehensive strategy.

United States policy should therefore be aimed at what we can do to strengthen the moderates and marginalize the extremists and radicals, be they secular or religious. This will require all the tools of bilateral and multilateral diplomacy available to you for conflict resolution, public diplomacy, focused intelligence assessments, military assistance and training, special operations, helping countries build representative institutions, and facilitating political, economic, and social reforms and development. Overall, the wiser course will be to avoid imposing solutions from the outside. Instead, you should adopt effective policies and actions that promote solutions that are mainly the outcome of the efforts of the people and countries of the region themselves. Our helping to alleviate the causes of frustration, humiliation, and deep-rooted grievances in the region, which extremists and terrorists exploit for their own political ends, can do much to marginalize the radicals and terrorists and strengthen the moderates.

I was brought up in the school of diplomacy that advocates negotiating differences and, when possible, seeking peace with one's enemies and adversaries. That is the ultimate task of diplomacy, bolstered by our military credibility. Unilaterally isolating adversaries and breaking off communications deprives us of essential tools to pursue our national security interests. Talking with a clear purpose in mind is neither a concession nor a sign of weakness, especially for a global power such as the United States. At the same time, our diplomacy should never be carried out in a way that indicates a lack of United States resolve. While Ronald Reagan stigmatized the Soviet Union as the "Evil Empire," his administration negotiated in a determined manner with the communist regime and achieved positive results.

I had the opportunity in 1969, early in my career, to have a conversation with Ambassador Raymond Hare, a veteran Foreign Service officer. In diplomacy, he told me, it is essential to master your opponent's argument and position as completely as possible. You should then explain your opponent's position to him as completely as possible in terms better than he himself could express. Ipso facto, you have disarmed him to an important extent. Then, you explain, as comprehensively as possible, what areas of agreement may exist. The seed of compromise is planted. This method is much better than a mere statement of position, under instructions that may serve only to antagonize your interlocutors. Never put your opponent in a corner. Never force him to strike back—unless, of course, that is your purpose. Always allow him a way out, Hare concluded, preferably in the direction of your point of view and position. This is not a bad formula for any United States administration to follow in the conduct of its diplomacy.

The absence of dialogue and engagement with adversarial regimes and groups serves only to polarize situations and promote miscalculations, even conflict, especially in the broader Middle East. You should therefore have your secretary of state carefully prepare to engage Iran and Syria in a major strategic dialogue on all the issues between us, in a serious effort to determine what middle ground there may be to build on. Through such comprehensive engagement, with all the key issues on the table, the prospects for getting these countries to change their behavior and accommodate United States interests on such crucial issues as nuclear nonproliferation and Arab-Israeli peace could be greatly enhanced.

As I will contend in this book, the road to Arab-Israeli peace goes through Jerusalem, not through Baghdad or Tehran. Direct face-to-face negotiations between Israel and its immediate Arab neighbors—the Palestinians, Syria, and Lebanon—are the key to peacemaking. While the other countries in the region have an important role to play in bolstering peace efforts, the focus must be on the parties to the negotiations themselves. The core political issue in the Middle East remains the Arab-Israeli conflict, especially the Palestinian issue, which has strong resonance throughout the Muslim world. For too long this conflict has been exploited as a pretext for regimes in the region not to carry out major political and economic reforms and to secure their positions of power. Any United States administration that doesn't grasp these realities and the urgency of resolving this conflict will face recurrent crises that it will be forced to address on a case-by-case basis, often distracting the government from other priorities at times not of its choosing.

The most effective approach is to steer United States policy from conflict management to conflict resolution. Putting out intermittent fires between Israel, Lebanon, Syria, and the Palestinians is a short-term and insufficient strategy. Instead, the United States must take the lead within the international community and act in its traditional but tarnished role as an "honest broker" between the Israelis and the Arabs, seeking to bring the parties to the negotiating table under the principled framework of the Madrid Peace Conference and the "land for peace" formula embodied in United Nations Security Council Resolutions 242 and 338.

Mr. President, to succeed in this major effort, you must take the lead and invest the power of the presidency in peacemaking through whatever modalities you choose. When United States presidents have displayed the political will and courage and have engaged their administrations in serious peacemaking, there has been progress, as evidenced, for example, by President Nixon in the disengagement agreements in 1974 after the Yom Kippur War, by President Jimmy Carter and the Camp David Accords of 1978 and the Egyptian-Israeli peace treaty of 1979, and by President George H. W. Bush and the Madrid Peace Conference of 1991. President Clinton, while not achieving a peace settlement, did succeed in narrowing the issues between the Israelis and Palestinians at Camp David and Taba in 2000–2001. President George W. Bush's call for a two-state solution in 2002, with a state of Palestine living in peace and security next to the state of Israel, was an important policy statement that should be translated into deeds in the Israeli-Palestinian negotiations initiated at Annapolis in 2007.

While progress toward Arab-Israeli peace, or even the attainment of that peace, will not end extremism and terrorism, it will do much to eliminate a major cause that the extremists exploit for their own ends and put the onus on radical groups such as Hamas and Hezbollah to justify continued armed resistance and terrorism. It would also do much to restore America's standing and credibility in the Arab and Muslim world.

Too often, from one administration to another, United States foreign policy is diverted away from issues and regions of the world where we should be making a strong and sustained effort to get the job done. Afghanistan and Pakistan, the regional caldron, are prime examples of this unfortunate and costly tendency and the principle of unintended consequences. We succeeded only too well in supporting the mujahideen in Afghanistan after the Soviet invasion of that country in 1979, helping defeat the Soviets in their Afghan adventure and contributing to the demise of the Soviet Union a decade later. We enlisted the support of Pakistan as a key ally in that effort and worked closely with the Pakistani government and military as the conduit of our political and military support to the mujahideen, including the provision of Stinger missiles that caused havoc with Soviet airborne operations.

But once the tide had turned in Afghanistan, we directed our attention elsewhere and virtually outsourced our policy to our Pakistani and Saudi allies, who, in turn, facilitated the rise of the Islamist radicals and the creation of Al Qaeda, led by Osama Bin Laden. The Pakistani military's Inter-Services Intelligence agency (ISI), which has had close ties to the Taliban and also to Islamist groups since the 1970s, and ultraconservative Saudi Wahhabis played their role in these developments. This situation was further exacerbated by the takeover of the Afghan government by the Taliban, who provided safe haven to Al Qaeda, which authored the deadly attacks on our homeland on 9/11. We successfully overthrew the Taliban regime by force after 9/11, but our military action in Iraq in 2003 diverted us from paying close attention to Afghanistan and Pakistan, resulting in the Taliban's resurgence in 2006 and 2007 as a political and paramilitary force to contend with once again, while Osama Bin Laden and his lieutenant Ayman al-Zawahiri still remain at large, most likely somewhere in Waziristan.

One of the most important decisions you could take is to make South Asia a major foreign policy priority, with a sustained focus on Pakistan and Afghanistan. The stakes for regional peace and stability are dangerously high. Pakistan and India are nuclear weapons states with a serious unresolved territorial issue, Kashmir, between them. Since their partition in 1947, Pakistan and India have gone to war three times. A major effort must be made to resolve the Kashmir issue, lest an escalation of this conflict result in a nuclear confrontation on the subcontinent. The struggle for democracy in Pakistan is fragile, as evidenced by the threat of Islamic militancy within the country, the renewed activism of Al Qaeda from the border regions of Afghanistan and Pakistan, the assassination of former prime minister Benazir Bhutto by a suicide bomber in December 2007, and the confrontation between Pakistan's president Pervez Musharraf and the Pakistani lawyers' political movement in support of the rule of law and the judiciary.

The United States should actively encourage Pakistan's moderate political parties and forces, the government, and the professional military leadership (the guardian and guarantor of Pakistan's nuclear weapons) to all work toward forming a democratic coalition that could govern Pakistan and restore political stability made credible by the electoral process. Our key policy objective should be the legitimate transfer of power to elected civilian leaders in Pakistan.

Despite its being the top priority for NATO, Afghanistan continues to struggle against the narcotics warlords, the Taliban, Al Qaeda, and Islamic militants who have come back to the fore and are focusing increasingly on terrorist acts, suicide bombings, improvised explosive devices, and the targeting of schools and teachers. Their goal is to sabotage the state and impose their will on the Afghan people. It is a tense struggle between the advance of state institutions and services in the country under the democratically elected government and the armed resistance of the Afghan extremists. Because the institutions of the state are in a formative phase and are not robust, the extremists are more dangerous than their actual numbers would suggest.

Afghanistan is in a major transitional stage that will require sustained and comprehensive support and commitment from the international community. Security, stabilization, and developmental operations are the key to success or failure. A United States general said, "We aren't losing, but we aren't winning either." He underscored the need for building a national Afghan army and police force to establish the conditions of security that can enable economic and infrastructure development such as basic services and roads—a top priority for Afghans. He is quoted as saying, "Where roads end, the Taliban begins."

Mr. President, elections alone do not make democracies. Indeed, they are often exploited to perpetuate dictatorships. Let me share with you an uneasy anecdote that underscores the point. During a meeting with the late Syrian president Hafez al-Asad, I referred to his recent re-election by an astounding vote of 99.44 percent. I then asked him, with tongue in cheek, if he knew who the .56 percent were who did not vote for him. He smiled and quipped, "Ambassador, I have all their names."

Democracy promotion that focuses on elections without prior institution building and the development of the rule of law, the adoption of the principles of pluralism, and the alternation of power will, more often than not, lead to unwelcome outcomes. Democratization will not necessarily progress in a straight line. A wiser course may well be for the United States to support and encourage erecting the building blocks of democracy from within these societies. It is best to "make haste slowly" toward this long-term goal. The challenge of fostering democratic forms of governance in the Muslim world is great. United States engagement with moderate forces in these societies, including NGOs, political parties, professional associations, and governments, will require much more sophistication and sustained effort than we have demonstrated to date.

We must be clear that there is no room for dialogue with the Islamic radicals such as those of Al Qaeda, whose agenda is to overthrow the governments in the region, destroy Israel, and weaken the moderates and the quest for modernity in the Muslim countries, as well as to weaken "far enemies" such as the United States. We must, however, differentiate between the Islamic radicals and Islamist groups that do not engage in terrorism. Accordingly, you should authorize the secretary of state to have our diplomats contact and engage certain Islamist groups and parties in the Muslim countries, especially those that do not resort to violence, with a view toward determining firsthand what they really represent, what their goals are, what common ground there may be between us, and whether we can engage them constructively in the attainment of our foreign policy goals and national security interests.

The decision to wage war and commit the nation's blood and treasure is your heaviest responsibility and burden. Except in a case of imminent attack on our homeland and people, that must truly be your last option as commander-in-chief, after all other options have been thoroughly considered and exhausted. Although Colin Powell has told me that no "doctrine" was ever published in his name, despite the many public references to the "Powell Doctrine," the essential elements of his approach bear your careful consideration if you have to lead the country into military conflict. According to Powell's thinking, as you consider your options in times of crisis, including the possibility of the use of military force, your most important task is to have a clear understanding of the political objective you wish to achieve. In short, "What is the mission?" "What are you getting the military ready for?" "What force structure and levels are needed to accomplish the mission?" The failure to put enough "boots on the ground" in Iraq to restore law and order under an occupation caused many of the tragic difficulties we have faced in Iraq since the successful initial military operations. Our forces have had to deal concomitantly with conventional ground combat, counterterrorism, and counterinsurgency missions. On top of those challenges, our military has been largely involved in nation-building operations to help provide the population with basic services, including, as one U.S. general told the Iraq Study Group in Baghdad, "picking up the trash."

It is important not to confuse military objectives with political objectives. Establishing democracy in Iraq is not a military objective, but taking charge of the country and restoring law and order are essential first steps toward political solutions. The distinction between military action and occupation is critical and calls for distinctively different policies and force levels of both military and civilian personnel. Once the mission is decided, "overmatch" your enemy with decisive force and have that decisive force applied to a clear military objective. Another key question you must ask is "How will this war end?" That is more important than defining an "exit strategy." And last, it is inherent in this approach that if military action is going to last for any appreciable amount of time, you must assure domestic political support and, to the maximum extent possible, international support for the war effort. This approach worked in Panama in 1989 and in Desert Storm in 1991. It was not adopted in Iraq in 2003. Indeed, one of your most important priorities may well be to have a major review of United States military policy and doctrine to assure that we are prepared for current and future dangers to our national security.

In an NPR interview in 2007, a United States Army general in Iraq observed that we are "an Army at war, not a nation at war." He expressed the painful sentiment that "folks [at home] can do more to support the effort." During a September 2006 visit to Baghdad by the members of the Iraq Study Group, one of the most effective generals we met was Lt. Gen. Peter Chiarelli. In an article in the journal *Military Review*, he wrote, "The U.S. as a Nation—and indeed most of the U.S. Government—has not gone to war since 9/11. Instead, the departments of Defense and State (as much as their modern capabilities allow) and the Central Intelligence Agency are at war while the American people and most of the other institutions of national power have largely gone about their normal business."

This is an important issue that strikes at the heart of American society and the concept of public service and sacrifice. Senior military officers have told me that they prefer the all-volunteer armed forces because of the professionalism they can achieve within the ranks, without having to train new recruits drafted every two to three years. But we should give consideration to registering Americans for the possibility of a draft if we are faced with a major war that would require an all-out national effort. We should also consider creating a system of national service in civilian government operations and institutions, in lieu of military service. When we started the all-volunteer armed forces in 1970 during the Nixon administration, the U.S. military began to lose a vital link to the country and American society. The historic concept of "the citizen soldier" was weakened. When we go to war we should be "a nation at war," with the citizenry engaged in various ways and, to the extent possible, from the broadest levels of society, to defend our national security interests at home and abroad.

One of the major stakes in the struggle of ideas in the Muslim world is the geopolitical reality of the vast oil and gas reserves located in the broader Middle East. Destabilization in this region can lead to major global economic disruptions, especially at a time of limited excess oil capacity and growing energy demand, not only from the United States itself but also from the emerging global powers of China and India. Creating an energy policy for the United States that responds to the urgency of the situation and looks ahead toward balancing supply and demand and the need for conservation and alternative sources of energy is a compelling public policy challenge that you should address as a top priority.

Mr. President, you are the "Voice of America." Whether addressing national or international issues, yours is the most important single voice influencing attitudes toward the United States abroad. Our country's public diplomacy must have your stamp of approval, enthusiastic support, and long-term commitment. You are the ultimate director of our public diplomacy. Our public diplomacy has lacked strategic direction since the dismantling of the instruments of persuasion we used so effectively during the Cold War. The task now is to reinvent this role in an effective manner within the government. The enhanced definition of public diplomacy should be "to first listen and understand, and then inform, engage, and influence foreign audiences." This is the modus operandi of public diplomacy. Getting this done effectively, with clarity of purpose and vision, should be a key objective of any United States administration. Important organizational changes in public diplomacy structure, resources, programs, and operations have been made in recent years, and your administration can build on them. We often hear the criticism that "it's the policy, stupid; not public diplomacy." But the reality is that if policy and values constitute, say, 80 percent of how people perceive us for better or worse, then there is an essential 20 percent that constitutes the role of public diplomacy and how effectively we communicate with and inform foreign audiences about our policy goals, values, and who we are as a nation and people. Your public diplomacy team has to be an integral part of the foreign policy formulation process and a key instrument in the actual conduct of the policy.

There is an urgent need to build our professional cadres of civilian, military, and intelligence personnel to be proficient in the languages and the cultures of the Muslim world.

We need to emphasize sustained language training and cultural education programs, so that Foreign Service officers in our State Department will have the requisite fluency in, for example, Arabic, so that they can go on an Arabic satellite TV station such as Al Jazeera and express and debate United States policy effectively.

I outline in these pages a strategic game plan for the direction of America's public diplomacy. Given the criticality of words and images in any struggle of ideas, such as that being waged by the Islamic radicals and extremists, the manner in which the United

States conveys our values, interests, and policies in this part of the world is of utmost importance. America's greatness is embodied in the example it has historically set for our own people and the world. Extensive surveys show that majorities in the Muslim world admire and identify with such American values as liberty, freedom of speech and the press, freedom of association, the rule of law, social justice, human rights, women's rights, minority rights, pluralism, equality of opportunity, higher education, science and technology, and market-based economies and the economic prosperity they foster. To the extent that the United States can live up to these ideals we will have the moral power to influence—not decide—world events according to our core principles.

Too often, we are not present to explain the context and content of our national values and policies. As the congressionally mandated advisory group I chaired in 2003 on public diplomacy was told in Morocco, "If you do not define yourself in this part of the world, the extremists will define you." The United States simply cannot afford such an outcome.

The way forward in meeting the strategic challenge of the struggle of ideas in the Arab and Muslim world is fraught with both danger and opportunity. The human-development deficits in the region and the continuing specter of violence, bloodshed, terrorism, and unresolved conflicts that plague this region have consequences that extend beyond its borders and to our own homeland. This complex situation inevitably requires not only crisis management but, more important and in the long term, resolution of regional conflicts and real progress on the major issues and root causes of political, economic, and social instability that extremists and Islamic radicals exploit for their own political and ideological ends. Given the preeminent position of the United States in today's world, our country can do much, in concert with the international community and the countries of the region, to influence, but not decide or try to transform by ourselves, the future progress of the Arab and Muslim world toward a more peaceful, just, and prosperous future.

The struggle to determine the balance between tradition and the forces of modernity and change in the Muslim world will have to come from within the framework of their own culture and societies. But by formulating and pursuing enlightened policies along the lines discussed in this book, you have a unique and historic opportunity to influence the course of events toward positive ends. This will take strong political will and determination to get the job done. We must learn from the successes and failures of the past and have the humility and courage to recognize where we have gone wrong in order not only to not perpetuate failed polices, but to restore the power and standing of the United States of America in the world as a unique experiment in democracy, liberty, and freedom. The stakes are simply too high to do otherwise.

Respectfully,
Edward P. Djerejian

ONE

THE MERIDIAN HOUSE SPEECH

W hat went wrong with America's foreign policy in the Arab and Muslim world? This question leads to many others:

- Why is America's standing at such a low point in public opinion polls throughout the region?
- Why are America's policies in Muslim countries perceived to be hypocritical when compared with American values?
- Why is the "War on Terror" a misnomer?
- How can the seeming dilemma of "democracy promotion" and such unintended consequences as Hamas's coming to power in democratic elections be resolved?
- Why is the neoconservative contention that democracy can be imposed in the broader Middle East seriously flawed?
- What can be done to help strengthen the advance of democracy by tying it to long-term processes of institution building and the rule of law?

- How can we balance American values and national security issues in ways that truly reflect our strategic needs and concerns?
- What lessons learned in Iraq can we apply to our relations with regimes in Iran, Syria, and elsewhere?
- Why is it necessary for the United States to talk to and negotiate with its adversaries?
- Why is it essential for the United States president to actively take a sustained international lead in moving the Arabs and Israelis toward a negotiated peace?
- Why must the United States, as part of its strategic approach in the region, focus on South Asia, especially Pakistan and Afghanistan?

Americans must understand that all these issues are part of one of the most important challenges of our time: the struggle of ideas between the forces of extremism and moderation in the Arab and Muslim world. We must also understand that the outcome of this struggle will affect our national interests, that this is a generational struggle that goes well beyond terrorism, that there can be no early and definitive "victory" over terrorism, and that our more realistic goal will have to be to marginalize Islamic radicals within the context of a larger strategy.

We are engaged in a major struggle that most Americans never expected.

For more than four decades after the end of World War II, international relations focused overwhelmingly on the dichotomy between the Soviet Empire of dictatorial regimes and centrally planned economies and the Free World of democratic governments and market economies. The Cold War reverberated around the globe, affecting virtually everyone, everywhere. America's foreign policy, like that of many other free nations, was either driven by or derived from collective efforts to contain Soviet aggression and expansion. Then, "not with a bang but a whimper," in no small part because of the policies of the Reagan and the first Bush administrations, the Soviet Union broke apart and we had to adjust to a new international landscape.

Scholars, policymakers, journalists, and pundits began to lay out the lines along which they thought the future would unfold. Johns Hopkins political scientist Francis Fukuyama proclaimed an "end of history," in which liberal democracy would soon sweep away competing political systems around the globe. Less optimistically, Harvard political scientist Samuel Huntington foresaw a "clash of civilizations" in which the primary source of conflict would not be ideological or economic, but cultural. "Nation states," he predicted, "will remain the most powerful actors in world affairs, but the principal conflicts of global politics will occur between nations and groups of different civilizations. The clash of civilizations will dominate global politics. The fault lines between civilizations will be the battle lines of the future."

As assistant secretary of state for Near Eastern Affairs during the administrations of George H. W. Bush and William Jefferson Clinton, I helped craft United States policy toward the Middle East and the Muslim world at the time of this crucial transformation of the geopolitical landscape.

It was a moment for which my whole professional career had prepared me.

Having served as an American diplomat in the Middle East and the Soviet Union, I sensed that the reality we would face would be more complex than some of the cogently argued viewpoints that were beginning to emerge suggested. I was also increasingly concerned that, in search of a new enemy, we would begin to define Islam as the next "ism" the United States would have to confront. Given my responsibilities for Near Eastern Affairs in the State Department, I thought it important for the U.S. government to begin to enunciate its assessment of the forces at play in the Middle East and its approach toward Muslim countries in general.

The best vehicle for doing this, I thought, would be an official speech that could begin to frame the issues we as a nation had to face in this important region of the world and to test the reaction to these ideas both at home and abroad. Accordingly, I held a series of meetings with scholars, Middle East experts, U.S government intelligence analysts, and policy-level officials. Then, after preparing my basic thesis and policy recommendations, I sat down with two bright young Foreign Service officers on my staff to craft the outline of what became known in policy circles as the "Meridian House Speech."

I didn't even look at the first three drafts they prepared. Using a ploy I had learned from former secretary of state Henry Kissinger when I worked for him years earlier, I simply returned them with the note, "It's not good enough." When we finally agreed on a final version, I went to see Secretary of State James A. Baker, III. He was sitting in his private office on the seventh floor of the State Department. We had a close professional relationship that had been forged during the years when I was the United States ambassador to Syria and he was conducting the shuttle diplomacy between Damascus and Jerusalem that led to the Madrid Peace Conference in 1991. I briefed him on the substance of the speech I was to give and asked for his approval. He looked at me intently, asked some probing questions, and said, "Okay, Ed, but be careful." I left Baker's office with an uneasy feeling that, given the contentious issues dealt with in the speech, my career was on the line.

The major themes of the speech I delivered at Meridian House in Washington on June 4, 1992, were adopted rhetorically by the administrations of Presidents George H. W. Bush, William Jefferson Clinton, and George W. Bush and served as the basis for certain policy initiatives. This policy framework remains valid today, especially in light of the attacks against the United States on September 11, 2001, and the continuing challenge of terrorism, war, conflict, and instability in the broader Middle East region. The Meridian House Speech can be summarized as follows:

- The United States government does *not* view Islam as the next "ism" confronting the West or threatening world peace. That rejected perception is a simplistic response to a complex reality. Further, it plays into the hands of the extremists.

- The next "isms" we are likely to confront are terrorism and extremism, which may wear either a secular or a religious cloak.

- The Cold War is not being replaced with a new competition between Islam and the West. The Crusades have been over for a long time. Americans recognize Islam as one of the world's great faiths, practiced on every continent and counting among its adherents millions of U.S. citizens. As Westerners, we acknowledge Islam as a historic civilizing force, one of many that have influenced and enriched our culture.

- Throughout the Middle East and North Africa, we see groups or movements seeking to reform their societies in keeping with Islamic ideals. These ideals are expressed in diverse ways. Of approximately 1.4 billion Muslims in the world, 80 percent live outside the Arab world and differ from each other racially, ethnically, linguistically, and culturally. Large Muslim populations are found in South and Southeast Asia, China, and Africa. The Muslim world is also divided into two major sects—Sunni, (some 85 percent) and Shia (about 15 percent)—each of which has further subsects.

- We detect no monolithic bloc or international effort behind Islamic groups and movements, but we are seriously concerned over Iran's exploitation of extremist groups throughout the region. Coordination between such regimes and extremist groups that resort to terrorism demands our vigilance. In the last analysis, however, it is social injustice—the lack of economic, social, educational, and political opportunity and the failure to resolve regional conflicts, especially between Israel and its Arab neighbors— that helps provide extremists with a constituency to exploit for their own political ends.

• Those governments that seek to broaden political participation in the region will find us supportive, but we are wary of those who would use the democratic process to come to power, only to destroy that very process in order to retain power and political dominance. We [the United States] believe in the principle of one person, one vote. We do not support "one person, one vote, one time." (This phrase was widely translated as "one man, one vote, one time." I deliberately used the word "person" to connote the right of women to vote. In any case, the statement stirred up much controversy and was interpreted as a direct reference to the scheduled elections in Algeria in 1992, which the Algerian military canceled to thwart an electoral victory by the Islamic Salvation Front [FIS]. To be sure, we were seriously concerned at the prospect of this Islamist radical party's attaining power in that important country, with possible destabilizing effects on Morocco and Tunisia. But we were making a larger point that reflected our concern that certain Islamist parties and groups in the region would use elections as a vehicle to come to power only to undermine the democratic electoral process in order to stay in power and would refuse to relinquish power if future election results went against them. This issue remains an important consideration in efforts to promote democracy in the broader Middle East. Tragically, after the Algerian military's actions in 1992, the country descended into a civil war that left more than one hundred thousand people dead. A government amnesty in 1999 alleviated the worst tensions, but Islamic radicals are still active and engage in acts of terrorism.)

- We differ with those who, whatever their religion, practice terrorism, resort to violence, reject the peaceful resolution of conflicts, oppress minorities, preach intolerance, disdain political pluralism, or violate internationally accepted standards regarding human rights. Simply stated, religion does not determine, positively or negatively, the nature of our relations with other countries. Our quarrel is with extremism per se, and the violence, denial, intolerance, intimidation, coercion, and terror that accompany it.

- Within the framework of these considerations, basic United States foreign policy objectives remain consistent and clear. We seek a just, lasting, and comprehensive peace between Israel and all her neighbors, including the Palestinians. We seek viable security arrangements that will assure stability and unimpeded commercial access to the vast oil reserves of the Arabian Peninsula and Persian Gulf. And we seek to promote political and economic reforms in the broader Middle East, with a keen appreciation of the culture and traditions of the region's societies and countries.

The strategic thrust of the policy I outlined in the Meridian House Speech was, and remains, the promotion of political and economic stability and progress in the Middle East and the undermining of attempts by Islamic radicals to exploit these issues to achieve their own political ends, particularly their efforts to overthrow existing regimes in the Middle East—what they call the "near enemy"—and to establish radical Islamic states, as the Ayatollah Khomeini had done in Iran in 1979 and as Osama Bin Laden continues to try to accomplish throughout the broader region.

On a clear, sunny morning in September 2001, when Bin Laden's Al Qaeda terrorists struck the World Trade Center and the Pentagon, prime symbols of the "far enemy," America woke up to a reality that Middle Eastern experts have understood for years. The struggle of ideas in the Muslim world between those seeking to modernize their societies within an Islamic framework and those Islamic radicals who seek to impose a totalitarian system rooted in extremist religious beliefs will shape the future of the Muslim world and beyond. Since people in the region will determine the outcome of this struggle, it is essential that mainstream moderate Muslims prevail. To craft informed and effective policies toward the Muslim world that the American public will support requires that United States policymakers come to understand Islam in all its complexity, with special attention to the dynamics between tradition and modernity in Islamic culture.

AN ARC OF CRISIS

The need for a coherent framework for policy regarding the Muslim world has become compelling as foreign policy challenges emerge along an "Arc of Crisis" that extends from the Horn of Africa in the west to the Indian subcontinent in the east and into the Balkans, the Caucasus, North Africa, the Middle East, and Central and South Asia. Violent conflicts have erupted in Bosnia, Kosovo, Chechnya, Algeria, Gaza and the West Bank, Lebanon, Afghanistan, Iraq, and Kashmir. Each has its distinctive historical, ethnic, and political contexts, but the rallying cry "Allahu Akbar" ("God is Great") reminds us that a bright thread runs through each strand of a complex web: Muslims asserting their identity and political goals against both non-Muslims and fellow Muslims.

In the first category we have seen Muslims against Serbs in Bosnia and Kosovo, Chechens against Russians in Chechnya,

Muslim radical groups against Israelis, and Muslims against Hindus in Kashmir and India. In the second category we have seen Muslim groups oppose regimes in the Islamic world, as in Pakistan, Syria, Iraq, Algeria, Morocco, Jordan, Saudi Arabia, and Egypt. And in a third category, outside the Arc of Crisis, Muslim extremists engage in acts of terrorism that target non-Muslims:

- the bombing of the Israeli Embassy in Argentina in 1992,
- the World Trade Center bombing in 1993,
- the Air France hijacking in 1994,
- the Paris subway explosion in 1996,
- the United States Embassy bombings in Tanzania and Kenya in 1998,
- the attack on the USS *Cole* in 2000,
- the September 11, 2001, attacks on the United States homeland,
- the car bomb explosion in Bali in 2002,
- the hotel bombing in Jakarta in 2003,
- the Madrid train bombings in 2004,
- the Beslan school hostage crisis in 2004,
- attacks on the London public transport system in 2005.

Is this the "clash of civilizations" that Samuel Huntington foresees, or the manifestation of particular political, ethnic, religious, and cultural conflicts that have intensified in the post–Cold War era? I believe it is most likely the latter, but whatever the case, it is evident that policymakers must now address religious, ethnic, and cultural factors in a way that was not obviously necessary during the bipolar confrontation between the United States and the Soviet Union. In fact, the realpolitik approach to foreign policy that prevailed during the Cold War was based largely on balance-of-power considerations and is insufficient to deal effectively and comprehensively with today's realities.

The international community now finds itself without a coherent policy framework as it reacts to fires erupting along the Arc of Crisis and in individual countries. Given this new context, what should United States policy be toward Islam? How can the United States, in its leadership role, develop a considered, comprehensive policy toward that Arc of Crisis and toward the role of Islam across that arc?

As a starting point, the United States must recognize that the disturbing proliferation of local and regional conflicts in the arc threatens major, even vital U.S. interests. Of great importance to the United States and other industrialized democracies is the fact that approximately three-quarters of the world's oil and gas reserves, as well as critical points of pipeline delivery, lie within the arc. Conflicts in this region can have significant impact on energy supply, security, and pricing. The 1991 Gulf War was fought to reverse Saddam Hussein's aggression in Kuwait—but also to protect precisely such interests. As we look ahead in the twenty-first century, energy needs will increase, especially as China and India proceed with their economic development. A reliable and abundant energy supply is imperative.

Key areas within the Arc of Crisis pose particular dangers:

- Tensions between Muslim Albanians and Orthodox Christian Serbs can still lead to instability in the Balkans, with serious implications for European security, NATO, and Russia.
- The resurgence of conflict in Chechnya could weaken Russia's stability and divert Moscow further from moving toward democratization and economic reforms.
- A renewal of the struggle over Nagorno-Karabakh could drag Turkey in on the side of Azerbaijan against Armenia, risking Russian intervention and causing tensions in Turkey's relations with Europe and the United States.

- The resurgence of violence against the Algerian regime by the regrouped terrorist organization responsible for bombings in Algiers in 2007, now calling itself "Al Qaeda in the Islamic Maghreb," could create a dangerous precedent in the Maghreb and the Arab world, with serious implications for European countries, especially France, with its large immigrant population from the Maghreb.

- Most important, in the absence of timely and substantive forward movement in the Arab-Israeli peace negotiations, groups such as Hamas, Hezbollah, and Palestinian Islamic Jihad can be counted on to maximize their efforts to scuttle the whole effort. Failure to move the peace process forward would have serious implications for Egypt, whose peace treaty with Israel remains the cornerstone for the structure of Arab-Israeli peace, but which faces continuing internal threat from Muslim extremists.

- And in Iraq, few tears are shed over the removal of Saddam Hussein and a brutal dictatorship that caused major harm to the Iraqi people themselves and threatened the region with his aggressive policies. But U.S. military action in Iraq and mismanagement of the occupation at the outset gave radical Islamic extremists, who call themselves "Al Qaeda in Mesopotamia," a new territorial base of action, and the negative forces of sectarianism the war has spawned in that country have consequences for the region as a whole.

- The situation in Afghanistan, where the Taliban is rearing its head again, could negatively affect neighboring states and re-establish a haven for terrorist groups.

- Al Qaeda's regrouping in 2007 in Pakistan's remote Afghan border areas led to its attacks on the Pakistani government and military. The assassination of former prime minister Bhutto further emboldened Al Qaeda to try to destabilize Pakistan.

- The regime in Iran continues to support Islamic radical groups and enhance its influence in Iraq.
- Farther east, Kashmir remains a potential powder keg, where tensions between Muslims and Hindus could exacerbate Indo-Pakistani relations and lead to another military conflict, with, in the worst-case scenario, the use of nuclear weapons.
- And in India itself, Hindu-Muslim tensions worsened in widespread communal riots and killing in the state of Gujarat in 2002.

THE NEW/OLD WORLD ORDER

Understanding the stakes is just the first step toward developing an effective policy for the United States and its international partners. The Meridian House Speech was an attempt to move in this direction at an important historical juncture following the collapse of the Soviet Union and the beginning of what I would call a "New/Old World Order." Following World War II, with the rise of communism and the beginning of the Cold War, international politics were polarized between the two superpowers and their respective allies and client states. Foreign policy was a "zero-sum game" in which the United States and the Soviet Union competed on an international chessboard for influence and supporters throughout the world. The political nature of a regime was less important than whether it was in "my camp" or "your camp." For example, the period of the Eisenhower administration and Khrushchev's rule was marked by intense rivalry over getting Egypt into the Western or Eastern camp. The Soviets succeeded in getting Egypt into their camp, where it remained until President Anwar Sadat broke with Moscow and displayed extraordinary statesmanship in forging a strategic relationship with the United States and making peace with Israel during President Jimmy Carter's administration.

Within the Soviet Union, the central government forcefully repressed and consolidated ethnic groups and nations. The breakup of their empire sparked a burst of nationalism that expressed itself in newly independent states. It was as if we were watching an old black-and-white documentary film of the assassination of Archduke Ferdinand of the Austro-Hungarian Empire in 1914, triggering the outbreak of World War I, then freezing the frames of that film after the Bolshevik Revolution in Russia in 1917 and the subsequent establishment of the Soviet Empire. With the fall of the Berlin Wall in 1989, that old film started to roll again with the rebirth of nationalist striving throughout the former Soviet Union and Eastern Europe. Ethnicity, nationalism, culture, and religion came back to the forefront in international affairs.

The Soviet invasion of Afghanistan, just one manifestation of the beginning of the end of the Soviet Empire, had the unintended consequence of spurring Islamic radical movements, at first in the form of the mujahideen, zealous warriors who saw the fight against communism as a fight for Allah, and later in the form of the Taliban, who seized on the chaos left by the war to establish a repressive theocratic regime.

As in a long marriage in which the comfort of habit prevails, we had grown accustomed to a polarized world and were ill-prepared to deal with the disintegration of this world and the rebirth of ethnic, tribal, religious, and cultural forces that came back to influence the policies of nation-states in important ways.

In this new setting, the United States must craft policies that can more effectively serve our values and national security interests.

TWO

ISLAM AND DEMOCRACY

*We are friends of liberty all over the world, but we do not go
abroad in search of monsters to destroy.*
—JOHN QUINCY ADAMS, 1823

U.S. policy toward the Muslim countries, parties, and
movements should be one of differentiation, engagement, and
dialogue. The Muslim world is not a monolith. It is diverse
and complex, and our policies should reflect that reality. This
means understanding the role of religion in Islamic society, the
difference between moderate Islamists and Islamic radicals, the
different forms of governance in Muslim countries, and the difference between secularism and secularization as factors that affect the way Muslims will craft their own forms of representative
government and democracy. U.S. engagement not only with the
governments of Islamic societies, but also with political parties,
nongovernmental organizations (NGOs), professional associations, Islamists, and other entities will require much more knowledge and sophistication than we have demonstrated to date.

UNINTENDED CONSEQUENCES

The administration of George W. Bush failed to foresee the unintended consequences of promoting democracy or regime change through military force in Iraq, an approach that unleashed destabilizing sectarian, insurgent, and terrorist forces within the country and gave Iran a major opportunity to aggrandize its influence in Iraq and the region. Neither did it foresee that elections in the Palestinian Territories would result in Hamas's electoral victory in 2006. By subsequently boycotting the Hamas-led government, the administration created the impression in the Arab and Muslim countries that the United States was hypocritical in its quite public call for democracy in the region. A 2005 Gallup Poll found that while the spread of democracy has been the stated goal of the United States, majorities in virtually every predominantly Muslim nation surveyed disagreed with the statement that the United States is serious about the establishment of democratic systems in the region: Only 24 percent in Egypt and Jordan and 16 percent in Turkey said they trusted U.S. intentions. The greatest agreement occurred in Lebanon (38 percent) and Indonesia (48 percent), but even there, majorities (58 percent of Lebanese and 52 percent of Indonesians) disagreed with the statement.

SECULARISM, SECULARIZATION, AND PLURALISM

It was profoundly naïve not to have recognized that, in Muslim countries, Islamist parties and movements will play an important political role in the electoral process. In these countries, religion is a primary source of social identity, for the individual and the nation alike, and religion can be expected to play a pronounced role in their political affairs. The major challenge Muslim countries face in evolving toward broader political participation and democracy is crafting political structures that can reconcile Islamic religious precepts and secular governance. That task is complicated by the fact that, in the Muslim world, "secular" often carries the connotation of being against religion.

In his book *No God But God*, Reza Aslan emphasizes the importance of distinguishing between *secularism* and *secularization*. Citing Harvard theologian Harvey Cox, he observes that

> secularization is the process by which "certain responsibilities pass from ecclesiastical to political authorities," whereas secularism is an ideology based on the eradication of religion from public life. Secularization implies a historical evolution in which society gradually frees itself from "religious control and closed metaphysical world-views." Secularism is itself a closed metaphysical world-view which, according to Cox, "functions very much like a new religion . . ." What is important for Muslims to understand is that it is pluralism, not secularism, that defines democracy in a major way. A democracy can be established upon a normative moral framework as long as pluralism remains the source of its legitimacy . . . Islam has had a long commitment to religious pluralism . . . The foundation of Islamic pluralism can be summed up in one indisputable [Qur'anic] verse: "There can be no compulsion in religion" (Sura 2:256) . . . Grounding an Islamic democracy in the ideals of pluralism is vital because religious pluralism is the first step toward building an effective human rights policy in the Middle East.

What also needs to be conveyed more clearly to Muslims in the region is that the United States is a secularized country with full freedom of religion for all. Muslims need also to understand that, despite being both officially secular and astonishingly pluralistic, the United States offers full freedom of religion for all and is one of the most religiously vibrant countries in the world.

LONGING FOR THE GARDENS OF CÓRDOBA

The forms that democratic structures may take in Muslim countries will, more often than not, reflect the central role of religion in these societies. U.S. policymakers need to understand the history of Islamic civilization and its past achievements, in order to appreciate current widespread frustrations in light of lost greatness and the inescapable struggle with modernity. In the classic film *Lawrence of Arabia*, Prince Faisal, a descendant of the Prophet Muhammad whom T. E. Lawrence had seen as the best hope to lead the Arab revolt against the fading Ottoman Empire, says to Lawrence, "I long for the gardens of Córdoba."

Faisal did not mean he wished to be in Spain; he was recalling a lost Golden Age. Within a hundred years after Muhammad's death in 632 C.E., Islam spread from Arabia westward to Spain and eastward to India, consequently becoming the enlivening spirit of rich and flourishing centers of civilization. It was one of the more remarkable movements in human history, and its success was seen as proof that it was of God.

Over the next five hundred years, Muslim dynasties centered in Damascus, Baghdad, Córdoba, and Cairo created and presided over the world's leading intellectual and cultural centers. In an effort to gather and preserve existing knowledge, Muslim scholars translated the classic works of Greek antiquity into Arabic, thus preserving them for later transmission to the Christian West. But they were not simply archivists. Dedicated to education, creative Muslims made stunning advances in virtually every field of knowledge—philosophy, the sciences, literature and the arts, architecture, and, particularly, mathematics.

While most of the European continent languished in the intellectual wasteland of the Dark Ages, medieval Islam bubbled with intellectual and cultural vigor. Baghdad itself was said to have been home to three hundred schools, and of a reported seventy libraries in Córdoba alone, one is reliably believed to have housed four hundred thousand volumes. Prince Faisal knew of those days of glory. He asked the Englishman Lawrence if he was aware that "in the Arab city of Córdoba [there] were two miles of public lighting in the streets when London was a village?" Lawrence responded, "Yes, you were great." But Faisal's awareness that those days were gone was painfully clear in his wistful reply: "Nine centuries ago."

Córdoba's decline, usually marked from the fall of the Umayyad dynasty in 1031, was not, of course, the end of Islamic empire. Under the Abbasid Empire centered in Baghdad, Islamic culture flourished, new heights in philosophy and science were attained, and the period was widely seen as the "golden age" of the Islamic world. However, the Caliphate's authority slowly began to erode as regional power centers developed throughout the empire. The last Abbasid caliph was executed by Mongol invaders. The fifteenth and sixteenth centuries saw the rise of the Moghul Empire on the Indian subcontinent, the Safavid Empire in Iran, and the sprawling Ottoman Empire, which reached its apex under Suleiman the Magnificent, who governed from Istanbul from 1520 to 1566. One of history's largest empires at its height, it endured, though in a progressively weakened state, until its final defeat in World War I (in which Prince Faisal and T. E. Lawrence played a significant role) and subsequent formal dissolution in 1922.

The eclipsing of these great empires, and the attendant ascendancy of European forces, primarily French, British, and Russian, created an existential crisis in the Islamic world. It soon became clear that these European nations, once scorned by Muslims as backward and inferior—they were right at the time—had surpassed them in science, technology, commerce, and warfare.

How could such a thing be? If the early conquests and subsequent grandeur of Islamic empires had seemed almost miraculous, clear proof that God was on their side, were not defeat and humiliation a sign that God's favor had been lost? Success and power were dependent upon obedience to God's will. Departure from the straight path of Islam meant loss of God's guidance and protection. Divine revelation proclaimed this, and now it had happened. A crisis of such magnitude demanded a response. It received several, the most important of which continue to vie for dominance in the Arab and Muslim world.

SHARIA AND THE SUNNI-SHIA DIVIDE

The inescapable starting point for all these responses is the role to be played by Sharia, the basis of Islamic law. Sharia is not a single, never-changing, universally recognized set of codified laws, laid down by Muhammad. It developed over centuries as Muslims conquered new regions and encountered new or changing conditions. Because the Qur'an did not provide all the answers they needed, they appealed to the *sunna*, the behavior, practice, and sayings of the Prophet in Medina; the *hadith*, the sayings, spoken decisions, and judgments attributed to Muhammad; *ijma*, the consensus of the Medinan community during or shortly after the Prophet's time; and *qiyas*, analogies based on principles in the Qur'an or precedents established in Medina. Taken together, these constitute the major elements of Sharia, the "way" or "path" Muslims are obliged to follow.

Given a lack of certainty about what the Prophet and his Medinan disciples actually said or did, as well as the flexibility of interpretation based on analogy, it is hardly surprising that centuries of debate over its content and application have led to rival schools of legal theory and differing understandings of its requirements, as when some Muslim states forbid women to drive cars while others elect them to steer their nations (for example, the late prime minister of Pakistan Benazir Bhutto). Still, there is sufficient agreement over the great body of Islamic law that a government based on Sharia is likely to look and be quite different from one that is not.

The crucial division between Sunni and Shia also plays a role.

In general terms, the distinction between the two major divisions of Islam traces back to the issue of who should succeed the Prophet Muhammad after his death in 632 C.E. The Shia contend, with plausible reason, that Muhammad intended his mantle to fall on Ali, his cousin, closest disciple, and son-in-law, the father of his only male descendants, Hasan and Husayn, and that his leadership would be perpetuated through this line. But after Muhammad died, the leaders of the community chose another of Muhammad's Four Rightly Guided Companions, Abu Bakr. He was succeeded by the other two, Umar and Uthman, before Ali finally became caliph. During the fifth year of his caliphate, Ali was assassinated while at prayer. The term *Shia* means "party" or "faction" and refers to those who are of "the party of Ali," who regard him and his descendants as the divinely appointed successors to Muhammad and the only legitimate religious and political leaders of the Muslim community. The Sunni, those who accepted Abu Bakr and the practice of choosing the caliph on the basis of communal consensus rather than heredity, see themselves as following the true *sunna*, or words, actions, and example of Prophet Muhammad.

In 680 C.E., at the Battle of Karbala, in modern Iraq, Husayn, then the Shia imam, or supreme authority, challenged the Sunni caliph, Yazid, and was cruelly martyred, an event remembered annually by the Shia on a day of mourning known as Ashura. From the beginning, the Sunni have been the majority faction in Islam, comprising an estimated 85 percent of Muslims worldwide.

The Shia retain a sense of disinheritance and martyrdom. Unlike the Sunni, who have no formal central authority, the Shia clergy organize themselves into ranks, with imams of greater and lesser stature and, of course, with ayatollahs and grand ayatollahs, a structure that can facilitate political activity. The Shia are most numerous in Iraq, Iran, Yemen, Azerbaijan, Bahrain, and Lebanon, but have significant minorities in other countries, where they are often subject to discrimination by Sunni majorities. Not surprisingly, the hostility between the two factions can run deep, sometimes to the point of one side's denying that the other is even entitled to call itself Muslim.

IJTIHAD AND THE USE OF REASON

In the early centuries, scholars of Islamic law also relied on *ijtihad*, roughly the use of reason and deep thought, to reach legal decisions and interpretations in cases where Sharia is silent or ambiguous. By the tenth century C.E., however, the use of *ijtihad* fell out of favor, often referred to as the closing of "the door of *ijtihad*." Thenceforth, most pious Muslims depended on *taqlid* ("imitation"), accepting that true doctrine and law were complete and need only be explained and applied, not subjected to addition or revision. Given their belief in the authority of the imam, Shia Muslims never subscribed to this view as strongly as did Sunnis.

The alternative to Islam was the political religion of the twentieth century: nationalism. For many of the nationalist regimes in the Middle East, the goal was to obtain independence from foreign occupiers, especially the British and the French colonial powers. Once independence was achieved, however, the nationalists were reluctant to share power with other parties and factions in their countries. The very concept of a loyal opposition was alien. Internal reforms and democratic practices were neglected and the main preoccupation was simply to remain in power. This led to the corruption of power, and in many cases, the military stepped in to seize political power in military coups d'etat, as in the case of General Husni al-Zaim in Syria in 1949 and that of Colonel Gamal Abdel Nasser in Egypt in 1952.

The evolution of political development in the region ever since has been one of partial reforms and what can be called "electoral autocracies," with strong military and security establishments and a semblance of democratic trappings. In effect, there is a strong tendency toward one-man rule in many Middle Eastern countries in the form of monarchies or dictatorships.

For there to be sustainable political and economic reforms in the Muslim countries, consideration must be given to Islamic concepts that could create Islamic forms of democracy: namely, *ijtihad*, the exercise of informed and independent judgment; *bay'ah*, the oath of allegiance given to a tribal leader; *shura*, the practice of consultation between rulers and the people with a view toward elections of the people's representatives; and *ijma*, the concept of consensus as a basis of law and parliamentary rule. We should not expect that the strict separation of Church and State that evolved over time in different ways in the West will be replicated in the broader Middle East. There will be variations on a theme.

Even a cursory look at the history of Islamic political thought reveals robust debate over the proper relationship between religion and the state.

OTTOMAN REFORMS

Many leaders of Muslim lands favored widespread adoption of Western ways, including abandonment or at least a serious reduction in the role of Sharia as the basis for law and society. The Ottoman rulers themselves had admired aspects of Western political regimes and had initiated various reforms in efforts to slow the decline of their empire. The most notable of these were contained in the Tanzimat ["reorganization"] Edict of 1839, issued by order of Sultan Abdulmecit I and drawing on changes begun by his predecessor and father, Sultan Mahmud II.

The Edict called for, among other changes, reorganization of the financial and legal systems along the lines of those in France (whose good will the sultan sought), the establishment of modern universities and academies, and a prototype of a parliament. Perhaps most striking was the removal of disadvantages based on religion. From the time of Muhammad, Jews and Christians— "People of the Book"—had been tolerated in Muslim lands, often faring better than did Muslims in Christian-dominated areas. But they were still second-class citizens. In addition to other impediments, all non-Muslim men were required to pay a head tax known as *jizya*, in return for a measure of autonomy and safety. They were not, however, required to pay *zakat*, the tax paid by Muslims.

The Tanzimat Edict abolished *jizya*, referring to all inhabitants of the empire as "subjects," with equal guarantees of "perfect security for life, honor, and fortune." Going even further, the sultan declared that "the difference of religion and sect among the subjects is something concerning only their persons and not affecting their rights of citizenship. As we are living all in the same country under the same government, it is wrong to make discriminations among us." Abdulmecit's successor and brother, Sultan Abdulaziz, abrogated a number of these reforms, but important seeds had been sown.

KEMAL ATATURK AND THE MODERNIZERS

The following decades would see constitutions accepted and abrogated, parliaments established and disbanded, and the movement of reformers known as the Young Turks, who reinstated a constitution and greatly reduced what was left of the sultan's powers. The most dramatic break with the past, of course, was the thoroughgoing secularization achieved by Mustafa Kemal Ataturk, a charismatic military commander who drove the European occupiers out of Turkey and founded the modern Republic of Turkey in 1923. The Kemalist movement proved to be one of the most dynamic forces of change and modernization in modern Islamic history. The central factor of the movement was the disestablishment of Islam as the basis of the state, resulting in a radical alteration of the traditional role of Islam in the political, economic, intellectual, religious, social, and cultural realms.

In contrast to the Islamic ideal of the *umma*, a transnational

39

civilization and culture, nationalism was the keystone of the Kemalist regime. Turkey was established as a republic, with an elected president and parliament, with the power and authority of the state at least theoretically resting with the people, including women as equal citizens. The government played a large role in managing the economy and a form of étatism, or state capitalism. The schools were ordered to pay regular homage to Ataturk and the republic, but Islamic content was stricken from the curriculum. Religion was relegated to the individual level, but even here was subject to state control, as when Ataturk banned the wearing of traditional Islamic clothing in favor of Western styles.

No other Muslim country went nearly so far as Turkey in decoupling religion and the state, but several influential Muslim intellectuals and political activists, who came to be called Islamic Modernists, tried to articulate visions of authentic Islam that did not require repudiation of Western ideas and practices. Two of the most important of these were Jamal al-Din al-Afghani (1838–97), who claimed Afghanistan as his primary home but spent long stretches in Egypt and Paris and traveled widely in Europe, and Muhammad 'Abduh (1849–1905), a Sunni judge in Egypt who was influenced by Afghani and joined him in Paris, where they published a journal calling for reform. Afghani and 'Abduh contended that the surest way to regain Islam's lost glory was to return to the attitude and approach of their early Muslim ancestors (salaf), who, they said, were rational, practical people who used their reason and common sense (ijtihad) to adapt Islamic law and practice to changing conditions. They wanted Muslim states to be independent of Western control, but encouraged the practice of modern science and advocated adoption of democratic government and secular law, as well as education and greater freedom for women.

Among their more notable intellectual heirs were Muhammad Rashid Rida (1865–1935), a Syrian who rejected taqlid (imitation of the past) and the ossification that he saw in the ulama, or clergy, and Sheikh Ali abd al-Raziq, a senior professor at Al Azhar

University, usually regarded, at least by Sunnis, as the premier center of Islamic learning, who wrote approvingly of the Turkish revolution and its emancipation of government from religious authority. Going further, Raziq argued that adherence to Islam required neither the Caliphate nor any other specific political arrangement. Muhammad, he asserted, had communicated divine revelation regarding faith and religious behavior, but the political arrangements he instituted were appropriate for his time and situation; they had not been intended as a template for all political communities in all realms and eras. Modern Muslims are therefore free, he argued, "to organize the state in accordance with [existing] intellectual, social, and economic conditions."

Recounting Raziq's effort, British historian Antony Black notes that Raziq's views "received no support in religious circles," and that he was expelled from the university and stripped of his position as religious judge.

WAHHABISM AND MILITANCY

Such exceptions notwithstanding, the response of most religious leaders to the threats posed by modernity and Westernization was to proclaim that the only way to regain God's favor, and thereby also restore Islam's lost glory, was revival, a return to the path from which a faithless people had departed, seduced by the shallow blandishments of the West. By the middle of the eighteenth century, before the confrontation with the European powers became serious, Muslim societies were showing serious signs of strain, and reformers were beginning to call for a sociomoral reconstruction of society on the foundations of Islam.

The most important of these efforts was the Wahhabi movement, established on the Arabian Peninsula by Muhammad Ibn 'Abd al-Wahhab in the mid-1700s. The Wahhabis sought to purify and perfect the faith of individual believers and to call on rulers to assist in this effort. They also emphasized the universalistic character of Islam, the global community of the faithful—the *umma*. Wahhab enlisted the support of a local ruler, Muhammad al-Saud, forming a symbiotic combination of respected religious teacher and strong commander that proved advantageous to both. The Wahhabis helped the Saudis gain control of most of the Arabian Peninsula and, in the process, solidified "Wahhabism" as a major reform and revivalist movement in modern Muslim history, a movement with significant influence today.

The monarchy needs the cooperation and approval of the *ulama* (the religious authorities) to enhance its legitimacy. The *ulama* need royal support to maintain their privileges and wield some influence over policymaking. Considerable tension exists, as the royal family overlooks the excesses of the Wahhabis in return for their support, and the Wahhabis tolerate the royal family's policies in return for monetary and political benefits. Wahhabism today continues to call for the Islamization of society and the creation of a political order that gives appropriate recognition to Islam. It is the most enduring experiment within the broader mission of revival and has provided a standard against which other movements and states could be measured.

After the dissolution of the Ottoman Empire, vigorous Islamist movements arose in other countries. In Egypt, Hassan al-Banna and a handful of associates, none of them clerics, founded the Muslim Brotherhood in 1928. Concerned that Western social practices such as dancing and drinking alcohol, attending theaters and engaging in other questionable amusements would corrupt the morals of young people, they established educational and devotional programs designed to reaffirm commitment to Islam and thereby to reform the political, economic, and social life of the country.

Over the years, the Brotherhood became a significant force in Egyptian politics and has often been in conflict with the official regime, at times being officially suppressed, with its members imprisoned or even executed. The Brotherhood today includes many professional men and has expanded its activities to establishing medical clinics and small businesses and industries, actions that win approval from the people but increase tension with the government authorities by pointing up their failure to meet such needs adequately. Egypt remains the major stronghold of the Brotherhood, but other Arab countries have established branches of the movement.

During the 1970s, more militant Islamist groups arose, determined to overthrow the *jahili* (faithless, apostate) regime and attack other enemies of the faith. The most important of these have been Jamaat al-Islamiyya (Islamic Group), which was responsible for the killing of sixty tourists at Luxor in 1997, and Egyptian Islamic Jihad, sometimes called simply al-Jihad, the group involved in the assassination of Anwar Sadat in 1981. The spiritual leader of Jamaat is the blind cleric Sheikh Omar Abdel Rahman, convicted and imprisoned in the United States for involvement in the 1993 bombing of the World Trade Center. Al-Jihad's most infamous figure is Ayman al-Zawahiri, Osama Bin Laden's closest associate, who often appears on Al Qaeda videotapes delivering propagandistic messages aimed at "impious" Arab regimes, Israel, and the West.

These and other Islamist extremists have been inspired and inflamed by the writings of Sayyid Qutb (1906–66), one of the most influential of radical antimodernist Muslim thinkers. Qutb regarded the governments of all Islamic societies as faithless and urged their overthrow and replacement, by violent means if necessary, by leaders committed to rejecting Western values and ways and establishing a government based entirely on the Sharia.

In India, and later in Pakistan after it became an independent state, Abu Ala Maududi (1903–79), perhaps the most important Islamic thinker of the twentieth century and a significant influence on Sayyid Qutb, categorically rejected accommodation between the Sharia and modernity. For him, the Qur'an and *sunna* are all-sufficient and unchangeable and should be the sole source of Islamic society. While he claimed to be an advocate of democracy, his views have been characterized as "theodemocratic" or "nomocratic," meaning that voters had only the chance to endorse what the Sharia demanded. Rulers who deviate from a strict application of Sharia are to be marked as apostates, removed, and replaced. Maududi even went so far as to contend that Islam should seek "to destroy all states and governments anywhere on the face of the earth which are opposed to the ideology and programme of Islam regardless of the country or the Nation which rules it."

In 1941, before the partition of India and Pakistan, Maududi founded Jamaat al-Islamiyya, a religiopolitical organization that has been a significant force for militant Islam in Pakistan and has inspired similar groups in India, Bangladesh, Kashmir, and elsewhere. Maududi's continuing influence has been such that, whatever their private commitment to Islam, Pakistan's rulers have necessarily accorded great weight to Islamic law in their administrations. This tendency is further strengthened by thousands of Islamist madrassas, religious schools (often run by Wahhabis and financed by Saudi Arabia) that inculcate boys and young men with the extreme views Maududi espoused. In contrast to Turkey, where the military acts as a check on politicians thought to be a threat to that nation's official commitment to secularism, the Pakistani army has been supportive of Islamist leaders.

In Sunni-dominated countries, especially in the Middle East but elsewhere as well, a movement known as Salafism has gained prominence. The term refers to an effort to recover, as reform movements often do, the spirit and practice of the very earliest generations of the Islamic community, the time of the pious ancestors, or *salaf*. Islamic Modernists such as Afghani and 'Abduh claimed a similar goal, but pointed to the adaptability of the *salaf*. The contemporary version rejects that approach in favor of a much more slavish attempt to re-create what they believe to be the actual behavior of those original, pure, uncorrupted Muslims. This involves close attention to such matters as ritual and personal appearance, but can also foster extreme impatience with governments seen to be impure, as governments tend to be.

The similarities between Wahhabism and Salafism are obvious, so it is not surprising that Osama Bin Laden is regarded as both Wahhabist and Salafist, or that some observers describe members of Al Qaeda as Salafist.

The densely populated nation of Indonesia has the largest Muslim population in the world, estimated at more than 200 million, but it is not an Islamist state and seems unlikely to become one. Though traditional, even radical elements have some strength, especially in the province of Aceh, most Indonesian Muslims subscribe to a more moderate form of Islam that does not require the rejection of modernity. In 1945, at least partly in response to Muslim efforts to give Sharia law official standing in the nation's constitution, President Sukarno formalized a state philosophy or ideology known as Pancasila, whose principles included belief in one God, national unity, social justice, humanitarianism, and democracy. Such vague principles could be interpreted to suit the desires and aims of authoritarian rulers, but they have provided a substantial measure of religious freedom to six officially recognized faiths (Islam, Roman Catholicism, Protestantism, Hinduism, Buddhism, and Confucianism) and have established an ethos that enables political leaders to resist domination by Islamic radicals.

Another populous and diverse Southeast Asian nation, Malaysia, provides a somewhat different model whose viability is currently being tested. The Malaysian constitution clearly states that the fundamental rights it contains apply to all Malaysians, "regardless of religion, race, descent, place of birth, or gender." In practice, however, the Muslim majority—estimates vary, but most place the Muslim population at between 50 and 60 percent of the country's twenty-three million inhabitants—enjoy certain advantages and the top government leaders have overwhelmingly been Muslim. Non-Muslims are free to practice their religion, but are forbidden to attempt to convert Muslims and often meet resistance when seeking permission to build new churches or temples. In recent years, some states have begun to implement

Sharia as their legal code, though applying it only to Muslims. While non-Muslims are still adjudicated under the secular civil code, non-Muslims view such developments as possible predecessors to more Islamist policies. Interestingly, some moderate Muslims, including organizations of progressive Muslim women, have joined with moderate Muslims to resist efforts by Islamists to move the country in a more theocratic direction and to insist on closer adherence to what is essentially a secular constitution.

The above examples are of Sunni-dominated regions, but the most notable contemporary event in the political history of the Islamic world is obviously the Iranian Revolution of 1979, when Shia militants led by Ayatollah Ruhollah Khomeini successfully overthrew the rule of Shah Muhammad Reza Pahlavi and installed a theocracy based on the "Guardianship of Islamic Jurists," a small group of clerics, or mullahs, led first by Khomeini and later by his successor, Grand Ayatollah Ali Khamenei. Although this regime has often been harsh, even ruthless, in instituting its policies and silencing dissent, it has allowed a measure of democracy. Its citizens, male and female, can and do vote in elections at all levels, albeit only for candidates approved by the mullahs. The rights of women have been severely restricted in some areas, but they are permitted to attend school and university, to hold public jobs, even to serve in elected office.

Iran has attempted repeatedly to export its revolution, calling on Muslims to replace secular or apostate rulers with Islamic government and giving substantial financial and military aid to Shia populations and organizations in Iraq and Lebanon. Even in Sunni lands, with Palestine as a key example, they have provided support to Islamic radical groups such as Hamas.

While by no means a full listing of Muslim countries or of the varied types of relationships between religious and political forces within the Islamic world, I trust these examples do make it clear that we must approach and deal with the Islamic world as, to use Vartan Gregorian's felicitous phrase, "a mosaic, not a monolith."

TRADITION AND MODERNITY

The mainstream debate over tradition and modernity, where the future of the Muslim world will be decided, is likely to revolve around the question of whether Sharia is only one source of law or the one and only source of law in Muslim countries. The Turkish model of rigorous secularism seems unlikely to spread beyond Turkey in the foreseeable future and, indeed, is under considerable strain even there. Since 2001, the Gallup Organization has interviewed tens of thousands of respondents in thirty-five predominantly Muslim countries, yielding unprecedented information regarding Muslims' thoughts and feelings about a number of critical issues. In their 2007 book, *Who Speaks for Islam? What a Billion Muslims Really Think*, John Esposito and Dalia Mogahed assert that

> the emphasis that those in substantially Muslim coun-
> tries give to a new model of government—one that
> is democratic yet embraces religious values—helps
> to explain why majorities in most countries, with the
> exception of a handful of nations, want Sharia as at least
> "a" source of legislation. In only a few did a majority
> say that Sharia should have no role in society; yet in
> most countries, only a minority want Sharia as "the only
> source" of law. In Jordan, Egypt, Pakistan, Afghanistan,
> and Bangladesh, majorities want Sharia as the "only
> source" of legislation.

In the Meridian House Speech, I used the phrase that has been translated into "one man, one vote, one time," in juxtaposition to the principle of the alternation of power through democratic elections and the concept of a loyal opposition, both of which are critical to the success or failure of democratic models in the Muslim world. This issue remains a major point of discussion and debate, especially in the context of the Bush administration's major policy initiative of democracy promotion in the broader Middle East.

Elections are but one major element of democracy. Its core concepts also include the constitutional rule of law and the consent of the governed. That means, among other things, that when one political group or party gains executive power in elections, it must be ready and willing to relinquish that power if the ballot box goes against it the next time around.

The policy statement in the Meridian House Speech was made in view of the upcoming elections in Algeria in 1992 and the prospect of the Islamic Salvation Front's coming to power through the electoral process. My phrase in that speech has been often quoted and referred to both positively and critically. Some have erroneously interpreted it, for their own political ends, to mean that the United States was and is categorically opposed to having any Islamist parties come to power in the region and is interested only in stability in the broader Middle East region, to the benefit of dictatorial regimes. To the contrary, the whole thrust of the policy statement was the compelling need for meaningful political and economic reforms in the Middle East and resolution of the Arab-Israeli conflict—not only as intrinsic goods, but also to marginalize the extremists in the region, whether secular dictators such as Saddam Hussein or Islamic radicals such as Osama Bin Laden. Political and economic reforms are a necessary prelude to the evolution of the Muslim and Arab countries toward democratic systems tailored to their own cultural context and traditions.

It is therefore more meaningful and realistic to talk about broadening political participation in the Middle East as a building block toward democratic systems in the future. Promotion of democracy without the necessary antecedents of the rule of law, political parties, elaboration of civil society, the rights of minorities, and other major reforms will, more often than not, be doomed to failure. This will be a long-term, generational process.

In this context, we must correctly analyze and differentiate among the Islamist groups. Let me be clear: Some groups and movements are beyond the pale and should be strongly opposed and marginalized. Islamic radicals such as the Al Qaeda network and the Salafist jihadists who target both the "near enemy" (the "impious" regimes in the Muslim countries) and "the further enemy" (the United States, other Western countries, and Israel) promote an extremist agenda and resort to violence. Olivier Roy, the noted French expert on Islam, argues that Al Qaeda does not actually have an ideology and that its advocacy of Sharia law does not constitute an ideology. Neither Osama Bin Laden nor Zawahiri are ideological thinkers, according to Roy. He characterizes Al Qaeda as "an attitude of revenge" with no real societal program. It is basically a nihilistic organization promoting violence and suicide bombings with no day after, at least not on Earth. So elevating Al Qaeda as central to the struggle of ideas in the Muslim world is giving it much too much credit, according to Roy. In my view, irrespective of its ideological status, Al Qaeda must be confronted with all means for what it is—an Islamic radical terrorist organization with a political agenda to establish its totalitarian brand of the caliphate.

But some Islamist groups and parties represent important Islamic schools of thought that have been and could be engaged to participate in the political process and, possibly, persuaded to abide by the rules of the game. In this category we can include parties such as the Justice and Development Party in Turkey, which won the elections in 2002 and has governed the country under the leadership of Prime Minister Recep Tayyip Erdogan; the like-minded Party of Justice and Development in Morocco; the Muslim Brotherhood in Egypt and Jordan; and the Prosperous Justice Party in Indonesia.

Another distinction that needs to be made concerns groups and parties such as Hamas and Hezbollah, which have a radical Islamist agenda and resort to terrorism but are also closely identified with territorial goals, namely, opposition to Israeli occupation. Developments on the ground between the Israelis and Palestinians, such as former Israeli prime minister Ehud Barak's unilateral disengagement of the Israel Defense Forces (IDF) from southern Lebanon in 2000 and Ariel Sharon's unilateral withdrawal from Gaza and four West Bank settlements in 2005, help diminish this territorial raison d'être, with mixed results, as recent events in Lebanon and Palestine have demonstrated, until a comprehensive peace settlement is reached.

The challenge with Hamas and Hezbollah is whether they are willing to transform their policies away from violence and toward political participation in both Lebanon and Palestine, an effort that surely should be supported, but without illusions about the complexities involved, especially given their ideological platforms.

In this regard, I concur with the insight of former Israeli foreign minister Shlomo Ben-Ami, who said:

> A dialogue with political Islam, in the form of Hamas, for instance, is an unavoidable necessity. Ostracism and banning is a recipe for disaster, as the example of Algeria shows. Creating a space for legitimate political activity by Islamic parties, including recognition of their right to govern, is the way to encourage moderation. The challenge therefore is not to destroy the only Islamic movements that can claim authentic popular support in parts of the Arab world, but rather to solidify their fragile transition from radical jihad to the politics of compromise.

Contact has occurred between U.S. diplomats and representatives of the Muslim Brotherhood in Egypt. This dialogue should be pursued. In 2005, Muhammad Akef, supreme guide of the Brotherhood, was asked if the organization was prepared to talk to the Americans: "Yes," he replied, "but they should forward the request to the Egyptian Foreign Ministry." His point was that the Brotherhood was operating in the open and not as an entity alienated from the Egyptian government.

James Traub, writing in the *New York Times Magazine*, reported that Magdy Ashour, a member of the Muslim Brotherhood, told him, "We want to establish the perception of an Islamic group cooperating with other groups, concerned about human rights. We do not want a country like Iran, which thinks that it is ruling with a divine mandate. We want a government based on civil law with an Islamic source of lawmaking."

Similarly, Hazem Farouk Mansour, head of the foreign policy committee of the Brotherhood's bloc in the Egyptian parliament, said of the Camp David peace agreement between Egypt and Israel, "We accept it as an agreement, whether we like it or not." (The Qur'an, in Sura 8:55, instructs Muslims to honor treaties.) Of course, such statements of intent cannot be taken at face value, but must be tested. In this case, the major question is whether, given the Muslim Brotherhood's opposition to the Camp David Accords and peace with Israel, it would renounce these treaty obligations if it did come to power.

DIFFICULT CHOICES

The task of engaging Islamist parties and groups will require difficult choices, incentives, and disincentives, in the first place, by the countries in the region directly involved, and secondly, in the shaping of policies of the international community, especially the United States, given its major role in the Middle East and globally. As I stated in the Meridian House Speech:

> We differ with those, regardless of their religion, who practice terrorism, oppress minorities, preach intolerance, or violate internationally accepted standards of conduct regarding human rights; with those who are insensitive to the need for political pluralism; with those

who cloak their message in another brand of authoritari-
anism; with those who substitute religious and political
confrontation for constructive engagement with the rest
of the world; with those who do not share our commitment to peaceful resolution to conflict, especially the
Arab/Israeli conflict; and with those who would pursue
their goals through repression or violence. [At the same
time,] Those who are prepared to take specific steps
toward free elections, creating independent judiciaries,
promoting the rule of law, reducing restrictions on the
press, respecting the rights of minorities, and guarantee-
ing individual rights, will find us ready to recognize and
support their efforts, just as those moving in the opposite
direction will find us ready to speak candidly and act
accordingly.

This approach to nonradical Islamists is one of the major
components of the challenge of democratization in the Arab and
Muslim world. As a first step, there must be engagement between
the region's governments and the Islamists, to try to bring them
into the political mainstream, where they will be required to assume responsibility in governmental affairs and be held accountable in the complex business of decision-making. In addition,
countries outside the region can encourage and support, by word
and deed, structural economic and political reforms, broader political participation, transparency and anticorruption programs,
and the promotion of the rights of women, as well as other human rights.

The United States and other leading countries should consider the merits of engaging in contacts with Islamist groups that
would be prepared to forgo violence and that might be willing to
consider positive involvement in broadening political participation in the Middle East. Nothing is lost by such contacts and,
at a minimum, we might gain some better understanding of the
dynamic forces at play in the Muslim countries. Indeed, this ap-

proach can enhance our ability to formulate policies to facilitate broader political representation and economic reforms.

ISLAMIST POLITICAL PARTIES

In 1992 I had a discussion in Washington with veteran Egyptian ambassador Raouf Reedy about the use of Islam as a political vehicle. He said that some Islamic movements seek to become political parties in order to gain political power. They start as religious movements and do not reveal their political motivations initially. They will try to participate in elections or try to take over by force. When the Muslim Brotherhood in Egypt started in 1928, it did so as a socioeconomic organization, emphasizing God and religion as the refuge of the poor and disenfranchised. In Jordan, the Brotherhood also started as a social organization, but declared itself to be a political party in 1940. In its Syrian incarnation, what started as a cultural association grew into a major political force that tried to topple the regime of Syrian president Hafez al-Asad, who moved against them decisively in Hama in 1982 in a military action said to have killed at least twenty thousand people, in effect decapitating the movement. In the Sudan, the Brotherhood infiltrated the military and shared power in a military coup d'etat.

I asked Reedy if it might not be in the interests of the international community to have these Islamic groups participate in the electoral process, in the hope that, with the view that once they shared political power and were forced to focus on issues of governance, they might moderate their views and behavior. Reedy was categorically negative: "They are dictatorial organizations that will never permit democratic processes."

I related to him that, in 1991, an Algerian ambassador had told me that the elections in Algeria should proceed and the Islamic Salvation Front (FIS) should be allowed to come to power if it won a majority of the vote in the upcoming elections. In his view, the FIS did not have the answers to Algeria's serious economic and social problems and would, therefore, fail in office and discredit itself. But another Arab diplomat told me that the risk was too high and that the Muslim Brotherhoods throughout the Arab world would exploit the democratic process for their own ends and, with the aid of their military wings, would establish "fascist and Leninist" "democratic centralism" regimes. He continued that, indeed, because the established regimes do not have viable answers to the widespread poverty and other social ills in their countries, truly free elections would likely see the Muslim Brotherhood come to power in most Arab countries.

THE POLITICAL GAINS AND LOSSES OF ISLAMIST PARTIES

Islamist movements are gaining ground in some Arab countries, albeit with periodic rising and falling fortunes at the polls. The Muslim Brotherhood in Egypt went from fifteen to eighty-eight independent parliamentarians in the 2005 election and is the most important opposition group in the country. In Morocco, the Party for Justice and Development has also become the largest opposition party in the country. In Algeria, the Movement for a Peaceful Society has been working with Algerian president Abdelaziz Bouteflika's government. The Islamic Action Front in Jordan had seventeen of 110 members in parliament. In Jordan's latest general election in November 2007, however, the IAF's share of the votes fell to 5 percent, down from almost 15 percent in the elections in 2003. The group, linked with the Muslim Brotherhood movement, managed to keep only six of its seventeen seats in the National Assembly. The Muslim Brotherhood is part of the parliamentary opposition in Yemen, Bahrain, and Kuwait.

It is important to point out that the decisions by various governments in and out of the region have had the effect of bolstering the position of the Islamist parties. Some have argued that

Anwar Sadat made a mistake by bringing the Muslim Brotherhood into the political process to offset the Egyptian communists and leftists. But Sadat opened up Egyptian society and allowed public debate, which had the result of generating open public confrontation between Muslim extremists and more moderate elements of that society. While allowing the establishment of political parties, Sadat did not allow religious groups and movements to organize into political parties. This was considered to be a smart move.

The Algerians made the mistake of allowing political parties to organize on the basis of religion. This led to the tragic violence in Algeria after the 1992 election.

The Israelis supported Hamas as a rival to the PLO in the 1980s, and many years later had to face the consequences of Hamas's wining the elections in 2006 and threatening the Palestinian moderate leadership of Fatah and Palestinian Authority president Mahmoud Abbas.

The United States supported the mujahideen fighters in their effort to repel the Soviet invasion in Afghanistan. That was a successful strategy that helped defeat the Soviets, but it also led to the creation of Al Qaeda.

JOBS AND EDUCATION

It is important to note that political, economic, and educational reforms in the region must go hand in hand. In my many discussions with Arab interlocutors on the political role of Islamists in the Arab countries, a common narrative persists. Repeatedly, they told me that it's all about "jobs, jobs, and jobs" and education for both men and women, coupled with participation in civil society and the political life of the country. A significant part of the success of the Muslim Brotherhood was its founding of social institutions such as hospitals, schools, and pharmacies, and achieving prominence in such job-creating industries as plastics.

At times, a key reason for the Egyptian government's extensive subsidies for major segments of the population has been to avoid popular discontent and also sideline the Muslim Brotherhood, which was engaging in extensive grassroots political organization while providing needed services to the people.

According to a joint Organisation for Economic Co-operation and Development (OECD) and regional study, approximately half of the 300 million people in the Middle East are below the age of twenty, and the rate of unemployment in many countries is in double digits. An estimated 80 to 100 million jobs have to be created by 2020 and the region's economies will have to grow by at least 6 to 7 percent to meet these demographic demands. There is, however, modest reason for optimism. Foreign direct investment in the Arab countries grew to $19 billion in 2006, in comparison to $4 billion in 2001. Inter-regional investment has also increased since 9/11, when Arab investors and businessmen sensed an unfriendly climate, especially in the United States, and began to look for opportunities within their own region. Bolstered by the high price of oil and gas, Arab energy-producing countries are actively beginning to diversify their economies. Middle East stock markets are opening up, accompanied by a creative reinter-pretation of Islamic financial regulations, such as the prohibition of interest on loans, that have inhibited economic development. The availability of financing for different strata of the economy is also key. Responding to the needs of the street is essential.

Reform of the educational system is a critical necessity and priority for the modernization of the Middle East. My contacts stress that the education system in the Arab world needs to be more rigorous and students should be kept in school for eight hours a day with extracurricular activities. The goal is to provide a balanced education that will produce viable entrants, men and women, into the labor force. That means education in econom-ics, the natural sciences, engineering, and other disciplines that provide direct preparation for employment. Conversely, religious education and training by extremist clerics and teachers must be curtailed. A telling anecdote comes from a Saudi mother as published in a Saudi newspaper:

> My older son came home from school one day a few
> years ago and said to me, "Mommy, did you know that
> Osama Bin Laden is a hero?" The day after 9/11 my
> younger son told me that his art teacher asked him to
> draw the planes as they hit the World Trade Center. We
> kept our children from watching these violent scenes
> on television at home, but apparently the teachers had a
> different point of view. For four years I suffered silently
> about all of this. And then the day came when terrorists
> attacked the Saudi interior ministry in Riyadh. As we
> were eating lunch, we saw the names and pictures of the
> attackers on TV. My son said that he recognized one of
> the men. Tamer Al-Khamis was a teacher at his school!
> This is the kind of man who was teaching my children.
> How can a mother send her children to school, knowing
> that they might fall prey to a terrorist teacher?

The crisis in the educational system in the Arab world cannot be separated from the struggle of ideas in the Muslim world and the political regimes in each country. This cultural war is being fought in the classrooms of the region between modernizers who seek constructive engagement with the world and advocate teaching critical thinking and religious zealots who adhere to a strict and extremist interpretation of Islam.

Among the modernizing forces are secular public educational institutions in Arab countries, such as the American Universities of Beirut and Cairo, which have produced leaders in various professions throughout the Arab world. At the bold new Education City in Qatar, branches of world-renowned universities offer courses in science and engineering, international affairs, and medicine. The Qatar Foundation has also established the Qatar faculty of Islamic Studies. Al Azhar University in Cairo, the leading Islamist institution of higher education, has much influence in the Sunni world as the voice of Islam, although Saudi-financed Salafist institutions have challenged its influence in recent years. Al Azhar could help spread the message of moderate Islam and oppose extremist views. It should focus on training moderate clerics and creating mainstream Muslim clergy for the Sunni world. If local religious leaders and mosques are strong, the extremists can be marginalized.

On the extremist side are the madrassas, such as those in Pakistan that have been incubators of Muslim radicals and Wahhabi influence, spawning waves of young people inculcated with anti-Western sentiments. Adding to the difficulty of reform is the influence in the Arab world of the Egyptian and Saudi models of education and curricula, which in many instances have reflected strong tendencies in the past toward strident Arab nationalism or radical interpretations of Islam.

Furthermore, as the 2003 United Nations Development Programme report on education in the Arab world pointed out, a significant number of Saudi students study religion and literature; too few study science and engineering, economics, or other disciplines that can make them eligible for the job market and equip them to assume the obligations of citizenship in their country. These educational systems cry out for curriculum reform, a challenge that is not only technical but cultural, because of the influence of radical ideology. Education reform remains integral to political and economic reforms, as well as to other aspects of the larger societal crisis.

A DIFFERENTIATED DIALOGUE

Obviously, there are no guarantees that dialogue will actually further the attainment of greater understanding and resolution of differences, and we cannot assume that the motives of those with whom we are able to establish dialogue will always be beneficent.

Two personal examples come to mind. In the early 1990s, while I was assistant secretary of state for Near Eastern Affairs, I had a conversation with Hassan Al-Turabi, a prominent Sudanese political figure. Early in his political career he joined the Islamic Charter Front (ICF), the Sudanese branch of the Muslim Brotherhood, and became the secretary general. Dressed in a three-piece suit, Turabi in my Washington office appeared to be no different from many affluent, sophisticated Middle Eastern businessmen I had known in Beirut and Damascus. As we talked, he displayed wide knowledge and deep understanding of a range of issues common to Middle Eastern states and their relationship to the United States and the West—no surprise, given that he holds a doctorate from the Sorbonne and speaks fluent French and English. After all, he had talked of healing the breach between the Sunni and the Shia, and of expanding the rights of women, and had spoken positively of at least some form of Islamist democracy. He was also, however, the same man who founded the Popular Arab and Islamic Congress (PAIC) and, appearing in his traditional Arab headdress and robes, hosted militant Islamist leaders from around the world.

Similarly, after my Meridian House Speech, I received a long letter from Rachid Ghannouchi, an outspoken Tunisian Islamist who fled to London in 1989 to escape a sentence of life imprisonment as an enemy of the Tunisian regime. In his communication with me, Ghannouchi expressed his pleasure that the United States was signaling that it did not regard Islam itself as an enemy. He wrote as follows:

> Muslims harbor no ill feelings for you or for your superpower status, but we want our freedom in our own countries; we want our right to choose the system we feel comfortable with. We want the relationship between you and us to be based on friendship, and not subordination. We see a potential for an exchange of ideas, for a flow of information and for cultural ex-

change in an era governed by the rules of competition
and cooperation rather than the rules of hegemony and
subordination. We call on you to halt your aggression
against our people and against our religion. We invite
you to a historic reconciliation, to rapprochement and
to cooperation.

I was fully aware that Ghannouchi hoped I might help him
obtain a visa to enter the United States, which we in the State
Department had repeatedly denied, but his statements reflected
what the United States should want to hear from a dedicated
Islamist if there were reason to believe his assertions were genuine. But, like Turabi, whom he greatly admires, Ghannouchi has
often shown another side. Though a Sunni, he supported the
Iranian Islamic Revolution led by Ayatollah Ruhollah Khomeini
and echoed Khomeini's designation of the United States as the
"Great Satan" and the first Bush administration as "the greatest
danger to civilization, religion, and world peace."

At the time of Desert Storm, the 1991 Gulf War occasioned
by Saddam Hussein's invasion of Kuwait, Ghannouchi sided fervently with Saddam, declaring in a speech that "we must wage
unceasing war against the Americans until they leave the land
of Islam, or we will burn and destroy all their interests across the
entire Islamic world. . . . Muslim youth must be serious in their
warning to the Americans that a blow to Iraq will be a license
to strike American and Western interests throughout the Islamic
world." Subsequently, he has been an ardent supporter of Hamas
and has spoken out against the Arab-Israeli peace process, con-
demning any nation that "extends a hand to the Zionist enemy"
and urging Palestinians not to accept any compromise.

It is possible that Ghannouchi and Turabi, and others like
them, are simply double-tongued deceivers, telling Americans
what they want to hear but venting their true, anti-American
feelings to their real constituency. It is also possible, however,
that, since they know the appropriate responses to their own ar-

guments, they may genuinely have been seeking opportunities to engage. Whatever their motives, objective engagement and dialogue could at a minimum test their true intentions.

The growing influence of Islamist parties in the Arab world, as evidenced by their electoral successes in Jordan, Egypt, Morocco, Palestine, Yemen, Kuwait, and Algeria, argues for the differentiated approach I recommended earlier toward these parties and movements. Accordingly, the United States should engage and open a dialogue with certain Islamist organizations and parties to learn firsthand who they are and what they profess; to differentiate between those that resort to violence and advocate extremist ideologies and those that do not; and to determine what common ground there may be between us. Such a dialogue should focus on the position of these groups on such matters as the Sharia as only one or the one and only source of law, on women's rights and human rights generally, on the alternation of power in an electoral system, on the rights of political and religious minorities, on the resort to violence and interpretations of jihad, and on Arab-Israeli peace and conflict resolution.

The purpose should be not merely to "improve America's image" in the Muslim world, but, by engaging with relevant parties and organizations in the Muslim countries, to promote our national interests and foreign policy goals. At the same time, we must recognize that our influence in the evolution of these Islamist groups and movements will necessarily be limited. We can help shape the outcome, but we cannot determine it. The renewal of Muslim society must come from within if there is to be a meaningful accommodation with other cultures and societies. In this respect the Qur'an (13:11) states: "Verily, Allah does not change the condition of a people until they change what is in themselves."

While pursuing dialogue with selected Islamist groups, we must, at the same time, be vigilant in countering the radicals and extremists with all the instruments we have in our domestic and foreign policy and our national security organizations. Our diplomatic, intelligence, and security services must coordinate closely with one another in combating Islamic radicals and extremism both at home and abroad. We must be clear-eyed in seeing that Islamic radical groups have declared a holy war against their enemies and have made clear who those enemies are. As Osama Bin Laden and his associate, Dr. Ayman Al-Zawahiri, have reiterated in many statements, the "near enemy" is the impious regimes in the Arab and Muslim world, which do not conform with their concept of a totalitarian Islamic state, and the "far enemy" is the United States, European countries, and Israel.

Still, the United States must distance itself from the hubris of trying to solve the democracy, economic, educational, and human rights deficits in the broader Middle East by outside intervention and military action. This is not a productive way to facilitate political, economic, and social reforms and change in the region or to counter the threat of Islamic extremism. Instead, it plays into the hands of the Islamic radicals and extremists. Marginalizing the Islamic extremists and radicals by strengthening the position of the forces of moderation throughout the region by the deft use of "soft and hard power" is a key objective. Change in the Islamic world will have to come from within, but we can help influence the direction of that change by informed policies that will serve our national interests and avoid a so-called "clash of civilizations."

It is difficult to measure success in such a long-term struggle — and a struggle is what it is, not a war in the classic sense of the term. Ironically, Secretary of Defense Donald Rumsfeld, one of the major proponents of the wars in Iraq and on terror, gave a realistic metric with which to measure success or failure: "Are we capturing, killing, or deterring and dissuading more terrorists every day than the madrassas and the radical clerics are recruiting, training, and deploying against us?"

That question still hangs ominously in the air.

THREE

BEIRUT

I first saw Beirut in 1965, through the window of an airplane landing in the thick of the night. For a young American diplomat on his first foreign assignment, the glittering array of lights, sharply edged by the darkness of the Eastern Mediterranean, was captivating.

Beirut at the time was a thriving metropolis, a multireligious society of Christians, Muslims, and Jews at the crossroads of the Middle East. Virtually every political current in the Arab world was present, and the city bustled with financial, intellectual, and cultural activity. East melded with West, and multilingual conversations flowed without pause. Mosque, church, and synagogue coexisted, in mutual respect for all "People of the Book." A wide spectrum of political factions and parties from left to right advocated their causes inside and outside the Lebanese Parliament.

Beirut in the 1960s was also an important listening post and center for spies in the Middle East, a microcosm of inter-Arab politics, the Arab-Israeli conflict, and Cold War rivalries. The image of Beirut and Lebanon in those last of its best years was that of a tolerant country, at ease with different cultures and religions.

The Department of State sent me to Beirut, first to study Arabic and later to take up an assignment in the political section at the American Embassy. After a year at the Foreign Service Institute Arabic Language School, I became a third secretary in the political section of the Embassy. My duties included serving as the ambassador's interpreter and acting as the Embassy's primary contact with the many Muslim, nationalist, pan-Arabist, and leftist groups in Lebanon's changing political landscape.

It was an exhilarating time for a young American diplomat—interpreting for the ambassador with the leaders of the country, contacting radical Arab political parties and groups as well as religious leaders, and socializing at night in Beirut's sensational "political salons" and nightclubs. One of my early impressions of the contrasts of life in Lebanon was my first visit to the Casino du Liban—a luxurious gambling and entertainment spot in Jounieh on the Mediterranean coast north of Beirut. I would walk into the game room of the casino to witness a dazzling array of stunning beauties cajoling comfortably seated sheikhs from the Gulf, resplendent in their traditional robes and headdresses, trying their luck at playing roulette while the less daring would be engaged in a serious bridge game with actor Omar Sharif, whose tailor fitted me impeccably for my first tuxedo, which after all these years I recently had to replace, with feelings of nostalgia. Meanwhile, a major floor show from the Lido de Paris was featured in another hall. I soon realized how sharp the contrast was between these vivid scenes and the complex and dangerous situation we were then dealing with in Lebanon and the region as a whole.

One of Lebanon's distinctive features was the "confessional" system of government established in the National Pact of 1943, whereby Lebanon's largely Christian, Muslim, and Druze communities were apportioned their respective quota of seats in Parliament based on the 1932 census whereby the ratio of six Christians to five Muslims, including Druze, remained in place for decades. (The Druze, a Middle Eastern sect, has roots in Islam but incorporates religious and philosophical tenets from other movements and sources.) Given the implications of possible reapportioning of political power, Lebanon has not conducted a comprehensive census since 1932. The Ta'if Accords, which ended the Lebanese civil war in 1989, revised the National Pact ratio for Christian and Muslim sects in Parliament and the cabinet from 6-5 to 50-50.

According to this religion-based apportionment of positions, the president of the republic is a Maronite Christian, the prime minister a Sunni Muslim, the Speaker of the Parliament a Shia Muslim, and so on. The political bargain struck in the National Pact reflected a compromise between the Christians who did not want to be engulfed by a larger Arab Muslim entity (Greater Syria) and the Muslims who did not want Lebanon to be under the influence of the Western (Christian) powers.

BEIRUT SHATTERED

While Lebanon at the time was considered a model of multiconfessional coexistence that, on the surface, seemed to work well, I rapidly grew to appreciate the fragility of the situation. My feeling was that if one scratched the surface, one would find lurking below feudal and sectarian demons ready to emerge and cause great harm. The country was on the edge of turmoil, with demographic growth that favored the Muslim population, shifting political alignments, external intervention by Syria and Israel, and prolonged conflict just over the horizon.

Tragically, the beguiling image of Beirut was soon shattered, as Lebanon became the victim of regional forces and its own internal political and confessional factions. The 1967 Arab-Israeli Six-Day War, in which Israel stunningly defeated the forces of the Arab countries arrayed against it, seizing control of all of Jerusalem, the West Bank, Gaza, and the Sinai Peninsula to the south, and the Golan Heights to the north, was a devastating blow to all Arabs everywhere and heightened anger toward the United States, Israel's key ally and supporter.

In December 1968, I stood looking from hills outside Beirut at the Beirut International Airport in the distance, as streams of smoke rose into the air from fourteen Lebanese civilian aircraft destroyed on the tarmac in an Israeli airborne commando operation launched in retaliation for an attack by the radical Popular Front for the Liberation of Palestine (PFLP) on an El Al airplane at Athens airport. A member of the PFLP was from Lebanon and a statement claiming responsibility for the incident had been issued in Beirut. So Israel had struck back.

I was with two young Lebanese Jewish friends on this occasion. As we gazed at the smoke from the burning planes below, they turned to me and asked what they should do. I hesitated, then said, "I think much will change now. It would be wise for you and your families to leave Lebanon. It can get ugly." They were of the same mind, but sad to have to uproot themselves from what they considered their country.

In the aftermath of Black September, a failed 1970 uprising against King Hussein of Jordan, highlighted by the hijacking and dramatic televised destruction of several airliners by Palestinian terrorists, thousands of Palestinians flooded into Lebanon from Jordan. The country subsequently became a major base for the Palestine Liberation Organization, prompting Israel to invade the country in 1982 to drive the PLO out, leaving much of Beirut in ruins. And beginning in 1975, the country was torn for nearly fifteen years by civil war among its various religious and secular factions.

In 1976, the Maronite Christian president Sulayman Franji-yah, greatly concerned that the Muslim factions would overrun the Christian forces, appealed to Syrian president Hafez al-Asad to intervene and send Syrian military forces into Lebanon to help stabilize the situation. Asad was only too happy to oblige, thereby consolidating Syria's grip on Lebanese affairs. By 1989, when the internal fighting finally ended with the signing of the Ta'if Accords in Saudi Arabia, countless lives had been sacrificed, Beirut's image had been destroyed, the Lebanese system had crumbled, and a new word had entered the political lexicon as intrastate conflicts elsewhere in the world came to be described as "Lebanonization."

MEETING IMAM MUSA AL SADR

In 1966, I had an important meeting with a remarkable Muslim leader who opened the door to my and Washington's understanding of the plight of the Shiites who would play an increasingly important political role in Lebanon and the region as a whole, as seen in Iran's revolution in 1979, the emergence of Hezbollah, and Iran's aggrandized position in the Middle East following the Iraq War in 2003.

Although I had studied Islam at Georgetown University and felt I had a good understanding of its history and key beliefs, my assignment to Beirut provided me with my first actual experience of the importance of the division between Sunni and Shia, the major "denominations" of Islam.

As explained in the previous chapter, the distinction between them arose in the quarrel over who should succeed the Prophet Muhammad after his death in 632 C.E. The Shia ("party" or "faction") of Ali, Muhammad's son-in-law and father of the Prophet's only male descendants, felt that leadership of the Muslim community should perpetuate through that line. The Sunni, who see themselves as following the true *sunna*—the words, actions, and example of the Prophet Muhammad—disagreed. Since the showdown battle between the two sides at Karbala in 680 C.E., at which the Shia imam, Muhammad's grandson Husayn, was killed, the Sunni faction has dominated, comprising more than 80 percent of Muslims worldwide. With the exception of a few countries such as Iran and Yemen, where they are strong both numerically and politically, the Shia often suffered discrimination by Sunni majorities and, as dominated peoples will, felt a deep-seated sense of grievance. Such was the case in Lebanon.

Concentrated mainly in the Bekaa Valley and around the city of Tyre, in the southern part of Lebanon, many of the Shia were poorly educated farmers, living in areas without schools, health care, decent roads, or other basic amenities. Those who moved to Beirut often wound up living in slums; many of the more able and ambitious left the country. By the 1950s, as Lebanon grew more prosperous, the Shia, as well as other marginalized groups, grew more restive. Some joined Marxist or other leftist secular political groups; others were attracted to pan-Arabist movements.

The most intriguing Shia figure to emerge in this unstable atmosphere was a cleric named Musa al Sadr. Though he was born and educated in Iran, Sadr's ancestors had once lived in Lebanon, so he was not actually an interloper, although questions about his reasons for moving back to his ancestral home never quite went away. In any case, after arriving in Tyre in 1959, he quickly established himself as the leader of Lebanon's Shia community, a figure who had to be taken seriously by the government in Beirut. His family's claim of descent from the Prophet Muhammad no doubt added to his appeal among the Shia.

With modest cooperation from the government of General Fouad Shihab, who had become president in the aftermath of a 1958 civil war, Sadr was able to obtain a few benefits for his people, such as a vocational training school in Tyre, built with funds from the government and Shia businessmen. But he wanted more—not only for the Shia, but also to help create a more stable country, difficult when a sizable segment of its population lived in conditions of deprivation. In Lebanon's multicultural political economy, major groups such as the Maronite Christians, the Sunni Muslims, and the Druze were represented by organizations, similar to political parties, that promoted their interests.

Seeing that the Shia had no such body, Musa al Sadr led in the formation of the Higher Shia Council and, in 1969, was named its leader for life.

It was during the early stages of Sadr's campaign to bring the Higher Shia Council into existence that I became aware of his growing influence—and also of the fact that some members of the political and religious establishment did not know quite what to think about this charismatic figure who was encouraging his Shia followers to demand a greater role in their country's affairs. I decided that I had to meet him, to learn firsthand about the situation of Lebanon's Shiite community. Most of the Embassy's contacts were with the established political, sectarian, and economic elite of the country: the Christian, Sunni, and Druze establishment. Neither we nor Washington had much information about the political, economic, and social conditions of the Lebanese Shiite population, and it was apparent that it was becoming increasingly important.

I made some discreet queries in the Shia community, asking for an audience with Musa al Sadr, which would be the Embassy's first official contact with him. After several weeks of waiting, I received a telephone call from one of Sadr's aides, who told me the imam would see me, but that I would have to come in my personal car and without any escort. I was instructed to go to the ancient city of Tyre, to a high school where there was an empty soccer field. I would find a stone bench underneath a tree and I was to wait there until the imam appeared. I was delighted with this news, but I knew that if I asked my superiors in the Embassy for permission, they might consider it too risky and ask me to cancel the meeting for security reasons. I decided to proceed on my own.

On the appointed day and hour in October 1966, I drove from Beirut to Tyre in my Peugeot 404 and arrived at the designated place. I waited for over an hour and a half and began to think that I had been set up. Finally a black Mercedes sedan came down the dusty driveway to the soccer field. Two bodyguards got out and opened the rear door and a tall, powerful-looking figure with piercing eyes and a full black beard, wearing a black turban and flowing robes, emerged. I must admit that I was intimidated as I walked toward him to greet him in Arabic. He reciprocated warmly and, after exchanging brief pleasantries, we began our first discussion, which lasted almost three hours. The conversation was wide-ranging, touching on the plight of the Shiite community in Lebanon, the political situation in Lebanon and the Arab world, and the Arab-Israeli conflict.

I complimented the imam on his efforts to build social and educational institutions in southern Lebanon, such as the vocational training center in Tyre, which I had visited during an earlier visit to southern Lebanon, and told him I had found it quite impressive. I inquired whether efforts to establish light industry could be helpful to his people. He thought not, indicating that increased mechanization of agriculture held more promise. Families were being separated and broken because of the poor conditions of the countryside and young people were being forced to leave for the urban areas and for Africa. The social problems that resulted were daunting. For example, serious health problems among the population could be prevented by timely medical attention, but the villages and towns of the south were without medical facilities.

Sadr then spoke of a major concern that had great significance for the future of Lebanon and, indeed, for the region as a whole. He stressed that, from his perspective, the most dangerous element in the Lebanese situation was the psychological outlook of the Shiite community itself. After so many years of neglect by the government, the south had become a depressed area not only materially but also psychologically. As a religious leader of his community, Sadr said he felt obligated to restore the spiritual values of his people and to give them a sense of self-respect. He stressed that the psychological element was probably the most depressing consequence of the poor economic and social conditions that prevailed in the south.

In articulating these themes of dispossession, denial of equal opportunity, and humiliation, Musa al Sadr ably captured the daily struggle of his followers, not usually addressed in the traditional lexicon of Lebanese politics, which centered on confessional, local, and regional Arab issues. As a charismatic religious leader, Sadr promoted an activist political agenda. As he has been quoted as saying of himself, "I took the man of religion, *rajul al din*, into the social realm . . . I removed him from the dust of the ages."

BLACK TURBAN AND WHITE TURBAN

Despite his efforts to use political means to improve the lot of his religious community, Musa al Sadr was no sectarian radical, bent on the destruction or subordination of those who did not share his religious convictions. To the contrary, he repeatedly sought to tear down barriers that divided his country and the Arab world.

In an insightful account of Sadr's life and political significance, Johns Hopkins professor Fouad Ajami tells of several steps Sadr took to underscore his conviction that "all men were brothers, whatever their doctrinal differences." When speaking to Muslim clerics, he said there was no difference between the black turban of the Shia and the white turban of the Sunnis.

One Friday, after preaching in Tyre's main mosque, Sadr announced that he was going for a walk after the service, essentially inviting the congregation to join him. Then, with a sizable crowd in train, he made his way to an ice cream stand that most Shia had avoided because it was owned by a Christian, which in their minds made any food he handled impure. In an act reminiscent of Jesus's attitude toward arbitrary social boundaries, Imam Musa asked the owner, "What sort of ice cream are you giving us today?" Christians, he said by his actions, are neither impure nor to be shunned.

TYRANTS IN THE NAME OF RELIGION

In a more pointed example recalled by Professor Ajami, Musa al Sadr spoke at a Catholic church during Lent in 1975, at a time when sectarian tensions and violence were threatening once again to erupt into civil war. His remarks on religion and politics reveal not only his ecumenical spirit, but also acute awareness of the tendency for religious leaders, if they are able to gain political power, to commit the same abuses of power that they had condemned in secular leaders.

"Oh, our God," he began, "the God of Moses and Jesus and Muhammad, the God of the weak and of all creatures, we thank you for sheltering us, for uniting our hearts with your love and mercy. We are assembled today in a house of yours, at a time of fasting . . . Our hearts yearn for you; our minds derive light and guidance from you . . . We've come to your door, we have gathered together to serve man. It is man that all religions aspire to serve. All religions were once united; they anticipated one another; they validated one another. They called man to God and they served man. Then the different religions diverged when each sought to serve itself, to pay excess of attention to itself to the point that each religion forgot the original purpose—the service of man. Then discord and strife were born, and the crisis of man deepened.

"Religions," he continued, "sought to liberate men from 'the lords of the earth and the tyrants,' to provide sustenance to the weak and the oppressed. But when the religious orders triumphed, the weak found that the tyrants had changed their garb, that they now wielded power in the name of religion, brandishing its sword."

This was and still is a significant statement, not only in the context of the imminent and bloody civil war Lebanon would endure, but in the larger context of the contemporary Middle East and the Muslim world. The events of 9/11 brought that struggle to the American homeland and it continues to manifest itself in many regions of the world. The outcome of that struggle within Islam will have major implications not only for the Middle East and the Muslim countries, but also for the United States and the international community as a whole.

Unfortunately, Musa al Sadr was denied the opportunity to pursue his goal of a united Lebanon in which religious leaders would promote "the service of man" over narrow sectarian interests. In 1978, while on a trip to Libya, Sadr mysteriously disappeared. Though his body was never found—causing some of his Shia followers to believe he is still alive and will one day return—it appears certain that he was abducted and assassinated, most likely by the Libyans, because his political activities posed a threat to established factions and leaders, both religious and secular, in Lebanon and other parts of the Arab world.

HEZBOLLAH AND THE ROAD TO TERRORISM

Given the Shia conviction that its leaders—Muhammad's legitimate successors—would always be the target of unrighteous opposition, Musa al Sadr joined the line of martyred heroes who have inspired their followers to fight and die in the struggle for their God-ordained cause. But given the turmoil of the times, they did not maintain his commitment to peaceful ecumenism and coordinated efforts on behalf of the whole. Instead, they turned in a more sectarian direction, culminating in the founding, in 1982, of Hezbollah ("Party of God"), a militant organization that aspired to transform Lebanon into an Islamic state modeled after Iran under the revolutionary government led by Ayatollah Ruhollah Khomeini.

From its beginnings, Hezbollah has engaged in armed jihad and resistance and acts of terrorism to achieve its goals. The party's spiritual guide since the mid-1980s, Muhammad Hussein Fadlallah, has said that "the pious strong man is more meritorious in God's eyes than the pious weak man," noting that Muhammad was both a ruler (caliph) and religious guide (imam). Contending, in keeping with Islam and most religions, that "it is legitimate to defend self and land and destiny," he said that "one must face force with equal or superior force" and that "all means of self-defense are legitimate." Although Fadlallah included suicide bombing among these legitimate means, it is worth noting that he immediately condemned both the attacks of 9/11 and the March 2004 Madrid train bombings.

Far from the Imam Musa al Sadr's vision in the 1960s and 1970s, the Shiite militancy and radicalism that emerged in those following tumultuous years in Lebanon and the region, including the devastating terrorist suicide attacks against the United States Embassy and Marine barracks in 1983, were a manifestation of increasing radicalization in the broader Middle East. After the Israeli invasion of Lebanon in 1982, Hezbollah emerged as one of the most powerful paramilitary forces in the region. Many militants in the Middle East who oppose a negotiated settlement with Israel have taken up its call for "resistance" against Israeli occupation.

It is no accident that when the Israel Defense Forces finally withdrew from Lebanon in 2000, Hezbollah's secretary general, Sheikh Hassan Nasrallah, made a public appeal to Yasir Arafat not to enter peace talks with Israel, claiming that the path of resistance, not negotiations, was the only successful one, as evidenced by Israel's withdrawal from Lebanon and Hezbollah's role in that outcome. Further, by actions that precipitated the Israeli-Lebanese conflict in summer 2006, Hezbollah demonstrated that it is a force to contend with in any settlement involving Lebanon and Israel.

AN AMERICAN COMMITMENT

My early assignment to Lebanon ended in 1969. Many years later, as assistant secretary of state for Near Eastern Affairs, I accompanied President Clinton to his first meeting with Lebanese prime minister Rafik Hariri in New York City during the Special Session of the United Nations General Assembly in September 1993. After I had briefed the president on the range of issues we had with Lebanon, he asked me what was the most important message he should deliver during the meeting. I had known Hariri since my years of service in Damascus as U.S. ambassador to Syria (1988–91) and had established a close working and personal relationship with him over time. He was dedicated to Lebanon's independence and to getting Lebanon out of the morass of its brutal and tragic civil war from 1975 to 1990. Hariri, a self-made billionaire, became the engine for Lebanon's economic recovery and provided hope for the future. He also knew that for Lebanon to be truly independent, Syrian influence over its political and economic life had to be substantially alleviated. A comprehensive Arab-Israeli peace settlement could do much in this respect.

It was in this context that I suggested to President Clinton that the main message to deliver was that, under his administration, United States policy would remain fully committed to Lebanon's political independence, sovereignty, and territorial integrity. Further, nothing the United States would do as the interlocutor between Israel and Syria in peace negotiations would contravene this policy. Namely, we would not help strike a deal between Israel and Syria at Lebanon's expense. Hariri was clearly bolstered by the president's assurances.

RETURN TO BEIRUT

With the signing of the Ta'if Accords in 1989 in Saudi Arabia, which ended the civil war, Lebanon was able to start the long and painful process of trying to heal its wounds. I have had occasion to visit the country several times since the end of my tour there, both in an official and in a personal capacity. In 1993, I flew over Ras Beirut in a helicopter as I accompanied Secretary of

State Warren Christopher on our way to the presidential palace in Ba'abda. What I saw was devastating—the destruction of the inner city, the bombed-out shells of buildings, the dark, gaping holes of what I had remembered as a glittering city full of life.

In February 2000, when I was no longer in government, I landed once again at Beirut International Airport and, after dismissing my bodyguards, walked alone in the streets of Beirut as in the old days. I revisited Ain Mreiseh on the corniche where I had an apartment in the 1960s. The building was still there, pockmarked by shells but not destroyed. I remembered the mass demonstrations in the street below during the 1967 Arab-Israeli war when President Nasser of Egypt brought crowds out into the streets all over the Arab world by falsely accusing the United States of responsibility for the swift and devastating destruction of Egypt's air force. Since the nearby United States Embassy was the target of the demonstrators, the decision was made that key embassy personnel would temporarily relocate off site with our communication equipment. The deputy chief of mission (DCM) and the political counselor established temporary quarters in my apartment. Among the essentials they brought along was the DCM's silver martini shaker, after he ascertained that I had a sufficient emergency supply of gin in my flat.

Now those were the days of the traditional Foreign Service!

The beautiful, old Arab villas, the American University of Beirut, the St. George Hotel, Hamra and Bliss Street all reminded me of a happier past. I went into a pharmacy in West Beirut, the Muslim quarter, to buy sundries. The shopkeeper looked at me and asked his son to get the items I asked for. He stared at me for a moment and said in Arabic, "I know who you are." I thought to myself that I should have kept those bodyguards with me. He said in a very somber tone, "You are American ambassador Demerjian [*sic*]. We have seen you on the television and in the newspapers. What are you in Lebanon for?"

Given the latest eruption of anti-American sentiment in the country, especially among the Muslims, I thought I should make a quick move to the door and not become another hostage. But before I could devise an "exit strategy," he stretched his hand over the counter to shake mine and said, "We need you. We need America to help us stop the bloodshed and fighting. Help us to make peace. It is the only way out of this endless violence." It was yet another poignant reminder of the perception of America's influential role in the region. All I felt I could do was to reassure him that America would remain engaged in the difficult pursuit of Middle East peace.

A LETTER FROM THE PRIME MINISTER

When I walked to the restored Parliament building, the Grand Serail, and other major sites nearby, I was impressed and encouraged by the vast reconstruction of the center of the city—the Solidere Project—which Lebanese prime minister Rafik Hariri had initiated. It gave me hope that Beirut, indeed, all of Lebanon, would not only rebuild materially but would also rediscover its unique identity. After I returned to the United States I wrote a short essay about my trip for *Insight* magazine, expressing my guarded optimism about the country's future. Not long after the article appeared, I received the following letter from Prime Minister Hariri:

> I read your article in *Insight* magazine with great pleasure and thoroughly enjoyed your reminiscences about Beirut and its golden days with its "glittering lights" on the "shores of the Mediterranean." It is this vision of Beirut that drives us to do all we can to recreate and improve this city that you describe. As you know, the image of Lebanon and Beirut suffered during the awful war years and it is a good sign that the wider perception of Lebanon is changing to be more positive, a change of impression helped by articles like yours.

We have tried to realize this dream for our people through reconstructing the heart of Beirut, a point you yourself make in the article. This wasn't an easy task, not because of the difficulty of the job, but the difficulty of convincing others that their dream is our vision of Beirut. The heart of Beirut is beginning to beat again, with the pulse of the hundreds and thousands of Lebanese who visit it every day. This pulse quickens at night, with people going there to listen to music, sample food or relax with a *narjilah* [water pipe] in the dozens of new cafés. I visit my favorite café a couple of nights a week across the street from the Parliament with friends and journalists. There we rediscover the heart of our city and create new memories to fill our own hearts and wipe away the memories of war.

Thank you for your kind words about Beirut and its rebuilding. I am looking forward to seeing you again in Lebanon, maybe have a cup of coffee in downtown Beirut, in my favorite café?

I was never able to take up my friend on his warm offer. Rafik Hariri was brutally assassinated in February 2005 in Beirut. Tragically, the very forces that worked against Lebanon's independence put an end to his life, but not to the cause of Lebanon's independence as a multiconfessional and democratic nation. His son, Saad Hariri, took up his father's political mantle.

After the general elections in 2005, the political confrontation that erupted between the parliamentary majority, represented by Prime Minister Fouad Siniora's government, and the opposition, led by former general Michel Aoun and Hezbollah, coupled with a string of additional political assassinations, led to a dangerous stalemate that paralyzed political life in Lebanon. The dangerous situation continued throughout 2007, and the opposing factions continued to struggle to try to reach agreement on the election of a new president, formation of a national unity government, and reform of the electoral law for the 2009 elections. Finally and under the effective auspices of the government of Qatar, a concensus was reached in May 2008, and Michel Sleiman, the former commander of the Lebanese Armed Forces, was elected president. The immediate crisis was defused, but serious strains remain within Lebanon's body politic. Nevertheless, the Lebanese were able once again to strike their traditional "*Ni vainqueurs, ni vaincus*" ("neither winners nor losers") compromise with the hope of living up to their history as a multiconfessional crossroads in the Middle East—one that they and, with them, the international community, must not abandon.

In the last analysis and more than any single factor, a comprehensive Arab-Israeli peace settlement would remove many of the negative forces at play both inside and outside Lebanon that have used that country as a venue for proxy wars and conflicts.

FOUR

DAMASCUS

I felt a chill in the air that morning in October 1988, when I left the Embassy residence in Damascus. As the new American ambassador to Syria, I was on my way to present my letter of credence from President Ronald Reagan to Syria's President Hafez al-Asad, formally identifying me as the accredited, official diplomat representing President Reagan and the United States to President Asad and Syria. (A letter of credence is a formal letter sent by one head of state to another head of state, formally requesting acceptance of the diplomatic accreditation of an ambassador.)

A Syrian military aide, in the full dress uniform of the Presidential Guard, escorted me to the awaiting bulletproof limousine, with American and Syrian flags flying on the front bumpers in deceptive harmony. The Embassy conducted its business largely through the chef de cabinet of the Syrian foreign minister, and access even at that level was quite limited. High-level visits by Secretary of State George Shultz, Assistant Secretary of State for Near Eastern Affairs Richard Murphy, and a small number of

members of Congress were important, but provided only intermittent access to the Syrian leadership.

The dialogue between the two countries had dwindled to a
form of stasis that served neither side's interests. Memories of
the USS *New Jersey*'s lobbing massive shells onto Syrian gun
and surface-to-air missile sites in the Lebanese mountains in
1983—in retaliation for the targeting of unarmed U.S. recon-
naissance planes—had not faded. The May 17, 1983, agreement between Israel and Lebanon, following Israel's invasion
of Lebanon in 1982, was stillborn and totally undercut by Asad,
since he saw it as a direct threat to Syria's political and security
interests.

Overall, the political context was not promising: Next door, to
the west, a bloody civil war had torn Lebanon apart. To the east,
the Iran-Iraq War continued to take its horrendous toll. And in
the south, attempts to revivify Arab-Israeli peace talks were going nowhere. Furthermore, the serious issue of terrorism marred
United States–Syrian relations, especially in the aftermath of the
attempted bombing of an El Al flight from London to Tel Aviv
in 1986, a plot in which the Syrian government was directly implicated.

Both the letter I was carrying from President Reagan to President Asad and Secretary of State George Shultz's instructions
to me stated my mission succinctly. My major task was to pave
the way for a sustained and effective high-level dialogue between
the two countries, so that United States interests in the Middle
East could move forward. Without Syria, we could not help end
the tragic civil war in Lebanon, move the Arab-Israeli peace process forward in a comprehensive manner, curtail certain terrorist
groups, control drug trafficking, promote regional security, and
advance our human rights agenda. Secretary Shultz said I must
look for common ground and try to build on it, but I must never
forget my primary role, which was to represent my country—and
by telling me the story of new ambassadors and his big globe, he
had made sure I wouldn't forget which country that was. This

was especially important in an assignment to Syria, where our relationship was both adversarial and controversial.

THE SPHINX OF DAMASCUS

After my first overseas diplomatic assignment in Beirut, in the mid-1960s, Hafez al-Asad had emerged as a major player in Syria and the region. I knew that, as the new American ambassador, my first meeting with him would be critical to the success or failure of my mission. After my Senate confirmation hearings in Washington earlier in 1988, I thought long and hard about how I would handle this initial encounter. I read all the limited in-formation on Asad that I could get my hands on and talked with colleagues and others who had dealt with him or knew much about him.

Asad was only nine years older than I. He was born in 1930 in the village of Qurdaha in the northwest of Syria. His fam-ily belonged to the heterodox Shiite Muslim sect known as the Alawites. The "crucial turning point" of his life, he once told the British biographer Patrick Seale, was when, at age nine, as a mountain boy from a minority Muslim community, he had come down to the coastal city of Latakia to attend school. It was the beginning of his formal education and his first step on the long path to Damascus and the presidency.

At the time of my assignment, Asad had already been ruling Syria with an iron hand for eighteen years since 1970, when he had come to power in a bloodless coup that overthrew the more leftist, socialist faction of the dominant Syrian Baath Party. He became president in 1971. Asad was a career military man and rose rapidly through the ranks of the Syrian Air Force and the Syr-ian Baath Party to become minister of defense, where he played a crucial role in the Arab-Israeli Six-Day War in June 1967. The sudden Arab military defeat on the Egyptian, Jordanian, and Syr-ian fronts came as a traumatic shock. In the space of six short days, he witnessed the destruction of the Syrian Air Force, the Israeli occupation of the Golan Heights and Mount Hermon (giving Israel a dominant position to oversee the whole Damascus plain), and the Israeli destruction of the Druze town of Qunaytra.

Syria regained Qunaytra after the 1973 Yom Kippur War, but Asad deliberately kept it in its pillaged state as a symbol of the unfinished work of war and peace. Over the years, Asad overcame the humiliating setback of 1967, consolidated his grip on power in Syria, and carved out for himself and his country a major strategic role in the Middle East.

Ironically, the most valuable advice I got was from Yitzhak Rabin, who was visiting Washington in 1988 as Israel's minister of defense. I was then the principal deputy assistant secretary of state for Near Eastern and South Asian Affairs, and Secretary of Defense Frank Carlucci invited my wife and me to an official dinner in Rabin's honor. Carlucci introduced me to Rabin and told him I would soon be assuming my new post in Damascus.

Rabin, never known for small talk, looked at me, paused, puffed on his cigarette, and said, "You will be dealing with perhaps the most intelligent ruler in the Arab world. He is beyond a doubt the most difficult Arab leader to negotiate with and you will have to be careful to avoid loopholes in any agreement you may reach with him because he will drive a truck through them. But whatever he agrees to and commits himself to, he will live up to and you can count on it. That has been our experience." Rabin took another puff on his cigarette, gave me a brief smile, shook my hand, and wished me good luck.

The motorcycle escort sped us through the tree-lined streets of Abu Roumana on that October morning, skirting the foot of Jabal Qassioun, the small mountain that overlooks Damascus and is considered sacred by Muslims, who believe Adam may once have lived there and that Abraham learned the doctrine of the unity of God there. Though he did not enter Damascus, Muhammad the Prophet is also said to have visited the mountain. We passed Asad's official residence and offices and proceded toward the Muhajarin Palace (Qasr al-Muhajarin), a small and beautiful example of old Damascene architecture that had later become the residence of the first president of Syria.

The car stopped at the entrance of the old building. I got out, walked a few steps toward the honor guard, then stopped and stood at attention. The officer of the guard, in his colorful uniform, sharply marched toward me in a goose step, reminiscent of the Soviet military. Barely a few feet away from me, he drew his gleaming sword up to his eyes in a short arc, the blade passing only inches from my face, and shouted an honorific welcome in Arabic. I will never forget how close that blade came. He did an about-face and I followed him to review the honor guard. The chief of protocol then escorted me into the building and up to the second story, where President Asad, members of his government, and my Embassy's country team, heads of sections at the Embassy, were present.

I walked toward Asad and, facing him in the center of the reception hall, introduced my colleagues to him. Flanked by his government ministers and aides, Asad smiled. I read my letter from President Reagan and handed it to him. We shook hands and he invited me, along with one of his closest advisors, Minister of State for Foreign Affairs Nasser Qaddur, into an adjoining room for a private discussion that was scheduled to last only twenty minutes according to strict diplomatic protocol. In another room, five other ambassadors were waiting to present their credentials, but our conversation kept them waiting for well over an hour and would be the prelude to many long meetings and negotiations over the next three years.

After a brief exchange of pleasantries over Arabic coffee and sweets, Asad noted my Armenian name and asked me about my family origins. I recounted how, as youngsters, my father and mother had escaped the Turkish massacres during the 1915–18 period, when the Young Turk government was pursuing its genocidal policy against the Armenians, and how they had fled to Syria, where they were given refuge. My mother's father, a police official in the Armenian town of Kharpout, was executed, and her mother succeeded in bringing her and her two sisters to Aleppo, in northern Syria, for a short period, then took them to the coastal town of Jbeil (Byblos) in Lebanon, where there was a Danish orphanage for Armenian young girls. In his upper teens, my father escaped the "Death March" that forced Armenians to travel on foot from their homes in eastern Turkey to the Syrian Desert town of Deir az-Zor, an ordeal during which hundreds of thousands died.

His flight from his family's village of Hadjin in eastern Turkey eventually took him to Aleppo, where there was a large Armenian community. There, he was given refuge by an Arab family and became their stable boy. During this period, he performed a courageous act, rescuing two young Armenian girls who had been taken into the harem of a Turkish notable in Aleppo. Incensed by their captivity and marked by the horrible experiences he had witnessed, he decided to try to save them. He took two horses out of the stable one night and arranged to have the girls escape from the Turk's household, then took them to an Armenian church in the city, where they were given a haven.

Those two girls eventually made their way to the United States, where they had an elder brother in Worcester, Massachusetts. Their brother, who was an American citizen, was later instrumental in sponsoring my father to immigrate to the United States and to become an American citizen himself.

In the meantime, my mother had sailed to Havana, Cuba, to go to school and await the opportunity to go to America. Based on a photo he was shown, my father eventually went to Havana to meet and marry my mother and bring her to the United States to start his own family.

"So you see," I told Asad, "it is because of my father's deeds in Aleppo that my brother and I were born in America. If someone had told that young Armenian boy in Aleppo during those tragic and desperate times that one day he would have a son who would become the American ambassador to Syria, my father would have considered that person to be out of his mind. This is the greatness of the United States of America. I am the son of refugees. We are a country of immigrants and a land of great opportunity. I know that you have engaged with United States presidents, secretaries of state, congressmen, and senators, but it is unfortunate that you have never visited the United States yourself and do not know it firsthand. I love my country and I am privileged to serve as its representative to your country, Syria, which has a rich and ancient history and which has and continues to play an important role in the Middle East today."

Asad was visibly moved by these remarks. Continuing, I informed him that my wife also had family ties to Syria. Françoise's mother was born into an Armenian family in Aleppo and lived there until the age of nineteen, when a young and handsome French military officer stationed in Syria, a French Mandate at the time, stole her heart and they decided to marry. Asad quipped that the Damascenes were going to be jealous of our family's ties with Syria's second-largest city, Aleppo. The mood became relaxed. Asad remarked that the Armenian community in Syria had distinguished itself in the professions and in commerce. Most important, he noted, the Armenians had proven themselves to be good and loyal citizens of Syria—as well, I commented, as of the United States.

I then referred to my formal remarks at the ceremony in the ornate hall, where I had outlined my mandate from President Reagan. I asked Asad if I could speak candidly. He nodded affirmatively. "Mr. President, my government is serious about initiating a high-level dialogue with your government on the key issues I have mentioned. Both of our countries play an important role in the Middle East. The United States had no hidden or secret agenda regarding Syria. Our relations have been difficult and even adversarial. We have serious problems between us. However, where we can find common ground and mutual interests, let us try to build on them. Where we have problems, let us try to resolve them. But let me make it clear that we are not interested in a dialogue simply for the sake of a dialogue. We want to achieve positive results."

At this point, I threw the protocol book out of the window. Knowing full well that it was a roll of the dice that could lead either to an opening of a dialogue or to spending the rest of my assignment to Syria as little more than a pro forma bearer of official messages, I said the following: "Mr. President, for us to initiate such a dialogue, my Embassy and I need to have direct access to you and your ministers and ranking officials. You can easily relegate me to enjoying living in the beautiful ambassadorial residence in Damascus, attending one diplomatic and official reception after another for the next three or so years of my assignment here. I can report to Washington what others tell my staff and me that you are thinking and what your government's policies are. I would prefer not to do it that way, Mr. President. I was not sent to Damascus for that. If we are truly serious about improving our relations, there is another road we can take. We can deal with one another directly and authoritatively. I hope you will agree with this approach."

I stopped at that point and nervously awaited Asad's response, not knowing if I had gone too far. The so-called "Sphinx of Damascus" gazed intently at me with the piercing look that, as I later came to recognize, was so characteristic of him when he pondered an issue before speaking. After an awkward moment of silence, he turned toward Minister of State for Foreign Affairs Nasser Qaddur and said, "I agree with the ambassador. Let us proceed accordingly!" He got up from his chair, we shook hands, and he wished me success in my diplomatic mission.

I thought to myself that now, having both Rabin's and Asad's best wishes, there might be a chance to work for peace.

That work would prove to be quite difficult and frustrating, but this was a beginning, and over the course of the next three years we were able to achieve a structural improvement in United

States–Syrian relations and the positive results we sought on some key issues: the Ta'if Accords, which ended Lebanon's bloody civil war and gave that country the chance to start rebuilding; Syria's joining Desert Storm, the political and military coalition led by the United States against Saddam Hussein after his invasion of Kuwait; Asad's critical decision on direct face-to-face negotiations with Israel, which allowed us to proceed to the Madrid Peace Conference; Syria's key role in the release of American hostages held in Lebanon by Iranian-supported groups; Asad's agreement to give Syrian Jews the same freedom of travel enjoyed by other Syrian citizens; and engagement with the Syrians on the contentious issues of terrorism and human rights. While the road to Damascus was a difficult one, it did prove to lead to certain destinations that I believe served the interests of the United States.

PEACE WITH YOUR ENEMIES

The United States must engage its adversaries. That is the task of diplomacy.

The heart of the Arab-Israeli conflict is the issue of Palestine, but the geopolitical core is the Israeli and Syrian front. Without an Israeli-Syrian agreement, there will be no comprehensive peace between Israel and its Arab neighbors. A Lebanese agreement would quickly follow if there were progress on the Israeli-Syrian track. Therefore, the initiation of peace talks between Israel and Syria should be a high priority for the United States president and secretary of state. Ever since the Madrid Peace Conference of 1991, much progress has been made in the Syrian-Israeli negotiations under both Republican and Democratic administrations on the key issues of land, peace, normalization of relations, security arrangements, and access to water. Both Syrian and Israeli negotiators have told me that they and their predecessors had thoroughly discussed at least 85 percent of the issues and had either resolved or narrowed areas of disagreement. The United States has been the essential interlocutor for the two sides in these negotiations and is the repository of the negotiating history.

It is useful to understand how this role developed. In 1991, President George H. W. Bush and Secretary of State James A. Baker, III had a broader strategy in mind than just reversing Saddam Hussein's invasion of Kuwait and not letting that kind of aggression against another state stand in the immediate aftermath of the end of the Cold War. They knew that the geopolitical landscape in the Middle East had changed with the demise of the Soviet Union and that the anticipated liberation of Kuwait by a broad-based international coalition could facilitate creation of another opportunity to advance the Arab-Israeli peace negotiations. Accordingly, and before the victory of Desert Storm, they began an intensive diplomatic effort to prepare for a breakthrough in the Arab-Israeli status quo.

In Damascus, I was instructed to help prepare the groundwork with President Asad, to get him to begin to move off his intransigent positions vis-à-vis Israel.

FROM "ZIONIST ENTITY" TO ISRAEL

In my first meetings with him, Asad would never refer to Israel as such, calling it instead "the Zionist entity." I soon realized that his knowledge of Israeli society and domestic politics was very limited. He had an elderly and distinguished advisor of Palestinian origin, Assad Elias, who spoke and read Hebrew and who would counsel him on Israeli affairs. Elias's room in the presidential palace was stacked from floor to ceiling with dusty Israeli newspapers and journals. He obviously longed for his former homeland, and his views had been frozen in time, which affected Asad's understanding and outlook.

During my meetings with President Asad, I made a point of discussing Israeli policy and domestic politics whenever possible, to inform him of the dynamics at play in Israel. He would listen carefully, then launch into one of his characteristic long historical monologues, including tracing the history of Israel's population not to biblical Middle Eastern origins but to the ancient Khazar Empire in Eastern Europe, whose inhabitants converted to Judaism in the eighth century C.E., migrated to Poland, and formed the base of Western (Ashkenazi) Jewry. In his historical view and as a pan-Arab nationalist, he opined that the Israelis were largely foreign and Western transplants in the Arab world. He considered them akin to the French and British colonialists who carved up the Middle East between 1916 and 1922 according to the Sykes-Picot Agreement.

Asad's thinking did evolve during the years I was in Damascus, at least on contemporary Israeli politics. He became conversant with the complex coalition politics in Israel and the significance of such factors as the influence of the ultraorthodox Shas Party and its spiritual head, Rabbi Ovedia Youssef. He stopped referring to Israel exclusively as the "Zionist entity" and started calling it by its proper name, but he continued to expound on the role of the "Jewish Lobby" in the United States and its hold on U.S. administrations, reflecting a widespread perception in the Arab world that the American Jewish community exerts major political influence on American foreign policy in the Middle East. During one congressional delegation meeting with Asad, I introduced the delegation and pointed out to him that two private individuals in the delegation were what he would consider part of the "Jewish Lobby." My friends in the delegation were aghast, but I knew Asad had a sense of political humor, and he laughed and said he would be interested in hearing what they had to say. The exchange was candid but cordial, and I felt that another minor psychological barrier was being breached, if only slightly.

THE SYKES-PICOT AGREEMENT

During my three years in Damascus, Asad subjected me to countless narratives about how the Sykes-Picot Agreement was the origin of all the ills of the contemporary Middle East. He would explain that the British and French colonialists drew lines in the sands of the region to stake out their respective territorial mandates. Sykes was the British agent and Picot the French agent who colluded in this master imperialist scheme. The French had an interest in creating "Greater Lebanon" and consolidating a multireligious state, giving the Christian community there a prominent political role among the Sunni and Shiite Muslim communities and the Druze community. This "scheme," according to Asad, was at Syria's expense. He considered Syria and Lebanon one nation, which is why he never moved to permit the opening of a Syrian Embassy in Beirut or a Lebanese Embassy in Damascus. For him, both countries constituted Greater Syria, one Arab nation.

Asad harbored a deep-seated resentment against the French colonialists. He once mentioned how, as a young boy, he had felt angry at seeing French troops in Syrian streets and humiliated by their occupation of his country. He was equally resentful of the British mandate over Palestine and the creation of a Jewish homeland, regarding these as further manifestations of Western imperialism in the heart of the Arab world. As for Iraq and Kuwait, he would comment on how the British drew the borders in the Arab Gulf and note that Iraqis considered Kuwait the nineteenth province of Iraq. In this overall context, Asad delighted in rambling on at length, usually concluding that the conflicts in Lebanon, the tensions between Israel and its Arab neighbors, and Saddam Hussein's invasion of Kuwait could all be traced to Sykes-Picot. Only after these historical narratives were conveyed would we be able to address current issues.

I learned early on that what seemed to be ramblings were more often than not, at least in his mind, poignant political messages, directed especially to Western interlocutors. In one of my first meetings with Asad, he described in detail the representations that Special Middle East Envoy Philip Habib had made to him at the height of the Israeli invasion of Lebanon in 1982.

The Israeli forces led by General Ariel Sharon pushed into Lebanon with the goal of evicting Yasir Arafat and the PLO from that country, where they had created a state within a state. Ambassador Habib had assured Asad that the Israelis had told him they did not intend to attack and enter Beirut. Asad's great concern was that the Israelis would establish a pro-Israeli regime in Beirut and sideline Syria and its interests, which would have been a political and strategic setback for him. When the Israelis proceeded to do just that, Asad fought back. He told me that at various times Israeli aircraft would overfly Damascus to pressure him to stay put, but, he said, his eyes were on the combat situation on the ground in Lebanon, and he knew that the Israelis would not be able to hold their own, especially politically. He did everything possible to sabotage Israeli plans in Lebanon and, for the most part, succeeded.

Israel eventually withdrew from its positions in southern Lebanon in 2000.

The point Asad was making to me at that meeting was, "Don't bring me false messages." He made it clear that, if I did so, he would no longer consider me a valid interlocutor in those circumstances. This was particularly poignant for me personally because what Asad did not know was that Ambassador Habib had my highest respect as one of the best career diplomats we had, was one of my mentors in the Foreign Service, and actually recruited me into the service when I was a young lieutenant in the U.S. Army Counter Intelligence Corps in South Korea in 1961. I told Asad that I thought Habib was accurately informing him of what he was being told by the Israelis and others.

DESERT STORM

In November 1990, the Bush administration was making a major effort to put in place the political and military coalition for Desert Storm, to reverse Saddam Hussein's aggression against Kuwait. President Bush, displaying his understanding of the history of Arab politics and culture, made it clear to his national security team that he did not want to have American troops invading an Arab capital—in this instance, Kuwait City.

Secretary Baker asked me what it would take to convince President Asad to commit Syrian troops to the Coalition forces. I said that we had already made a major breakthrough in getting Asad to make the political decision to join a United States–led Coalition against his rival Saddam Hussein, but to get him to commit Syrian armed forces to the Coalition would likely require a summit meeting between President Bush and President Asad. Baker's response was typically decisive and quick: "Okay, start arranging it from your end."

After much effort, we were able to organize a summit meeting in Geneva, which took place on November 23, 1990. A few days before the meeting Baker called to tell me that he would not be able to accompany President Bush to the Geneva meeting. He was on his way to Latin American capitals to round up UN Security Council support for the Coalition's military action in Kuwait. He instructed me to accompany the president on *Air Force One* and to brief him on how to deal with Asad, to help assure that we got a positive response.

President Bush was returning to the United States from a trip to Asia and was stopping off in Cairo to meet Egyptian president Mubarak. I had to leave Damascus for Cairo urgently, and my Embassy staff booked me on the last flight to Cairo that day. As the plane was getting ready to taxi for takeoff, the pilot of the Egypt Air flight announced on the speaker system that the air space over Cairo international airport had been closed because of the arrival of the United States president. I panicked, and the first thought that came into my mind was that Secretary Baker would never understand why I missed getting on *Air Force One*. I asked to speak with the pilot and showed him my diplomatic passport. I explained that I was the American ambassador to Syria and was on a critical mission to travel with President Bush to meet with the Syrian president in Geneva. I asked him to call the authorities in Cairo to see if we could get permission to land.

Miraculously, it worked. We got to Cairo in time for me to board *Air Force One* just minutes before the president got on the plane, and we took off for Geneva.

Brent Scowcroft, the national security advisor, came into the back cabin where I was sitting and, as the plane was taking off at a steep angle, gestured to me to get into the president's conference room to start the briefing. For the next several hours I had the unique opportunity to brief President Bush on what to expect from Asad, the issues he would most likely raise, his tough negotiating style, and the role of his aides. I also suggested how the president should deal with Asad and that, when the time came to make the pitch on Syria's military commitment to the Coalition forces, he should ask to speak with Asad privately with only Brent Scowcroft with him; I was sure, of course, that Asad would have Foreign Minister Shara accompany him. This gesture would underscore the importance the president attached to the military request. I also suggested that, in that private meeting, the president underscore the central role we saw Syria playing in the administration's initiatives for Arab-Israeli peace. This would dispose him to say yes to our request.

The meeting in Geneva proceeded as anticipated, with Asad bringing up hardline positions but ready to come to an agreement. President Bush worked Asad effectively and came out of the private session with Asad and whispered to me, "I did it."

"Well done, Mr. President," I replied with some awkwardness, since I wasn't used to complimenting presidents on their performance.

President Bush succeeded in getting Asad to agree to commit Syrian military units to participate in the Coalition military action, but only in a defensive capacity. At the end of the day and with further efforts by Baker in Damascus, the Syrian forces did join the Coalition forces in entering Kuwait, but in a largely supportive role at the rear of the battlefield. This represented a historic achievement for President Bush and Secretary Baker. To persuade Asad to commit Syria politically and militarily to join a United States–led coalition against a neighboring Arab state and, subsequently, to have Syria engage in direct, face-to-face negotiations with Israel was no mean feat.

A TEST OF ENDURANCE

During Secretary Baker's long but successful shuttle diplomacy between Damascus and Jerusalem we dubbed these long meetings and encounters with Asad "Bladder Diplomacy." I had forewarned Baker that President Asad prided himself that he would never get up to go to the restroom, no matter how long the sessions lasted. Furthermore, the room where we would meet was often stuffy and warm and many rounds of Arabic coffee and a sweet lemonade would be served. If one drank too much, the inevitable call of nature would occur. Baker looked at me and said, "Ed, I'm the secretary of state of the Free World. If Asad can do it, I can do it!"

Baker lived up to his boast. I, however, proved less resolute. During the longest nonstop meeting we had with Asad—nine hours and forty-six minutes on April 23, 1991—I failed to follow the advice I had given the secretary of state and drank too much coffee and lemonade. In the sixth hour I passed a note to Baker reminding him to raise an issue, but the real intent of the message was my second suggestion that, if he so wished, he could take a break. Baker looked at the note and gestured with his hand that he was fine and crossed his legs. I began to sweat. Fortunately, Asad gave me a way out by embarking on his Sykes-Picot narrative, which I knew by heart, so I could leave the room without missing any important substantive exchange. I gestured to Syrian Foreign Minister Farouq al-Shara that I had to make a telephone call. He nodded and I left the room. When I returned, Asad was winding up his story and I thought my plan had worked.

Only later did I learn from Shara that after I had left the room, Baker remarked to Asad that Djerejian had to go to the bathroom to make a phone call. Later that year, at a ceremony at the State Department in Washington, where I was sworn in as assistant secretary of state for Near Eastern Affairs, Secretary Baker referred to that incident and said that President Bush and he had decided that they had to call me back and send someone to Damascus "who could hold his water."

WINGED BULLFROGS AND SHUTTLE DIPLOMACY

At that same marathon meeting, Asad, for the first time, invited us to have lunch with him in the adjoining dining room in his presidential office suite. The exchanges of the morning had not been promising. Asad was hanging tough on his positions, especially avoiding movement toward direct negotiations with Israel and insisting upon full participation of the United Nations and a conference permanently in session until agreement was reached—conditions the Israelis would not agree to.

We sat down at the table: I was next to Asad and Baker was opposite him, with an interpreter and the foreign minister. Copious Arab hors d'oeuvres called *mezzeh* were served. When Asad reiterated his stance, Baker quipped, "Where I come from in Texas, they would say to that, 'If a bullfrog had wings, its balls wouldn't scrape the ground when it landed.'" The interpreter hesitated and Asad turned to me and asked me in Arabic what Baker's expression meant. Baker smiled at me and said, "I guess that doesn't translate." I said he should try another phrase, and Baker looked at Asad and said, "If the dog hadn't stopped running, he would have caught the rabbit." Asad still looked confused, understandably, and we got back to work after lunch, only to face more obstacles.

At one point during the negotiations, after Baker had gotten Asad to agree on several important issues, Asad started the exchange as if nothing had been agreed to previously. Baker looked hard at him across the table, slammed his leather portfolio shut, and said, "Mr. President, I don't think we can do business together." Asad's minister of state, Nasser Qaddur, leaned over to Asad and said in Arabic, "He is angry." Asad seemed surprised that his negotiating tactics elicited such a strong response from the American secretary of state. Nevertheless, Baker's masterly negotiating tactics worked. Asad drew back and Baker got him to leave the door open for a compromise on the two sticking points.

On May 3, I called Baker to inform him that Syrian foreign minister Farouq al-Shara had conveyed Asad's acceptance of Baker's compromise offer of a United Nations observer to participate in the peace conference and that the conference could be reconvened by consensus. The path was now open to work with the Israelis and the Arab parties.

In an exercise in intensive shuttle diplomacy, Baker made sixteen trips to Damascus. Only on that last trip did Asad finally agree to participate in the international peace conference that took place in Madrid in October 1991. Leading up to that point of decision, Baker called me from Washington and told me he would be in Lisbon in a few days and had a letter from President Bush to President Asad. To underscore this letter's importance, he wanted to deliver it directly to Foreign Minister Shara. In effect, it was the basic United States proposal for Syria to accept face-to-face, direct negotiations with Israel in the framework of an international conference convened by the United States and the Soviet Union, with the United States assuring that the conference would be based on the two key UN Security Council Resolutions, 242 and 338, and the principle of land for peace; namely, that Israel would withdraw from territories it had occupied in 1967 in exchange for peace with its Arab neighbors. In staccato tones, Baker asked me to get Shara to travel to Lisbon in the next few days.

Getting the Syrians to make quick decisions was no easy matter. I called Shara and explained the situation to him. He grumbled about his schedule, said it was impossible, and that in any case he would obviously have to get the approval of his boss. I kept pressing him and after a couple of days he answered positively. I was relieved and informed Baker. Then I realized there was no way I could get to Lisbon in time for the meeting on scheduled commercial flights. I asked Shara if I could hitch a ride with him in his official Syrian aircraft. When he agreed, I had to rush to get State Department approval for me to travel on the host country's aircraft. At the Lisbon meeting Shara grasped the importance of President Bush's letter, and Baker explained to him that this could be a turning point in Arab-Israeli peace efforts, depending on Syria's response.

On our return to Damascus after the meeting in Lisbon, I began the hard work of answering the multitude of questions Shara and Asad posed about the substance of the letter. They scrutinized every word and called key points into question. My discussions with Shara were intense and at times erupted into angry exchanges. We were both under pressure—he by Asad's dissecting the United States proposal and I by daily calls from the State Department, saying that the secretary and the president wanted to know if the response from Asad was in hand.

Finally, I was asked one evening to come to the Syrian Foreign Ministry to meet Shara. I actually thought that, given the lateness of the hour, it might mean a United States hostage in Lebanon was being released and I was happy at the thought. When I arrived in Shara's office he was remarkably relaxed and smiling. He said, "I've got good news," and handed me a sealed white envelope addressed to President Bush. I thanked him and remarked that I hoped it was a positive response. He handed me a copy of the letter and asked me to read it, saying that he wanted to have my reaction. I told him that my reaction was not important, but those of President Bush and Secretary Baker would be. He laughed and said he understood, but that President Asad and he wanted to know what I thought. I read the letter. It was a few pages. Then I began to reread it.

Shara said, "Why is it taking you so long to read the letter?" I looked at him, smiled, and said, "I'm looking for the Syrian loophole!" He chuckled and asked, "Have you found it?" I replied that he had now made me nervous because I found none.

"What do you think?" he asked.

"Mr. Minister," I said, "please tell President Asad that I think he has made a historic decision for peace."

I was elated and rushed back to the Embassy to send the text of the letter to the State Department for Baker and the president. Indeed, it was a clear acceptance of President Bush's letter. Asad's only cautionary clause in the letter was that if this initiative failed, he would reserve the right to revert to his past positions, with the UN's role central in any negotiations.

Asad was buying into the United States initiative.

More work would have to be done to nail all this down, but the corner had been turned, leading, under the aegis of the United States, to face-to-face, direct negotiations between Israel and Syria, a goal Israel had been seeking for some forty years. This decision by the leading Pan-Arab Baathist leader on Israel's northern border was a breakthrough.

While my Embassy communications people were preparing to send the cable to Washington, I called Secretary Baker on my secure line. Baker's assistant, Caron Jackson, answered the phone, and I asked to speak to the secretary. She told me he was in a meeting with Soviet foreign minister Bessmertnykh. In an atypical reaction I said, "Caron, I don't care who he is with, get him to the phone. This is important!" She paused and asked if I was all right. I said I was fine but needed to talk to him urgently.

A short moment later, Baker got on the phone and said, "This better be important, Ed. What's up?" "Mr. Secretary," I replied, "I just met with Foreign Minister Shara and he handed me President Asad's reply to President Bush's letter. It is an unqualified acceptance of the president's letter." "Are you sure?" Baker asked. I said I was certain and that the text of the letter was on its way by cable. Baker paused, said, "Well done, Ed!" and hung up.

Following their meeting, Baker and his Soviet counterpart gave a press briefing. Baker decided that before they discussed their meeting, he wanted to announce that he had just received a call from me and that, "according to our ambassador," President Asad has responded positively to President Bush's letter concerning peace negotiations. When I heard this, I knew that my bottom was on the line until Baker had read the text of Asad's letter himself and ascertained that Asad's response was unqualified. I later jokingly told Baker that he really had me hanging in the wind until he verified what I had told him.

He replied, "You got it!"

My tenure in Syria (1988–91) coincided with the collapse of the Soviet Union. These extraordinary historic circumstances had particular repercussions in the Middle East, where the superpower competition during the Cold War was acute. Syria was in the Soviet camp and a key beneficiary of Soviet weapons and assistance. The fall of the Berlin Wall, the breakup of the Soviet Empire, and the fall of communist leaders such as Nicolae Ceausescu of Romania, who was executed in December 1989, had a powerful and negative impact on the Syrian leadership. It had lost its superpower patron almost overnight and its ties to an increasingly vanishing and weakened communist bloc were fast becoming a liability. In this context a new dialogue was evolving at all levels of government of the two superpowers, from President George H. W. Bush and President Mikhail Gorbachev to American and Soviet diplomats in the field. Damascus was the ideal terrain for this unprecedented dialogue. My Soviet colleague, Ambassador Alexander (Sasha) Zotov, and I established a substantive and constant professional dialogue and a solid personal relationship. Zotov was a highly competent diplomat and Middle East expert. In fact, to mark this new relationship, my wife, Françoise, had the idea of our hosting a surprise birthday party in honor of Zotov. Guests included many members of the Syrian Foreign Ministry and our diplomatic colleagues. It was quite a party, and many weeks later the Syrian foreign minister, Farouq al-Shara, said to me, "You know, we are not disturbed at all by your close relations with your Soviet colleague in Damascus." Indeed!

One amusing incident occurred during the 1990 visit to Damascus by a Soviet colleague and top Middle East expert, Yevgeniy Primakov, whom I had known since my early days as a diplomat in Beirut in the 1960s. At the time he was a journalist and KGB operative. In subsequent years Primakov rose to the highest offices in the Soviet Union, including that of prime minister. In the early 1990s, while he was a member of Mikhail Gorbachev's Presidential Council and served as the Soviet president's special envoy to Iraq in the run-up to the first Gulf War, he would meet with Saddam Hussein and also visit Damascus. We agreed to get together on one of these occasions. We met at a café in a hotel in downtown Damascus. No sooner had we sat down and ordered coffee than a bevy of waiters surrounded us, obviously trying to pick up what we were discussing. Yevgeniy, ever the seasoned intelligence officer, wasted no time in waving them off and made it clear we wanted privacy. A few minutes later a waiter appeared with a potted plant and ceremoniously placed it in the middle of the table. Yevgeniy looked at me and smiled, then called the waiter back and said, "We didn't order flowers. Take them back!" With the flower-concealed microphone removed, we continued our conversation. "Yevgeniy," I quipped, "you trained them all too well."

FREEING AMERICAN HOSTAGES IN BEIRUT

Working directly at the highest levels with the Syrian government to obtain the release of the American hostages in Lebanon was a mission I found both challenging and personally rewarding. One of the most dangerous and wanted terrorists in the world was Imad Mugniyah, who was indicted by the U.S. government for the hijacking of TWA flight 847 in 1985 by Hezbollah operatives. Before his death in a car bomb blast in Damascus in February 2008—Israel, Syria, factions within Hezbollah, and several Arab states have all been suspected of arranging his death—Mugni-yah navigated between Iran and Hezbollah and reportedly had close links with the Iranian Revolutionary Guard Corps and Iranian intelligence. The U.S. government had pursued him since 1983, the year of the tragic bombings of the U.S. Embassy and the Marine barracks in Beirut. He was implicated in kidnapping Westerners in Beirut in the 1980s and in other operations under Hezbollah's aegis, using the name al-Jihad al-Islami (Islamic Jihad). Two of the hostages, Lt. Colonel William Higgins and CIA officer William Buckley, were brutally killed. Others were released at various times until the last American hostage held in Lebanon, Terry Anderson, was freed in December 1991.

On my watch, I was involved in the efforts for the release of three hostages: Mithileshwar Singh, an Indian-born United States resident who was chairman of the business administration department of Beirut University College, was released in 1988; Robert Polhill, a professor of business studies at the Beirut University College, and Frank Reed, the American director of the Lebanese International School, were released in 1990. Each release was a drama and each hostage faced his captivity in his own courageous way.

Since Syria had an important presence in Lebanon and close relations with Iran, it was well placed to aid us in getting the Iranians to use their influence with the hostage takers to release them. It was an arduous and often frustrating process with many false hopes and leads, but when we were successful, there was nothing more exhilarating than receiving a freed hostage into American hands. From the president on down, the U.S. government worked tirelessly to free our hostages, based on the principled position, during the time of my involvement overseas, of calling and working for their unconditional release. We never negotiated or made deals with the hostage takers. My job was to keep pressing the Syrian government to use all its influence in Lebanon and in Iran to obtain positive results. My main interlocutor was Foreign Minister Farouq al-Shara, with whom I had a close working association. Overall, our improved and growing relationship with Syria helped us get them to approach their various contacts on our behalf.

Each time one of the three was released, I got a late-evening call from the Foreign Ministry to come to see the minister. I immediately informed the State Department that there could be a possible freeing of an American hostage, since we had some preliminary information. When I arrived in the foreign minister's office, we waited together for the arrival of the individual being freed. Neither he nor I knew who the person would be; the Syrians got control of the hostages only when they were physically handed over to them in Lebanon. After they reached Damascus, I could hear the sound of armored cars pulling up to the Ministry and voices shouting out commands—they were the military intelligence personnel who had brought the hostage over the road from Beirut to Damascus.

Then there was more waiting, which seemed like an eternity, during which time the Syrians had the hostage change into an ill-fitting suit from the bazaar. Only after he had donned this faux chic garment would the door to the minister's office fling open. The minister introduced me as the American ambassador, and each time I got very emotional, extending my hand and saying, "Welcome back, you are on your way home!"

Each freed hostage reacted to his moment of liberation differently. Mithileshwar Singh was stoic when I brought him to the Embassy residence, where his and my wife and our devoted and able Embassy nurse, Birgit Khatib, were awaiting the liberated American. Though our cook had prepared a hearty meal, Singh, who radiated an incredible degree of calm, asked only to drink some tea.

Frank Reed had suffered painful beatings and made no effort to hide his justifiable anger at his captors. Robert Polhill was frail but displayed a sense of relief and humor that was contagious. When I welcomed him and said, "I'm so happy to see you," he came right back and replied, "You can't be more happy than I am to see you, Mr. Ambassador!" When we drove to the residence, I mentioned to him that President Bush had called me earlier and would like to speak directly with him, but only if he felt up to it. Polhill's voice was very weak and hoarse and he was concerned that the president might not be able to hear him. After a champagne toast with our wives, we made the call, and the president graciously expressed his happiness to Polhill over his release.

What Polhill did not know was that before I left for the Foreign Ministry, President Bush had called me from a boat off the coast of Florida and asked me for a status report on the situation and what I planned to say to the press and TV journalists that had gathered around the residence and the Foreign Ministry. After I briefed the president he said, "Good. And I'll be watching you, Ed, on the TV from the boat." That made me feel a little nervous. Marlin Fitzwater, the White House spokesman, made a statement in Florida that "we are pleased at the news that Robert Polhill has been freed by his captors. . . . We also wish to thank those who had a hand in his release, particularly the governments of Syria and Iran, whose efforts have contributed to the release of this hostage. . . . We have a number of difficulties with Iran and the terrorists, certainly, who took these hostages in the first place. . . . There are still seven remaining hostages and we will continue to press for their release. . . . There were no deals, no negotiations with the hostage takers. . . . In the case of Syria, they have provided us with information on a continuing basis about the possibility of the release. They helped facilitate the release in the final hours."

THIS PLACE CALLED BROOKLYN

Our dialogue with the Syrian leadership included discussion of the status of Syria's Jewish community. We sought the lifting of discriminatory restrictions on travel and the disposition of property. President Bush raised the issue with President Asad at the Geneva summit meeting and Secretary Baker had discussed the matter several times with Asad, as did numerous congressional delegations that traveled to Damascus. At the end of one of my meetings with President Asad on other subjects, I stopped as we were walking to the door and asked him if I could raise another matter. He said yes. I referred to my contacts with the Syrian intelligence officials on the status of the Jewish community and said I felt we were getting nowhere. This is not, I said, a political or security issue but a humanitarian one. It is not linked to other issues involving Israel, so it should not be perceived as any sort of concession to Israel. All we were asking was that Syrian Jews be granted the same travel rights as other Syrian citizens. I asked Asad if he would designate a trusted aide with whom I could continue our discussion on this issue. He reflected for a moment and said I should work with Nasser Qaddur, the minister of state and his trusted confidant. This encouraged me, because I knew that Qaddur could get things done.

In the ensuing months I had several meetings with Qaddur and met with the Syrian Jewish community leaders. Sometimes, to be more discreet, I would send my wife, Françoise, to carry messages to them. We focused on granting visas for unmarried Jewish women and reuniting divided families, on lifting restrictions on the sale and purchase of property, and also on the release of the Soued brothers, who had been arrested and incarcerated on charges for trying to travel to Israel, which was illegal because Syria was in a state of war with Israel. Asad once told me he didn't want the Syrian Jewish women to leave Syria for Israel and joked that there were plenty of Syrian men around, so they didn't have to get Israeli husbands. He stipulated that he had no problem with Syrian Jews going to "this place you call Brooklyn," where there is a large American-Syrian Jewish community, but that he would reverse his decision if he saw that Syrian Jews were emigrating to Israel.

Finally, after much effort on all sides, Asad made an important symbolic gesture when he met with key leaders of the Syrian Jewish community in Damascus, including Rabbi Abraham Hamra, chief rabbi of the Syrian Jews, and Dr. Nassim Hasbani.

Subsequently, the Soued brothers were released from prison and all members of the Syrian Jewish community were accorded the same travel rights as those afforded to all other Syrian citizens.

We welcomed these decisions as another result of the high-level dialogue we were conducting with the Syrian regime.

FAREWELL CALL ON ASAD

Near the end of my tour in Syria, I visited the city of Hama, a Muslim Brotherhood stronghold where government forces had killed an estimated twenty thousand people in a furious reaction to a Brotherhood revolt against the regime. With its main street erected over the rubble from the attacks, it reminded me of a Potemkin village. Though it was nearly a decade since the attacks, the bloody legacy of the past was palpable. With the exception of the days of Desert Storm, when we learned that Saddam Hussein's security services had dispatched a small team to Syria to kill me because of our having persuaded Syria to join the Coalition against Iraq, I never saw such intense alertness and agitation on the part of the local security guards assigned to me. When I made it clear that I wanted to venture into the streets of the city, they formed a human fortress around me.

In Damascus, the elite Marine Corps detachment that protected the Embassy assured our security. I felt particularly moved when one of our young Marines told me he would put his body between a bullet and me. Fortunately, we never faced such a situation, but danger was a frequent feature of life in Syria. The Syrian leadership from the top down relied heavily on a complex web of protection that resulted, among other things, in planting guards armed with Kalashnikov machine guns every hundred feet or so on the main residential streets of Damascus. One neighborhood in Damascus, where my daughter, Francesca, went frequently to attend her piano lessons, was particularly challenging since it housed, compliments of the Syrian government, a plethora of heads of terrorist organizations. This danger-infested environment, which the Syrians navigated and tolerated day in and day out, was never far from our minds. In this respect, I was certainly glad to be bringing my family back to safe shores and the comforts of our home in Washington, D.C.

In an unprecedented gesture that reflected the enhanced state of United States–Syrian relations, President Hafez al-Asad invited me to the Presidency for a private farewell call on July 24, 1991. During the three and a half hours of that visit, I observed that my mandate from Presidents Reagan and Bush and Secretaries of State Shultz and Baker to engage in a frank and direct dialogue with him and his ministers had, despite all the difficulties, produced positive results.

Asad acknowledged the results of the dialogue and insisted that it continue in the same open manner. Then, as I had learned to expect, he went into a lengthy historical soliloquy to make two basic points: first, that the United States should not seek to impose its positions or definitions on others; and second, that the United States should realize that perhaps the U.S. model of democracy cannot be applied identically in every country in the world. Referring to the first point, on the imposition of definitions, he observed that Syrian actions the United States has labeled "terrorism" are, from Syria's perspective, actions carried out in a state of war and are justifiable attempts at "national liberation" of Arab territories occupied by Israel. In an obvious reference to our approaches to the Syrian government regarding the targeting of civilians in the Occupied Territories, Asad said that the U.S. approach should also take into account the loss of innocent civilian lives on the Arab side, citing Israeli Air Force strikes against civilian targets in Syria as far north as Latakia and in other urban areas where innocent Syrian civilians had been killed.

On the second point, regarding the universal applicability of the U.S. model of democracy, Asad went into a detailed account of recent Syrian history since independence, mentioning the frequent military coups d'etat and resultant instability that reigned in Syria. He did not mention that he had become Syria's leader by overthrowing his rivals in the early 1970s, nor that the Muslim Brotherhood had attempted to assassinate him in the 1980s, leading to the brutal assault on Hama.

Asad commented that, in the Third World, the first task of leaders is to bring stability to their countries and then expand the democratic process. He claimed that Syria was going through this process, admittedly at its own pace. I responded to Asad's two points by stating that it is not our approach to impose our ideas on Syria, or on any other country, for that matter. Rather, we seek to determine if there is common ground upon which we can build to obtain positive results, as we had in the recent past with Syria. We try to *persuade, not dictate*. In reference to his second comment, I said that, indeed, we Americans believe that the American democratic system represents "a City on a Hill" that people throughout the world look to as a model. We do not claim that our society or our system is perfect; far from it. But, I said, the beauty of the American system is that it is a living experiment in democracy that evolves with changing times and without coups d'etat. We recognize the diversity of political life in the world and different stages of development. We feel strongly, however, that the principles of American democracy are worthy of emulation.

I left it at that without any expectation that Asad, one of the most powerful dictators in the Arab world, would respond to my burst of patriotism. He simply nodded and we went on to discuss the next steps in the Arab-Israeli peace negotiations.

At the end of our visit, I told him that Yitzhak Rabin had spoken to me about him just before I left Washington to assume my duties in Damascus in 1988. With a slight smile of amused curiosity, he asked, "What did Rabin say?" I told him that Rabin had described him as the most intelligent and difficult Arab leader to negotiate with, but that "whatever he agrees to and commits himself to, he will live up to and you can count on it." I asked Asad, "Is he right?" He paused a moment, then said, "On *this* issue, I agree with Rabin."

FIVE

JERUSALEM

All the governments of Israel have decided that if we want
democracies to emerge in the Arab world to negotiate peace,
we will have to wait a hundred years.
—PRIME MINISTER YITZHAK RABIN, JANUARY 17, 1994

On January 12, 1994, five days before Yitzhak Rabin made the above observation, an important new, though brief, chapter opened in my life when I arrived at Ben Gurion Airport in Tel Aviv to begin my assignment as the United States ambassador to Israel. I was accompanied by my wife, Françoise, and our children, Gregory and Francesca. As the TWA aircraft taxied to the gate we were told to deplane first, since press and media were gathered on the tarmac, which explained the splash of spotlights on the plane.

Having memorized an arrival phrase, I said in Hebrew, "We are very happy to be with you." An Israeli friend who habitually polled taxi drivers to get a sense of public opinion later told me that this simple gesture had had a positive effect. This was our first direct exposure to the scrutiny of the very inquisitive Israeli press corps, and I quickly realized that the American ambassador to Israel is fair game, ranking just below the Israeli political leadership as a target for attention. The first serious question at planeside homed in on President Clinton's scheduled meeting with Syrian president Hafez al-Asad a few days later in Geneva. I said that we hoped for some substantive results that would enable the Israeli-Syrian negotiating track to move forward. We were then ushered into the VIP lounge where another battery of TV and print media photographers took photos of our family, with most of the focus on Francesca and the kitten she was protectively holding in her arms to shield him from all the commotion. The next day the newspapers carried these photos with the commentary that the new American ambassador's daughter was promoting *aliyah* (the return of Jews to Israel), since the cat had been given to Francesca by Jewish friends of ours in New York. Indeed, the American ambassador and his family would be the focus of great scrutiny in Israel.

I also quickly understood something else about life in Israel when Françoise, Francesca, and I (our son had returned to the States for college) were taken to a location close to the Embassy Residence to be fitted for gas masks. It was a mandatory precaution and it felt eerie to me—Israel and Jews under the threat of gas, despite Israel's overwhelming regional military superiority. Scud missiles fired by Saddam Hussein during Desert Storm were a brutal reminder of these vulnerabilities. At the location we had been assigned for this exercise, we were greeted by an Israel Defense Forces officer and a group of attractive young IDF female soldiers who briefed us in a quite professional manner on the use of the masks. They then fitted each one of us and showed us how to inject ourselves with the antidote if we showed signs of contamination. "Yellow side up to the sun, green side down to the earth," they explained. It seemed unreal, but recalling a visit to Auschwitz years before, where I had seen the teeth and clumps of hair and pieces of bones of Holocaust victims cremated after death by gassing, it had a profound effect on me.

SETTLING IN

The ceremony for the presentation of my letter of credence occurred on the day after my arrival at post, the immediacy underlining the significance of my mission. Before the ceremony, I met with the chief of protocol and top officials of the Ministry of Foreign Affairs, including Shimon Peres, the foreign minister. I asked to see Peres for a private discussion and underscored that my goal was to enhance the high-level dialogue between our two countries across the broad spectrum of the U.S.-Israeli relationship. I told him that I respected his unceasing quest for peace with Israel's Arab neighbors and recognized that we had much hard work to do together. Peres was gracious in his remarks and told me that Israelis were happy with my appointment. We discussed the Clinton-Asad meeting. Peres hoped it would help move that track forward on its own merits, and would also put pressure on Palestine Liberation Organization (PLO) chairman Yasir Arafat to restart the stalled Israeli-Palestinian talks on a "Declaration of Principles" on interim self-government arrangements regarding Gaza and Jericho. Peres expressed his disenchantment with Arafat and his control of the negotiations in an increasingly dictatorial manner, going well beyond the Declaration of Principles. Peres predicted inevitable delays in bringing the talks to a successful conclusion.

Unfortunately, this pattern of delays and missed opportunities would characterize the future course of Israeli-Palestinian negotiations.

We then departed for the president's offices for the ceremony — although the prime minister is the head of the government and exerts by far the most authority within the Israeli government, the president is the head of state and is thus the official involved in such matters of protocol. The day, like that on which I had presented my credentials in Damascus six years earlier, was crisp and sunny. My family and I stood at the end of a long red carpet alongside which were a military band and honor guard made up of regular Israel Defense Forces soldiers—the IDF did not have a separate honor guard unit. We stood at attention while "The Star Spangled Banner" played and Old Glory was raised on the flag mast. After reviewing the honor guard we went inside to the reception room, where President Ezer Weizman, Shimon Peres, and other officials were standing. I made my remarks and presented my letter of credence to President Weizman.

Weizman shook my hand warmly and expressed appreciation for my remarks, which he characterized as quite meaningful. I introduced my Embassy Country Team to the Israeli officials present and we proceeded to a reception room where champagne was served and President Weizman and his lovely wife Reuma chatted with our family. I congratulated Weizman on his illustrious military and political career and his remarkable role in Israeli history. I told Weizman that his special relationship with Egypt's late president Anwar Sadat, who, with then Israeli prime minister Menachem Begin, signed the first peace treaty between an Arab state and Israel in November 1979, took extraordinary vision and was a monumental achievement. This led to an interesting series of anecdotes concerning Sadat and Begin. Weizman characterized them as "men of theater" who knew how to foster the drama of history, offering, as example, Sadat's arrival in Israel in a "a pageant of Pharaonic quality," as well as his eloquent and impassioned speech before the Knesset on November 20, 1977, when he foresaw a time when Israel and "the Arab nation" could embark on "a new beginning, a new life, a life of love, prosperity, freedom and peace," contingent, not surprisingly, on a withdrawal of Israeli forces from territory occupied after the 1967 Six-Day War, establishment of a Palestinian state, and Jerusalem as a free city belonging equally to Jews, Muslims, and Christians.

In our private discussion, Weizman made it clear that he thought Israel should vigorously pursue peace with Syria. That would be the big prize. He thought Syria could still inflict real harm on Israel. He recounted how, after the October 1973 Yom Kippur War in which Egypt and Syria had colluded to launch a surprise attack on Israel, he had told Sadat, as one military man to another, "Congratulations! You gave us a bloody nose." Israel won the war in the end, but at considerable cost, and its leaders recognized the continuing threat posed by a hostile state looming just across its northern border. The importance of Israel's relations with Syria was no diplomatic secret.

At a full-court press conference immediately after I signed the protocol book, a journalist asked me, in Arabic, about the Clinton-Asad meeting. After translating his question into English for the benefit of the Israeli journalists who didn't understand Arabic, I commented that it was an important opportunity to determine the prospects for peace between Israel and Syria.

He then asked a second question, about the possibility of a summit meeting between Israeli prime minister Yitzhak Rabin and President Hafez al-Asad. To that, I gave, also in Arabic, the only answer I could: *"Al Itiqal al Allah"* ("That depends on God").

AN ARMENIAN IN JERUSALEM

After the press conference, we went outside and stood at attention at the playing of the Israeli national anthem, then exited on the red carpet while the band played the popular Israeli tune "Hava Nagila," whose decidedly unanthemic beat greatly amused our son and daughter. It had been a good start. I then had lunch with Ely Rubenstein, who was a top advisor to Prime Minister Rabin and in charge of the peace talks with Jordan at the time. Ely, one of the smartest and wittiest men I met in Israel, said I was the first American ambassador to Israel of Armenian origin, the first American assistant secretary of state for Near Eastern Affairs to become ambassador to Israel, and the first American ambassador to have served in almost all of the Arab states neighboring Israel (Egypt was the exception). He observed that my presentation of credentials ceremony was, according to what he had heard from journalists, unprecedented in its informality. He was also impressed with my making a policy statement, choosing to meet privately with the president, and then appearing at a press conference.

We discussed the Israeli-Jordanian talks and Rubenstein expressed his concerns over the Jordanian track's being stalled because of snags in the Israeli-Palestinian talks. He urged that we consider a format whereby the two sides could focus on resolving details of outstanding issues in working groups, so that when the other negotiating tracks made progress, the Jordanian track could move forward in a way in which problems in one negotiating track could not hinder progress in another.

YITZHAK RABIN

I paid my first call as ambassador on Prime Minister Rabin the next day in his office in the Ministry of Defense in Tel Aviv. In addition to heading the government, Rabin kept for himself the portfolios of minister of defense, minister of internal affairs, and religious affairs. He and his staff greeted me warmly and we had the traditional handshake for the TV cameras before sitting down for an extended discussion. I told Rabin that I had come to Israel to pursue the close dialogue between our two countries at this important juncture in the Arab-Israeli context and that I had two main goals: first, to help advance the peace talks between Israel and its Arab neighbors; and second, to continue to promote U.S.-Israeli relations at all levels, with emphasis on economic, commercial, trade, and science and technology cooperation. I expressed my great respect for him and told him how much I looked forward to working with him closely. Rabin graciously returned the compliments and said he also looked forward to working closely with me and would be available whenever necessary.

We discussed the upcoming meeting in Geneva between

Presidents Clinton and Asad, and I made it clear that the United States was not approaching that meeting at Israel's expense; namely, that we would not be telling Asad, "If you do x, y, and z, Israel will do a, b, and c." We would be focusing on what Syria needed to do to advance peace negotiations. Further, we would not depart from our commitment to face-to-face direct negotiations, which I knew was uppermost on Rabin's mind.

While Rabin knew that Israel had no closer friend and ally than the United States, he was uncomfortable with putting the fate of Israel on war and peace issues in others' hands without direct, continuous Israeli engagement. At this stage of diplomacy, however, the United States was playing its essential role as an "honest broker" between Israel and Syria to pave the way for direct talks, albeit with the United States in the room, because of Asad's insistence that we be there.

Rabin indicated that he was "comfortable" with our approach, but expressed his concerns. He thought that although some in Israel felt that Asad could exchange ambassadors and establish embassies, he was not prepared to establish normal relations. Normalization, he emphasized, poses perceptual problems. He thought Asad would find it difficult to accept the free flow of people in and out of Syria: "Can he handle fifty thousand Israeli tourists in the Souq al Hamadiyeh [the central bazaar] in Damascus?" Rabin hoped the Geneva meeting would provide a clearer definition of peace, but his doubts were clear in his shrugging comment, "We must wait and see."

Rabin expressed his total disillusionment with Yasir Arafat, who he said was still trying to parlay the Declaration of Principles exercise into a discussion of final-status issues. He thought Arafat perceived Israel's interest in moving forward to implementation as a sign of Israeli weakness. Arafat had to understand, he maintained, that we were still in the first stage of a two-stage process. The security issues involved in the transfer of authority—passes for moving between sectors, the building and use of bridges, and, preeminently, the settlements—continued to pose problems. Israel, Rabin insisted, had to maintain control of external security during this phase.

Rabin thought that postponing the upcoming talks in Washington by the heads of the Arab and Israeli delegations or having only the neighboring Jordanian, Syrian, and Lebanese delegations participate might help nudge Arafat toward a more objective approach. Rabin was very skeptical about Arafat's tactics. He thought Abu Mazen and Abu 'Ala, key associates of Arafat's in Fatah and the PLO, were more serious interlocutors, but that deep division within the PLO and a loss of a sense of urgency had resulted in critically missed opportunities.

As I left Rabin's office, I realized anew how difficult the path of Arab-Israel peace talks would be, given the deep suspicion Arabs and Israelis felt toward each other.

I saw this again when our negotiating team came to Israel to brief Rabin immediately after President Clinton's meeting with Asad on January 16, 1994. Rabin had watched the press conference at the conclusion of the meeting and told me he did not like what he heard. He had hoped that Asad would have said the same thing that President Clinton had said about Israeli-Syrian peace. That, in Rabin's view, "would have made a difference."

When Martin Indyk, special assistant to President Clinton and senior director of Near East and South Asian Affairs at the National Security Council (NSC), and Dennis Ross, special Middle East coordinator, arrived in Jerusalem, I let them know that Rabin was disappointed. When we joined him at his residence, Rabin listened carefully to the briefing.

Asad had made a basic judgment that he wanted to move forward, but he wanted to convince President Clinton that Syria had legitimate concerns and that it was important for the United States to understand Syria's perspective.

The U.S. objective for the meeting had been to obtain both a private and a public end. We wanted Asad to say something about ending the conflict and achieving peace with Israel, specifying "Israel" by name, to announce that he had made the strategic choice for peace and to get the term "normal relations" into his lexicon and remarks. Our briefers told Rabin that, when a journalist had asked Clinton whether he had heard Asad commit to normalization, the president had answered, "Yes."

But Rabin, who was fluent in Arabic, had told me earlier that Asad used different terms in Arabic for normalization: (*al 'alaqaat al 'aadiya* (ordinary relations), not *al 'alaqaat al ta'biyya* (normal relations). Rabin insisted that he could not proceed with negotiations with the Syrians unless there was a clearly defined package that spelled out the nature of peace, including the phasing of withdrawal from the Golan, security arrangements, and the role of the United States. He had in mind a phased withdrawal over a period of three years, similar to the Egyptian peace agreement.

Asad had replied to another question by saying that Syria would meet the "requirements of peace." I knew Rabin did not think this was sufficient and so I was not surprised when he said, "In Israel there was disappointment in his [Asad's] statement. The average Israeli would say that Asad didn't say anything new. Rightly or wrongly, Israelis who were worried about this meeting were relieved. [For Asad] to say full-fledged peace and normalization of relations in reference to [the return] of the Golan Heights would put Israel in a real bind. That would be another matter and we would have to respond." Rabin then made an important statement: "Under these circumstances, what we discussed cannot be brought up." Here Rabin was referring to a very closely held secret "deposit" he had given to Secretary of State Warren Christopher on August 3, 1993, to convey to Asad, offering a hypothetical proposal that, if Israel's requirements for peace and normalization of relations, security arrangements, and a timetable for implementation, were satisfied, Israel could consider withdrawing from the Golan Heights to the June 4, 1967, lines.

Rabin continued that Asad was linking everything to a comprehensive peace on all fronts, which leaves it all open—and much harder to achieve. Syria would not sign a peace agreement with Israel unless Lebanon, Jordan, and the Palestinians were on board, which, he said, "makes what we discussed irrelevant. If it cannot be concluded bilaterally with Syria, we cannot proceed on the basis we discussed." Rabin made clear he had to have something to meet his preconditions, in particular a full-fledged bilateral peace agreement.

He talked about the possibility of holding a referendum in Israel about peace with Syria, but said he was not yet at that point. Still, he reiterated, "Whatever was done in private has now become more complicated."

In Rabin's calculations, the negotiations with Syria were qualitatively different from those with the Palestinians. The price for peace with Syria was full withdrawal from the Golan Heights, with the phasing of any withdrawal quite restricted by Asad's demands. With the Palestinians, the approach was one of an interim agreement, not a final one. As Rabin acknowledged, the Israelis realized there were problems with the PLO in the negotiations but they were not giving anything up at that stage because of the interim nature of the negotiating framework. That was why he needed Asad to be privately and publicly declarative on the nature of peace with Israel, so he could have Israeli support for "coming down from the Golan"—a strategic piece of territory, albeit less so in the age of ballistic missiles.

Rabin was prepared to begin to explore the Syrian negotiating track, to see how far Asad would go and also, in his calculation, to make the Palestinians nervous that the Syrian negotiations could overtake theirs. In the context of his difficulties with Arafat and Asad in their negotiations and his concerns over having the United States "negotiating in our name" with Syria, Rabin began to look seriously at concluding a peace treaty with King Hussein of Jordan, especially since there were no major territorial problems between Israel and Jordan. In addition, a peace agreement would complement the Palestinian track, and, in turn, put some pressure on the Syrians.

Indeed, Rabin did enter into direct, face-to-face negotiations with King Hussein. On July 25, 1994, King Hussein and Prime Minister Rabin signed the Washington Declaration at the White House, terminating the state of belligerency between Jordan and Israel and laying out the framework of a peace treaty. The treaty was worked out largely in secret between Jordan and Israel and formally signed on October 26, 1994, on the Jordan-Israel border, grandly declaring "an end to the age of war" between the two countries.

CLINTON IN GENEVA, 1994

At the January 1994 meeting with Asad in Geneva, President Clinton said that Rabin had reconfirmed the commitment that he made to Asad through Secretary Warren Christopher and sought Asad's reconfirmation of his commitment to Rabin; namely, that the borders would be open to trade, commerce, and tourism, and that the two countries would establish diplomatic relations and exchange ambassadors. Clinton referred also to understandings that there would be adequate security arrangements.

Asad replied affirmatively, but said that security arrangements had to be equitable and pushed for "balanced security on an equal footing," noting that Damascus is closer to the border than either Tel Aviv or Jerusalem. Clinton said the United States was prepared to provide a security guarantee, including the presence of U.S. troops, if it would be helpful to both sides and worked out satisfactorily between them. He referred to the Israeli-Palestinian negotiations and said that while the objective was a comprehensive peace, progress on Gaza and Jericho would satisfy movement on the Palestinian track. Asad reportedly nodded, but made no commitment. As for timing, both sides would have to work this out.

Asad raised the question of Israeli motivations and his suspicions over whether Israel really wanted to deal with him; he did not want to be strung along. President Clinton had confirmed that he had talked to Rabin several times, that a deal with Syria was essential to a comprehensive settlement, and that Rabin was committed to a peaceful settlement. Asad had expressed his hope that President Clinton's confidence in Rabin was justified. Clinton had told him the United States would like to see an Israeli-Syrian Declaration of Principles (DOP) worked out in private and announced publicly only when the two sides agreed to it. Asad had said he would like to have a date when it could be announced. Clinton wanted the timing to be part of the negotiation. Asad raised the issue of the 1993 Rabin deposit, insisting that it would have to be binding.

Realizing that Asad was worried that Syria would commit to the process, only to have Israel walk away from it, Clinton assured the Syrian that this was not his impression of Rabin. He then told Rabin by phone that Asad was suspicious of any negotiations, especially after his experience with Henry Kissinger in the 1970s, when Syria was shunted aside and Israel and Egypt proceeded with their peace treaty. Rabin understood. In fact, he was indeed being urged at the time by some of his top advisors to concentrate on the Palestinian track and put the Syrian track on hold.

Asad talked about the DOP as a framework agreement with appendices that would be the basis of everything, with no ambiguities. Clinton assured him that this was his view and, he believed, Rabin's as well. In private, Rabin did agree, but he was concerned that any private commitment would be made public before details could be worked out, generating dissent that would scuttle any long-term deal.

"You are negotiating in our name," he told Clinton, "and this is a problem. I have agreed on certain terms—'bilateral agreement,' 'phased implementation.'" With Egypt, borders had been opened before Israel's complete withdrawal. Israel had a major problem with the Sea of Galilee and the Sykes-Picot Agreement on minor border adjustments—all of which could become major problems if they became public prematurely. Above all, with Egypt there was Sadat's appearance in Israel. Rabin felt that Asad had not made any major move toward a peace that people could believe in. Clinton recognized the validity of Rabin's concern and told Asad that public diplomacy was needed and that once Israel and Syria agreed to announce the DOP, he would need to meet with Rabin to formalize the agreement, and that he, Clinton, would host the meeting. He added that Rabin had already agreed to such a meeting.

BUILDING PEACE, BRICK BY BRICK

Asad observed that the situation in the region was deteriorating and that time was not on the side of peace. He asked Clinton to tell Rabin, "I do not know how much time we have. My situation is not getting easier." When Asad asked Warren Christopher if he thought six months offered sufficient time to implement the phases of the process, Christopher replied that it was up to Syria and Israel to work this out between themselves.

In my meetings with him, Rabin expressed his concerns over the status of negotiations. He emphasized that, to achieve comprehensive peace with its Arab neighbors, Israel would have to build it "brick by brick on a bilateral basis with each country"—Jordan, Palestine, Syria, and Lebanon. He had made commitments on a number of issues in the Palestinian negotiations, and if he lost out on the phasing and security arrangements in the Syrian track, he felt he would be "crippled" and could lose his bargaining power. "This is the problem when you work through a mediator," he complained. "When you state my readiness for full withdrawal, you destroy my bargaining power. Once they leak it and before we get everything we need, then I have a problem. Whenever something wrong happens to him [Asad], his system can compensate for him." In Rabin's view, Asad was making "oral commitments" that were general in nature and could easily be rescinded, while he, Rabin, was committing Israel to the tangible act of withdrawal from the Golan Heights.

THE DEATH OF BASIL AL-ASAD

On January 21, 1994, Prime Minister Rabin telephoned to inform me that the Israelis had unconfirmed information that Basil al-Asad, President Asad's son and political heir apparent, had been killed in a car accident. Rabin said, "Basil was loved by his father. If the information is true, we do not know what the implications will be. If confirmed, please convey my condolences as a humanitarian matter privately." I commented that Basil, whom I had met in Damascus, loved driving his cars fast. It would be important to determine how Hafez al-Asad's politically ambitious brother Rifat al-Asad would respond and what his role might be in the immediate aftermath of Basil's death.

In any case, I assured Rabin that I would try to confirm what the situation was and would share with him whatever information we received. I called our ambassador in Damascus, Chris Ross, who said that it was 90 percent certain that Basil was dead. There had been a car wreck on the road entering the airport that morning and it was believed Basil was involved. President Asad had been scheduled to meet an American congressional delegation, but Foreign Minister Shara had called the U.S. Embassy to say that the president had to cancel the meeting because of a family emergency. The loudspeakers of the mosque next to the Embassy and close to the president's office were lamenting the late Basil al-Asad, but the Foreign Ministry was not yet confirming the news of his death.

On the assumption that Basil had indeed been killed, I asked Chris to convey Prime Minister Rabin's private condolences to President Asad. We learned later that Basil was racing to the airport at over one hundred miles per hour in the early morning fog to catch a Lufthansa flight. The car had hit a curb and rolled over several times, crushing Basil's head. He was taken to Asad Hospital where his father arrived shortly afterward and sat alongside his son's body for some time.

When Asad emerged from the room, he showed signs of having cried at length.

I called on Prime Minister Rabin on Shabbat, January 30, 1994, to discuss the situation in Syria following Basil al-Asad's death and the possible consequences for the peace negotiations with Syria. Leah Rabin greeted me at the door of their small but comfortable apartment in Tel Aviv and asked me what I would like to drink. Since it was eleven-thirty in the morning I asked for coffee, black. Leah looked at me and repeated the question in such a way that I immediately changed course and asked for a scotch on the rocks. That was obviously the right choice because that was what the prime minister was having.

Rabin and I concurred in our assessments of the situation in Syria. Hafez al-Asad was in full control, but deeply grieved by Basil's death. He would keep his brother Rifat in check, so that he wouldn't try another grab for power as he had once done in the past when Asad was ill. Rabin emphasized, however, that it would not be an opportune time to push Asad to make critical decisions on the peace negotiations. "He needs to regain his focus and direct the negotiations," Rabin reasoned. "Some political space is needed."

Rabin was quite uncomfortable with the state of discussions between the United States and the Syrians. In a private meeting I had with him on February 17, 1994, he again conveyed his basic concerns and his strong desire for direct and secret Israeli-Syrian negotiations. He told me that the real problem was that "we [Israel] do not have a Syrian partner in the negotiations and this is done purposefully by Asad. He wants the United States as a go-between to deliver Israel, a classic Arab perception." Rabin reiterated what he had told Secretary Christopher, that there had to be an overall package approach to the negotiations and that decoupling the core issue—withdrawal from the Golan—from implementation of peace is a mistake by the United States. Israel would not address the core issue in any detail in the absence of a full package involving the nature of the peace that could be expected, the phasing and timing of Israeli withdrawal, and the implementation of peace and security arrangements.

This followed the precedent that had been set in the 1978 Camp David Accords between Israel and Egypt. Israel withdrew to Sharm el-Sheikh and Ras Muhammed and did not uproot Israeli settlements during that stage. Embassies were established in Tel Aviv and Cairo and normalization began. Complete Israeli withdrawal from the Sinai took two to three years. Rabin emphasized that his "deposit" was made only on the assumption that we were dealing with a full package — "I spoke in generalities but made clear that it was all interconnected."

I asked Rabin what would happen if the Syrians did not change their approach. He replied, "Asad has to make a decision. He wants the United States to do the job for him and he can be in a position to take a backseat. There are other issues: The Sea of Galilee is Israel's water reservoir. The Sykes-Picot Agreements did not give Syria any rights to 'our water.' We need phased withdrawal and security arrangements. We can't give up all our leverage up front."

I responded by telling Rabin that since his "deposit" had already been conveyed to the Syrians and we were the "repository" of his offer, and since we were proceeding on the understanding that nothing was agreed to by the parties until everything was agreed upon, Israel was not really giving up its leverage. How, I asked him, can we find a creative way around this deadlock?

Rabin had a ready answer: "What I propose is that Asad send someone to a place where we can explore these positions in depth and secrecy. If we could keep the talks with the PLO secret for five months, we can do it with Syria."

In my discussions with Israeli leaders, I was struck by how fervently they wanted to engage directly with the Syrians, and especially with President Asad. President Weizman told me that, as former Air Force officers, he and Asad could engage in the kind of frank dialogue that could produce results, akin to what had been achieved with Egyptian president Anwar Sadat. Shimon Peres also expressed continuing interest in direct talks, as did Ehud Barak. When Barak was the chief of general staff of the Israel Defense Forces he would urge me in private to help set up a meeting between him and the Syrian chief of staff, Hikmat Shihabi. Later on, the two men did meet, but their talks did not lead to positive results.

In any case, though Israelis looked at the United States as their only honest broker in Arab-Israeli negotiations, the stakes for them on questions of war and peace were so high that their clear preference was for direct face-to-face talks, exemplified by the secret talks between Israel and the PLO that led to the Oslo Agreements in 1993, and those leading to the Israeli-Jordanian peace treaty in 1994.

Rabin's caution regarding talks with the Syrians was pronounced. A few days later, at a dinner hosted by the Russian ambassador and Middle East expert Alexander Bovin to honor the famous Bolshoi Ballet dancers Vladimir Vassiliev and Ekaterina Maximova, Bovin advised me that Rabin's government should not be pushed too far too fast, especially on Syria, lest Rabin lose his political constituency. Bovin had a point, but every Israeli leader has to weigh domestic political concerns against the risks necessary to achieve peace.

SCHINDLER'S LIST

Françoise and I attended the gala opening in Tel Aviv of *Schindler's List*, Steven Spielberg's film about Oscar Schindler, the German industrialist who bribed Nazi officials to allow him to employ Jewish slave labor in his factories in Poland and Moravia, thereby saving the lives of more than a thousand Jews, even rescuing some who had already been dispatched to Auschwitz. The film depicted the horrors of the Warsaw Ghetto and Auschwitz in all their brutality, leaving the large cinema house absolutely silent throughout the film. We were seated next to Spielberg, and

I remarked to him what an extraordinary setting and audience this was for his film. Prime Minister Rabin, President Ezer Weizman, former president Chaim Herzog, Ehud Barak, and many other officials and religious leaders were there with their spouses. Spielberg agreed, saying that each individual would absorb the grief in his or her own way, and added that the impact on the audience in Germany had also been strong. After the film ended I told Spielberg he had made a powerful film and we both instinctively grasped each other's arms. Rabin congratulated Spielberg on his work, but words failed everybody.

As an American of Armenian origin, I was deeply moved by this experience and referred to Hitler's August 22, 1939, speech to his military commanders about dealing with "the Jewish question," in which he asked rhetorically, "Who, after all, speaks today of the annihilation of the Armenians?" Spielberg said the Holocaust was a "mural of horror" and his film but one depiction. He recounted to me that when the German actors put on their Nazi uniforms, he had had a hard time relating to them. Indeed, he was taking a year off from work to recover from the emotional stress of making the film.

As we left the cinema, Shimon Peres commented to me that, tragically, Jews became blind in the face of imminent danger. Days later at his home, President Ezer Weizman told me that, while the film was important, he felt it trivialized the Holocaust by treating its symptoms and not its causes and by focusing on one man's heroism.

UNDERSTANDING THE OTHER

As an American diplomat who had spent many years in Arab countries, I was impressed with the ability of some Israeli leaders—certainly not all and not the ideologues—who really tried to "understand the other." For example, Rabin, Weizman, and Peres, each in his own way, made a serious effort to understand the

Arabs. They knew the Arabic language, studied the history and culture, and sought direct contacts whenever and wherever possible. But the state of war between Israel and its Arab neighbors prevented them from sustained and in-depth exchanges and experience, and at times, hindered bolder policy formulation.

One evening when we were at the Peres home in Jerusalem for dinner, Shimon Peres went to his library, took out a book of poems by the Arab poet Nizar Kabbani, and started to read his poem "Who Are You?" I thought to myself that this was extraordinary: Here we were in the home of one of Israel's historic political figures, and he was reading Arabic poetry to us. After reading some romantic lines, he deftly brought home a political point that he wanted to make to underscore his recent frustrations with the pace of negotiations with the Palestinians and the Syrians. Arabs, he said, like to "ski on words."

Reciting Kabbani's words, "Every time my heart overcame my mind was my happiest moment," he wryly observed that Arabs like to use words as "ornaments" and not necessarily "a means of precise definition."

Of course, neither side was averse to the use of deliberate linguistic ambiguity when it suited their needs.

Arab-Israeli negotiations have often coincided with acts of violence and terrorism that have hindered, delayed, and scuttled forward movement in the quest for peace. In my public statements I repeatedly noted that it has always been a race between the violence and terrorism on the ground and the political path of peace negotiations. Arab and Israeli leaders must ensure that the path of negotiations is the road taken and that the terrorists and extremists are marginalized. This applies to both sides. Arab radical groups such as Hamas, Hezbollah, Palestinian Islamic Jihad (PIJ), the Popular Front for the Liberation of Palestine (PFLP), and Al Qaeda have committed brutal acts of terrorism to sabotage any peaceful settlement. Jewish extremist groups and individuals have also played a destructive role.

These groups seek nothing less than a maximalist solution.

For the Arab radicals, that means destroying the state of Israel and "pushing the Israelis into the sea." For their Israeli counterparts, it means keeping all the Occupied Territories, even transferring the Arab populations from that land. Rabin, who would pay with his life at the hands of a Jewish extremist for his efforts to achieve peace, had the courage and leadership to delineate the only acceptable way forward under these difficult circumstances: "We will fight terror as if there is no peace process," he said, "and we will take the peace road as if there is no terror."

THE SANCTITY OF LIFE

Rabin's policy was anathema to Jewish extremists. A few weeks after becoming prime minister in 1992, he made a speech at a military awards ceremony, stating that Israelis should "cast off delusions of a religion of a Greater Land of Israel. . . . Remember, there is a people of Israel, a society, a culture, an economy; that the strength of a nation is not measured by land, the lands under its control, [but] rather by its belief [in] its ability to foster its social, economic and defense systems." Rabin's political outlook faced a terrible challenge on February 25, 1994, when an American-born Jewish settler, Bernard Goldstein, clad in an IDF uniform, entered the mosque at the Tomb of the Patriarch in Hebron and opened fire with his Galil rifle on Muslim worshippers gathered for Friday Ramadan prayers. He killed at least forty people and wounded many others. Goldstein himself was killed and his skull crushed. In the midst of the Ramadan and Purim holidays, another brutal and senseless attack on innocent civilians rekindled deep-seated hatred and spawned mass demonstrations in the Occupied Territories and on the Temple Mount, further jeopardizing the prospects for continuing the Arab-Palestinian negotiations.

Yossi Beilin, the Labor Party peace activist, called me and said that this shameful act should be a catalyst to move the peace talks forward with more vigor and asked me to tell Washington that the United States should take the lead in doing so. When I saw Prime Minister Rabin leaving an emergency session of the Cabinet, his face was flushed and he remarked, "This is a situation of life and death. I, as an Israeli, as a Jew, am more than shamed that a Jew carried out this atrocity. I have no proof now that this was part of any organized operation, but I am not saying that there are not circles of settlers that see such incidents as a political act. . . . I can understand the reaction of the Palestinians. However, those who support Hamas will exploit this incident for their own ends and seek revenge. We need to find a way to separate those who perpetuate violence. . . . The only solution is political. I spoke to Arafat and expressed my disgust and said that the only solution is to accelerate the negotiations on the Declaration of Principles. . . . We will fight terrorism and continue the peace negotiations and not link the two. This is the main message."

The Arab extremists responded on April 6, 1994, in the biblical Israeli town of Afula, when a Hamas suicide bomber drove a vehicle full of explosives into a bus, killing nine passengers and wounding over fifty others. In a communiqué claiming credit for the attack, the Izzed-Din al-Qassam Brigades, the military arm of Hamas, made clear its opposition to peace negotiations: "We demand that Mr. Yasir Arafat suspend the negotiations with Israel's leaders for one year, because our brigades with the help of God shall in that time force Israel's leaders to unconditionally withdraw their soldiers and settlers from Gaza, Jericho, and Hebron as a first stage toward the liberation of the West Bank and Gaza. We shall guarantee Mr. Arafat the presidency over these territories if he rules according to God's Sharia and the Sunna of the Prophet. . . . It is a Holy War, either victory or martyrdom."

In an interesting insight into the role of religion in Israeli politics, Aryeh Deri, the charismatic leader of the ultraorthodox Shas Party, told me that Rabin had asked the influential orthodox rabbi Ovedia Youssef to have Shas join his coalition government. Rabin made clear that, without the Shas Party, he could not proceed on peace talks with Syria. If Shas aligned itself with the opposition, he would be facing a Knesset with a 61-59 split, denying him a mandate. He needed a Jewish majority. Deri said that Shas alone in the Jewish religious community was supporting the peace talks, and subsequently, Rabbi Ovedia's Halacha key ruling that the sanctity of life is more important than the sanctity of land (that is, holding on to the Golan Heights) enabled Rabin to pursue the Syrian track with domestic support.

Rabin told U.S. secretary of defense William Perry and the Joint Chiefs of Staff that no Arab leader would engage in serious negotiations with Israel as long as he thought he could achieve his aims through the military option or terrorism. This, Rabin concluded, was the true value of Israel's defense posture in the pursuit of peace. Israel needed armed forces that could deter or, if deterrence failed, win decisively and quickly. Rabin said that he did not accept the U.S. idea of having American forces on the Golan as part of a peace agreement. "I am proud that we never asked one GI to shed blood. If we have the means, we can do it alone. We will never ask the United States to have a defense pact with us." Rabin's focus was on the strategic relationship. According to him, Israel was capable of dealing with all the threats against it without becoming part of any military alliance. Israel's armed forces were structured in such a way as to cope with any form of military alliance arrayed against it, including, in the past, minimal participation by the then Soviet Union.

In Rabin's analysis, there were two conflicting trends in the Middle East: the quest for Arab-Israeli peace agreements and "Islamic fundamentalism," which he characterized as "Khomeiniism without Khomeini." Nasser tried to adopt the Soviet system and failed. Sadat and Mubarak tried Western democracy and also fell short. These failures sparked a return to the Qur'an and Sharia law. Iran was spreading an ideology that was not contradictory to Arab nationalistic ideas and was seeking to assume a regional superpower role. Rabin's analysis was prescient.

A STRATEGIC RELATIONSHIP WITHOUT A STRATEGIC DIALOGUE

Shimon Peres once implied that U.S. policy was not as visionary and assertive as it should be, though he praised President George H. W. Bush and Secretary James A. Baker, III for Desert Storm and the Madrid Peace Conference and said they had made a difference. Commenting on the strategic relationship between Israel and the United States, Peres recounted an amusing story about Golda Meir, who once complained to the American ambassador, Wally Barbour, that the United States could not treat Israel the way it had been doing.

"After all," she said, "we are an independent country." Barbour, after inhaling from his allergy sniffer, replied, "Madame, the United States was the first country to recognize Israel's independence. The question I have for you, Madame Prime Minister, is, 'Does Israel recognize the independence of the United States?'"

The U.S.-Israeli relationship is close and complex, but I have been struck by what high-level Israeli military and civilian officials told me, during one of my visits to Israel in 2007: Despite a multitude of channels and considerable coordination on specific issues and operations, there is little or no real strategic dialogue between the U.S. and Israel. They complained that there are many discussions, including biannual Israeli–United States strategic talks, but they are of a routine nature and do not constitute a real strategic dialogue. This is a dangerous lacuna, given the scope of the relationship and the high stakes in the Middle East. The United States and Israel should establish a high-level forum to share not only their respective assessments of the political, military, and economic situation in the region, but to address on a sustained basis key issues such as Arab-Israeli conflict management and resolution, terrorism, weapons of mass destruction and their regional proliferation, energy supply and security, Iran, and the role and influence of Islamist parties and Islamic radicalism.

This dialogue can facilitate a better understanding of each side's interests and approaches to major areas of concern and avoid misunderstandings of the sort exemplified by the exchange between Golda Meir and Ambassador Barbour.

FAREWELL TO JERUSALEM

Prime Minister Rabin and his wife, Leah, hosted a special dinner at the prime minister's residence in Jerusalem on the occasion of our departure from Israel in 1994. The ambience was warm, friendly, intimate, and substantive, and the Rabins were gracious hosts. They had invited a number of members of the government, academics, the Israeli writer Amos Oz, and some of our Israeli friends. Rabin gave a toast that touched me deeply. He said that he and Leah regretted our short tenure in Israel and considered us as friends who had done much to enhance the U.S.-Israeli relationship and to work for peace. Never, he said, had there been an American diplomat who had come to Israel after being the ambassador to Syria, a country that symbolized the essence of the problem and the hope for a solution. He raised his glass and thanked us for "all you have done to educate us about our Arab neighbors."

I truly appreciated that remark, and on the eve of my retirement from the Foreign Service felt that it summed up my diplomatic career of serving my country on both sides of the Arab-Israeli divide.

Ehud Barak, the IDF chief of staff at the time, confided to me that when he was head of military intelligence and I was ambassador to Syria, "We watched your activities in Damascus very closely ever since you arrived in 1988. At first we were concerned that your successful efforts to improve U.S.-Syrian relations would be at Israel's expense. Then, when we realized that you were influencing Hafez al-Asad more than he was influencing you, we began to relax and started to consider the U.S.-Syrian rapprochement as a positive factor."

Also soon before our departure, Françoise and I hosted over two thousand guests for the traditional July 4 reception at the residence in Herziliya. There had been a contentious debate that day in the Knesset in Jerusalem and Prime Minister Rabin and Likud leader Benjamin Netanyahu were engaged in lengthy and at times bitter exchanges, with Likud's having introduced three no-confidence votes against the government, which the Labor Party coalition defeated 57–47.

Rabin told me that he had finally taken the floor and asked Netanyahu, "Are we going to prolong this debate to the point that we all will miss the American ambassador's July 4 reception?" Netanyahu responded that Likud had no interest in boycotting the American ambassador's reception, and they both agreed to end the debate and sped down to Herziliya to attend the event. After the Rabins arrived, I made a few remarks commemorating American Independence Day, U.S.-Israeli relations, and the quest for Arab-Israeli peace, and also commended Rabin's statesmanship in taking great risks for peace. I quoted in Hebrew what Ben Gurion University president Avishay Braverman's father told him: "The three qualities a human being needs are patience, tolerance, and endurance." All these words, I noted, come from the same Hebrew root: *savlanut, sovlanut, koach-sevel,* and all were relevant to all Israelis during this time of testing. To the surprise of all, Rabin broke precedent and came to the podium and made an eloquent statement about the strategic relationship between our two countries, the importance of pursuing peace with Israel's Arab neighbors, and our role therein.

The politically tense atmosphere in the Knesset largely dissipated at the reception, and Likud and Labor leaders conversed easily throughout the evening, with General Ariel Sharon and Rabin shaking hands in a very friendly fashion, but Netanyahu and Rabin passed each other like ships in the night.

FAREWELL TO THE PALESTINIANS

The U.S. consul general in Jerusalem, Ed Abington, and his wife gave a farewell dinner in our honor at their residence in

Jerusalem with the Palestinian "Insider" leaders, who resided in the West Bank and Gaza. These leaders, while loyal to the PLO and Arafat, had a tradition of promoting democratic rule and not the authoritarian model of the Arab world that Arafat represented. They were critical of the "Gaza-Jericho Accord," an interim approach that gave the Palestinians a political and economic foothold in both areas as a step toward a more comprehensive agreement. They characterized this agreement as too narrow and as "peace for peace," not land for peace, which was the basis of the Madrid Peace Conference and UN Security Council Resolutions 242 and 338. In their view, that accord did not address basic questions such as settlements, legislative issues, and Jerusalem. Hanan Ashrawi, who was the spokesperson of the Palestinian delegation to the Middle East Peace Process from 1991 to 1993, said, "All is based on the sufferance of the Israelis." A major concern was whether the accord would be a building block for final status talks or an end in itself. Another major concern was the rule of law, avoiding the arbitrary diktat of the Palestinian Authority (PLO) and fostering respect for human rights. While they felt that general elections must be held in the Occupied Territories, they should be carried out without the presence of the IDF. They also voiced concern over the turnout of voters and the risks that Hamas and the PIJ would gain ground. I responded that the Gaza-Jericho Accord must be seen as a building block for the next stage of negotiations.

As for elections, I commented that I had always felt that the Palestinians were in a good position to build a democratic society and to demonstrate respect for human rights. Given their history and unique historical experience living next to Israel, they had the opportunity to build a Palestinian society based on democratic principles that, if successful, would have a major impact in the Arab world. Nonetheless, the challenge they faced was twofold: On the one hand they had to deal with the autocratic tendencies of Yasir Arafat; on the other hand, they had to appeal to the Palestinian population at large and provide them with the incentives to marginalize the growing influence of the Palestinian radical groups such as Hamas and Palestinian Islamic Jihad. The path of peace negotiations and building the economic and social base of the population of the West Bank and Gaza were all interconnected.

In a subsequent discussion, Prime Minister Rabin told me that "we support a democratic Palestinian state as a long-term goal, but in the Arab world democracy is in the hands of leaders with a gun and military, security, and intelligence services. Palestinians first need the basic necessities of life—food, jobs, health services, education; then they can think of democracy. Democracy in the Arab world is like waiting for the Messiah."

In a visit to Gaza in July 1994, I met with Yasir Arafat, who had recently arrived in Gaza under his title of chairman of the PLO and the Palestinian Authority. He asked me to ride with him to a dedication of a U.S.-government-sponsored housing project. It was a strange feeling to be in Arafat's car, with the PLO flag flying on the front bumper and with him waving to the crowds along the route. He was charismatic to his people and thrived on the public recognition. I asked him what he meant by "the peace of the brave"—a phrase he often used to describe Israeli-Palestinian peace. He said it meant that all—he stressed *all*—Palestinians and Israelis alike must forget much of the bloody history of the Arab-Israeli conflict.

He then decried the Israeli rule that banned Palestinian National Council members from entering Gaza because of their past actions against Israelis. He said that if he applied the same standards, he wouldn't be talking with Israeli leaders who fought the Palestinians in, for example, Lebanon. I made the distinction between military actions between armed forces and acts of terrorism against civilians such as the school massacre in Ma'alot by Palestinian members of the Democratic Front for the Liberation of Palestine that occurred on May 15, 1974, the twenty-sixth anniversary of Israeli independence. Some of the PNC members were reportedly associated with this incident. Arafat did not respond.

YITZHAK RABIN'S VISION

In June 1994 Rabin had given a tough speech at a conference in Israel, underscoring the importance to Israel of the peace negotiations and the need for compromises. Referring to Syria, he said it had "ground missiles of a quality and quantity that make what we suffered from Iraq during the Gulf War look like child's play. Those who tell you that we can achieve peace just for peace, peace without all the Golan Heights, lie to you. . . . How can they say that, for peace with Egypt, [we had] to return the last square inch. . . . But concerning Syria we can achieve peace just for peace? Total nonsense. Total nonsense! Whoever would say that he is for retaining all the Golan Heights has to prepare for war."

Rabin took a great deal of political heat for his stance on what he considered was required to achieve peace with the Arabs. Once, when I was accompanying him on an official visit to Washington, he was the keynote speaker at the American Israel Public Affairs Committee (AIPAC) convention. I was seated next to Eitan Haber, his loyal chief of staff and speechwriter. I noted that Eitan was revising Rabin's remarks during the lunch and commented that I would have thought he had that speech all prepared before leaving Israel. Eitan replied, "Yes, I did, but look at this crowd. I have to toughen up Yitzhak's remarks."

Nevertheless, in a Zogby International Poll in June 2007, asked if they supported a Palestinian state, close to 90 percent of American Jews agreed—whether strongly or somewhat so—that Palestinians have a right to a secure and independent state of their own; 96 percent of Arab-Americans polled supported the idea. And 86.6 percent of Jewish-Americans and 80.9 percent of Arab-Americans feel that achieving peace between Palestinians and Israelis is of vital importance to U.S. national security.

Upon receiving the UNESCO Peace Prize in Paris on July 6, 1994, Rabin made an eloquent speech that demonstrated his vision for peace and understanding of the risks involved. He quoted the recently deceased president of the Ivory Coast, Félix Houphouët-Boigny, who said, "Let us proceed slowly, for we are in a hurry."

Rabin continued, "Indeed, we have been proceeding along slowly. For over a hundred years, we have fought over the same strip of land: the country in which we, the sons of Abraham, have been fated to live together. Both peoples, Israelis and Palestinians, have known suffering, pain, and bereavement. . . . Both sides must calculate their steps slowly, with prudence and care. For a century of hatred does not dissolve suddenly, with a handshake in Washington. . . .

"Peace will be built slowly, day by day, through modest deeds and countless spontaneous details. It will be built step by step, by people. . . . We are going slowly and cautiously, one step at a time, because the enemies of peace are even more numerous than we imagined. Because extremists on both sides are lying in wait for us, and we—Israelis and Palestinians alike—must not fail. At every step we must think, consider, weigh, check, and beware. We are in a hurry because we have waited over a hundred years for this day. . . . We are in a hurry to spare another Israeli mother [from] weeping tears of pain and another Palestinian mother from shedding bitter sobs. We are in a hurry to see the light in the eyes of neighbors who, until now, have never seen a single day of freedom and joy. . . . We are in a hurry, and therefore we are proceeding slowly. We are moving very carefully. For not all of us will have another chance."

The following year, on November 4, 1995, Rabin was tragically gunned down by a Jewish extremist.

SIX

RETURN TO THE ROAD
TO DAMASCUS

Hafez al-Asad died in 2000 and was succeeded by his son
Bashar al-Asad, who was training to be an ophthalmologist in
London and had not been groomed for the presidency. That role
had been intended for his elder brother Basil, a military man
mentored closely by his father to take the reins of power upon
President Asad's death. I met with Basil only once while I was
ambassador in Damascus. I had requested many times to have
an appointment with him, without any positive response, until
one day my secretary at the Embassy received a call from the
presidential palace to arrange to have me meet the heir apparent.
At the appointed day and hour, I was to wait outside the Embassy
alone, without even my bodyguards. A blue BMW with smoked
windows would arrive to pick me up and take me to the appointment with Basil al-Asad.

When my regional security officer heard of these arrangements, he told me he could not let me go alone. I told him I

understood his concern, but the Syrian regime had no interest in having anything happen to the American ambassador. Still, I wrote a "memorandum for the record," stating that I had taken this decision contrary to his advice and, therefore, if anything happened he would be off the hook.

It was a short but interesting ride to the nearby presidential compound. As the BMW rapidly made its way toward the outer gates of the compound, a number of what I thought to be pedestrians on the sidewalks turned, snapped to attention, and saluted the car. The heavy gates opened automatically, and without a pause we were in front of the building and I was ushered into Basil's first-floor office.

Basil was in military uniform and exuded confidence. He had good knowledge of the foreign policy issues we were dealing with in the U.S.-Syrian relationship, obviously well briefed by his father. He seemed obviously ready to assume his destined role. But destiny had other plans. After his fatal ride to the Damascus airport in 1994, the mantle fell to Bashar, who became president after his father died in 2000.

I have met with Bashar al-Asad one-on-one several times in Damascus. He is a young, energetic, and educated man who speaks in a staccato rhythm. There was much doubt about his ability to take over from his legendary father, who ruled Syria with an iron grasp. Yet he successfully consolidated his position immediately after his father died and survived the political fallout of the withdrawal of Syrian forces from Lebanon in 2005. In my discussions with the Israeli military in 2007, they had a sense that he has successfully survived a number of political challenges and remains in control.

BAKER INSTITUTE'S U.S.-SYRIA DIALOGUE

In January 2002, I approached Bashar al-Asad to propose a United States–Syria dialogue under the aegis of the Baker Institute at

Rice University. I wanted to initiate a serious dialogue between current and former officials representing both countries, plus academics and private and public sector representatives. I have always thought that informal settings provide a favorable atmosphere for exploring candidly the stickiest issues encountered in adversarial relationships. Moreover, I knew the timing was right to advise our respective governments on our deliberations and on how some of these differences could be resolved. He agreed to authorize the Syrian participants to engage freely in this format, and we held meetings in both Houston and Damascus. The first session took place at the Baker Institute from May 20 to 22, 2002. Despite a few bureaucratic hurdles originating on the Syrian side, our dialogue started out well with constructive opening presentations by former secretary of state James A. Baker, III, U.S. senator Arlen Specter of Pennsylvania, Assistant Secretary of State for Near Eastern Affairs William Burns, and Syrian deputy foreign minister Walid Mouallem. An extensive exchange in the panel discussions on the bilateral relationship and on terrorism was direct and nonpolemical. While the definitional differences remained (for example, what constitutes "resistance" against an occupying state and what is "terrorism"), there was a detailed discussion on how to build on the then-existing intelligence exchanges and cooperation on Al Qaeda and other terrorist groups in a practical and focused manner. The Bush administration's public statement that "Syria's cooperation in this regard has been substantial and has helped save American lives, and for that reason serves U.S. interests" was favorably noted. At the same time the administration's comment, "More is expected of Syria," was also noted and there was much discussion of Hezbollah, Hamas, the Popular Front for the Liberation of Palestine—General Command, as well as Palestinian Islamic Jihad.

On the Arab-Israeli peace negotiations, Walid Mouallem gave an important narration of the history of the Israeli-Syrian track from the Madrid Peace Conference onward that provided important insights from the Syrian point of view of what was achieved and where opportunities were missed. There was a consensus that at least 80 percent of the key issues on land, peace, security, and water had been extensively dealt with in prior negotiations and that with the requisite political will by the concerned parties, these negotiations could be picked up and moved forward. The Syrian participants reiterated Syria's commitment to negotiate peace with Israel, based on this "legacy" of past negotiations that included Rabin's "deposit" on the June 4, 1967, lines.

The panel of private sector representatives on economic and commercial issues focused on the pressing need for economic reforms and streamlining the bureaucracy in Syria and for the public and private sectors to be on an equal footing to move the economy forward effectively. The Syrians complained strongly about U.S. sanctions against Syria. The panel on cultural dialogue and press and media focused on what both sides could do to improve communications between the two countries at all levels, with an emphasis on student and academic exchanges. In an interesting aside, one Syrian asked what they should do to improve their diplomatic representation and effectiveness in Washington. I looked at Dr. Imad Moustafa, the young Syrian technocrat across the table, and told Walid Mouallem that they should assign someone like Moustafa who was smart, dynamic, and fluent in English, to represent Syria. A short time later, Bashar al-Asad appointed Imad Moustafa as Syria's ambassador to the United States. Moustafa would later joke that both his president and I had appointed him to be ambassador to Washington.

We held the second round of the U.S.-Syria dialogue in Damascus in January 2003, a scant two months before the United States war against Iraq. We had a twenty-two-person delegation and the Syrians had an equal number from the public, private, and academic sectors. My overall impression of the meetings and discussions was that the Syrians continued to attach much importance to their relationship with the United States and that they would conduct a difficult balancing act to accommodate their "Arab interests" with their concern not to be singled out by Washington as a major problem country in the region. They were ready to engage on all the issues, and that provided an opportunity for us, in my view, to determine what common ground there was to build on. The Syrians emphasized that given the historically strained relations between the Syrian and Iraqi Baath regimes, they had limited political ties with Baghdad, and the relationship was based largely on economic interests. They claimed that they had gone to the Iraqis to press them to comply with UN Security Council resolutions to avoid war and also urged us to go for a second UNSC resolution and "not to go it alone." They expressed fear of sectarian violence in Iraq if military action was taken and that this would undermine the antiterrorism campaigns. They also stressed their major concern over refugee flows into Syria from Iraq—a concern that proved prescient, given some 1.2 million Iraqi refugees in Syria in 2007. In the Syrian analysis, Iraq was no longer a serious threat to its neighbors. Mouallem commented that "Saddam is finished and all he wants now is to survive."

On the terrorism issue we asked the Syrians if they understood what they needed to do to get off the terrorism list and if were they willing to enter into serious and substantive negotiations toward that end. Drawing on our first meeting in Houston and the Syrian distinction between "resistance" and "terrorism," one of our panelists noted, recognizing the legitimate right of the people of an occupied land to resist occupation, that resistance becomes illegitimate when it involves attacks against innocent civilians. It is impossible for the United States to condone an organization's action of the first sort when it also conducts actions of the second sort. He stressed that the bottom line is that violent attacks by nonstate groups against innocent civilians is terrorism and unacceptable to the United States. This was an important point to convey to burst through the "definitional" argument. When we focused on Hezbollah and Palestinian groups in Syria such as Hamas, Palestinian Islamic Jihad (PIJ), the Popular Front for the Liberation of Palestine (PFLP), and the Popular Front for the Liberation of Palestine—General Command (PFLP-GC), the Syrians reiterated their position that Syria hosts some four-hundred-thousand Palestinians who "were not invited" and who pose an economic burden. They argued that the relationships with the Palestinians are too strong and historical and that breaking them is not politically achievable.

In 1978, President Hafez al-Asad directed that there would be no operations from Syrian territory. It was for this reason that the Syrians moved the notorious terrorist Abu Nidal out of Syria after Jimmy Carter approached the Syrian government. Mouallem then repeated what he said in the Houston meeting, that "any evidence of operations planned from Syria will be acted on" and that "we are listening to you carefully."

On the prospects for negotiations between the Syrians and the Israelis, the Syrians reiterated their "strategic option" for peace. One of our panelists made a presentation noting that, from an American perspective and looking at the period that began with Barak's election as prime minister and ending with the Geneva summit in 2000 between Presidents Clinton and Hafez al-Asad, three key problems stood out in terms of the Syrian approach to negotiations: 1) a need for constant high-level communication with the Syrians to exchange informal ideas and proposals; 2) a need for concrete counterproposals from the Syrians, for example, on issues of access to water, security arrangements, and normal peaceful relations; and 3) a need for confidence-building measures. The Syrians repeated Hafez al-Asad's refrain that confidence-building measures ought to follow a peace agreement, not precede them. This reminded me of Asad's once telling me when I was urging him to make some public gesture to Israel that "you Americans are always pushing us to make love before the wedding ceremony." The Syrians also argued that they had engaged in a manner to satisfy negotiating requirements and criticized the United States for not offering any concrete proposals or substantive bridging proposals during the Clinton administration. They reiterated that a sine qua non of any future negotiations is the full withdrawal to the June 4, 1967, lines and referred frequently to the Rabin "deposit" of August 1993.

On bilateral relations, the Syria Accountability Act, which would impose sanctions on Syria, loomed large in the background of the Syrian participants' presentations. We fielded an excellent private sector group of American participants. We pressed the Syrians on the need to quicken the pace of economic reforms and underscored that the timing and sequencing of private market reforms and anticorruption measures are key issues that must be addressed if foreign investment is to be meaningful. We were disappointed that the Syrian participants were much more cautious in their advocacy of reforms in Damascus than they were in Houston. Perhaps they felt more constrained in expressing their views in Damascus than they did in Houston.

BASHAR AL-ASAD

I met with Bashar al-Asad again in August 2003 in Damascus. I referred to the work I was doing in the region as chairman of the congressionally mandated Advisory Group on Public Diplomacy in the Arab and Muslim world. Asad commented that this public diplomacy initiative was important and emphasized that it has to be a two-way street. "It is not advisable for the United States to explain its values and policies without understanding better the world it is dealing with, and the United States should make a real effort to understand the foreign audiences it is seeking to communicate with and convey its messages in terms those audiences could understand," he said.

Asad concluded that U.S. public diplomacy faces a real challenge because there is the perception of "a certain contradiction in America's execution of its policies and the interests and values of the American people.

"I admire the development of American society, its science and technology, and much more," he said, "but the conduct of policy has led to problems." He gave as an example U.S. policy on Iraq and its impact on U.S.-Syrian relations. I commented that I had been told that within Asad's inner councils he is being advised by some to "wait America out," with the expectation that the U.S. policies in Iraq and the Arab-Israeli context were likely doomed to failure, and advised him that given the strategic situation in the region today he should opt for engaging with the United States. The United States and Syria have important common interests as demonstrated in the past by what we achieved: ending the Lebanese civil war; political and military cooperation in Desert Storm; releasing American hostages in Lebanon; cooperation against Al Qaeda; potential U.S. investment in Syria to move the Syrian economy forward; and ultimately in a comprehensive settlement between Israel and Syria.

Rather than disengaging, I told him it might be more prudent for Syria to try to cooperate with us to determine where there is common ground and to deal candidly with the issues between us. If Syria contends the United States doesn't take into account Syrian interests, I noted, then he should put this on the table for discussion. Syria does have a regional role to play and can be a constructive player with the help of the United States. That means, however, sustained constructive engagement. There is an impression in Washington that Syria provides more words than deeds. This can be problematic. Syria should build on what we've done together in the past and avoid the worst-case scenarios. Syria needs to engage and not just wait for initiatives from the United States.

I remarked that Asad was doubtless aware of the Syria Accountability Act, which expressed a strongly held point of view on the part of members of Congress. The fact that this legislative act was looming and would likely pass later in the year did not bode well for U.S.-Syrian relations and made it all the more compelling to engage in the months ahead. Asad replied that he understood what I was saying, but that the United States had to understand that he, too, had his own interests, and internal political considerations to take into account, just as the U.S. administration had with the U.S. Congress. He indicated that Syria was ready to discuss the issues. At the same time, he said that the United States was now perceived as "a superpower whose vision is not clear to us." Further, the United States must not approach its relations with Syria solely fixated on its own interests without taking Syrian interests into account. Syria's interests had to be part of the dialogue. "We do not have a constructive dialogue," he stated. We have engaged "and agreed" on the Iraqi assets issue, on Hezbollah, and the Palestinian groups in Syria. But the United States approached Syria with a list of requirements, expecting that every item on the list had to be fully checked off. If we acquiesce to four out of five of the issues, a report goes back to the U.S. Congress that Syria has not met U.S. demands. He implied that the United States "shouldn't make the perfect the enemy of the good."

Asad elaborated on his thoughts concerning Iraq. He said, "We do not think that the United States is going to withdraw from Iraq early." Syrian policy toward Iraq is "pragmatic," he said, and "we do not live on expectations. I look at the United States and Iraq through Syria's interests vis-à-vis Iraq. We need a vision, but, nothing is clear now and we need hope and a clear path." Asad commented that there is a political vacuum now in Iraq and it would be wrong to make any decision regarding Iraq when conditions are moot. He said, however, "We are not waiting for the United States to fail or succeed in Iraq. We have a long-term relationship with Iraq and we have our point of view and the United States, on its part, should make the effort to try to understand where we are coming from." Regarding its five-hundred-kilometer border with Iraq, Asad reiterated that Syria does not have the capability of completely controlling the entire border. I urged that a maximum effort be made, nevertheless, to assert Syrian control over the border at this critical time.

Asad said that Syria does control parts of the border, including the border posts and checkpoints, but that smuggling along all of the border cannot be controlled and the United States with its military presence in Iraq must also play its role in border control. Asad then volunteered that Syria had expelled a number of Saddam Hussein's followers who took refuge in Syria, including his sons Uday and Qusay. He urged me to recognize that "we can never forget the role the Iraqis played in the 1980s when they supported the Muslim Brotherhood's uprising against the Syrian regime." He pointed out that Syria's cooperation with the United States on Al Qaeda continued after 9/11. The meetings are less frequent, but ongoing. He commented that Syria has much experience with Islamist extremists and terrorism and that the United States should appreciate the expertise Syria can offer in this domain.

I asked Asad if he has actually closed down the Hamas offices in Syria as requested by the United States and other countries, or if they had merely been relocated. Asad replied that "I will close offices, but we will not expel them from Syria because without them we cannot obtain a cease-fire [in the Palestinian territories]. He stated that the Palestinian offices have been closed but that the United States should understand that as long as the Golan is occupied by Israel, what Syria can do with the Palestinians is "limited in space and time."

Referring to the prospects for Israeli-Syrian peace talks, I said I assumed that Asad's commitment to peace as Syria's "strategic option" remained on the table and that Syria's position was to restart the negotiations from where they were left off. Asad confirmed that his commitment is firm and specified that it was Syria's "preference" that the negotiations be reinitiated from the point at which they ended. I found this an interesting subtlety in the Syrian position. Asad was not insisting that the talks had to start from the very point that they had been broken off in 2000, as Syrian officials had demanded. It was now a "preference"—a small but important point of flexibility.

I then touched on the sensitive issue of Syria's reform program under Bashar al-Asad, which he had trumpeted as one of his highest priorities when he came into office and which had instilled much hope in Syria among the people. Asad stated that he agreed with the importance of reforms, but he added that democratic reforms have to be carried out according to the history and traditions of each specific country. However it is labeled, the end result of democracy is important and it has to be achieved by consensus in society and with due regard to security. Asad indicated he was not in a rush. This was a clear stepping back from what had appeared to be the promise of a young reformist president.

DAMASCUS, 2005

In January 2005, I visited Damascus again and met with Bashar al-Asad, going over many of the issues we had discussed in previous meetings. U.S.-Syrian relations had become very tense, and Washington was particularly frustrated over Syria's nonresponsiveness to its requests to clamp down on the Iraq-Syria border, where foreign fighters were crossing into Iraq to join "Al Qaeda in Mesopotamia," and former Iraqi Baathists and exiled leaders who had fallen afoul of Saddam Hussein and had taken refuge in Syria for many years were aiding and abetting the Sunni insurgency with material and financial support. Washington had provided the Syrians with a list of the names of some of the most active Iraqi insurgent supporters and requested that Bashar al-Asad stop their activities on Syrian soil and deport them into the hands of the Iraqi authorities.

I asked Asad if he was planning to take action against them, and he vented his own frustrations and went into a lengthy discourse on the U.S. administration's demands and opposition to Syria. He cited the need for night goggles from the United States that Syria had requested to help patrol the Iraq-Syrian border and never received. He complained about the United States not providing technical teams from the U.S. Treasury that could help the Syrians control financial flows to the insurgents. He claimed that the identification data provided by the Americans on the reported Iraqi exiles in Syria were often incorrect and incomplete.

I gave him the name of one Iraqi individual who was of particular concern to Washington and, noting that I did not represent the U.S. government, took the liberty to comment that if Asad were to render this person into the hands of the Iraqi authorities, that action would be well received in Washington and by President Bush himself and could help get the relationship back on track. This was especially the case, I explained, since we were on the eve of the Iraqi elections at the end of January, which were a major milestone, and anything that could be done to help stabilize Iraq so that those elections could be held successfully would be recognized by Washington.

I advised, however, that it would be wise to take this action now, before the elections, to have its full impact on Washington. Asad took this all on board and did act along the lines suggested, but in February, after the Iraqi elections. This only reinforced Washington's view that the most they could expect from Damascus was always "too little, too late."

When I left Damascus I had an uneasy feeling that the bilateral relations between the United States and Syria were taking a real turn for the worse. The following month, on February 14, 2005, Lebanese prime minister Rafik Hariri was assassinated in Beirut and the finger of guilt pointed immediately to Damascus. I decided that the Baker Institute's U.S.-Syria Dialogue needed a hiatus. The road ahead had become even more arduous and troublesome.

2006—THE IRAQ STUDY GROUP AND SYRIA

The following year, former secretary of state James A. Baker, III and I met with the foreign minister of Syria, Walid Mouallem, and Syrian ambassador Imad Moustafa in New York City as part of the Iraq Study Group's work. Baker opened the discussion by explaining the mission of the ISG and its mandate to take a fresh look at the situation in Iraq and make recommendations on the way forward to Congress and the administration.

He related how, in the 1990s, Syria had become a coalition partner with the United States in Desert Storm. President Hafez al-Asad could trust us and made a strategic calculation that benefited the United States, Syria, Israel, and the region. We need a strategic approach to the region. If we have anarchy in Iraq, it will be terrible for Syria and the region.

Mouallem responded that Syria was ready to resume the dialogue if the U.S. administration decided to engage and not isolate. He opined that the United States needed to open a new page and not discuss "the old policies." He recalled that when I came to Damascus in early 2003, before the military action in Iraq, he warned me that if the United States invaded Iraq, the Iraqis would see us as occupiers. Baker typically was asking pointed questions on Iran and on what Syria would be prepared to do to improve the situation in Iraq and Lebanon and toward the eventual resumption of Israeli-Syrian peace negotiations. Mouallem's responses were positive on all the major issues, and we reflected this in the ISG report. In fact, we specified in some detail what the negotiating framework should be and what obligations Syria, as well as Israel, would have to assume on a number of issues to reach a viable Israeli-Syrian peace agreement.

Mouallem told us that the Syrian government was ready to resume negotiations with Israel on the basis of the Madrid Peace Conference and concluded that much had been done in the last ten years and could be brought to closure in a few months.

It would be, according to the Syrians, a win-win situation for President Bush. Unfortunately, the Bush administration did not adopt the ISG report's recommendations for a dialogue with Syria and engaging the Israelis and Syria in peace negotiations. The administration opted to pursue a policy of isolating Syria and imposing sanctions.

SEVEN

Arab-Israeli Conflict Resolution

An old frog was on the bank of the Nile River, getting ready to swim to the other side, when a scorpion approached him and asked if he could hitch a ride across the river on the frog's back. The frog looked at the scorpion and said, "Do you think I am suicidal? If I carry you, you could sting me." The scorpion replied, "Don't be ridiculous, if I sting you, we would both drown." The frog thought a bit and said, "You are right; hop on." Halfway across the river, the scorpion stings the frog and in great pain the frog turns his head and says, "Why did you do that? Now we will both drown." The scorpion smiles and replies, "Welcome to the Middle East!"

THE PERILOUS ROAD TO PEACE

Many regimes in the Middle East are becoming increasingly vulnerable to the public opinion of their citizens, who view their governments' inability to deliver on urgently needed economic reforms, broader political participation, and Arab-Israeli peace with increasing frustration. One factor in this equation is the desperate economic plight of the Palestinians, which plays into the hands of Palestinian extremists such as Hamas. The lack of employment, food, water, and basic services fuels anger and resentment against both Israel and the Palestinian Authority.

A second factor is the delayed promise of the historic Madrid Peace Conference of 1991, which had heralded a comprehensive peace between Israel and all of its Arab neighbors through direct, face-to-face negotiations based on the principle of land for peace and the central United Nations Security Council Resolutions 242 and 338, which call for the withdrawal of Israeli forces from territory seized in the 1967 war. In addition, the wide gap between elite opinion and popular opinion concerning the peace process has had a negative impact in the region. To many Palestinians, the prospects for peace are dim or nonexistent, and they perceive no change in the difficult circumstances of their daily lives. For many Israelis, there is neither peace nor security. The Oslo Process, with its focus on step-by-step diplomacy and interim accords, proved to be too protracted, without sufficient tangible results on the ground.

The Israeli-Jordanian peace treaty in 1994 was a major achievement, negotiated directly between the Israeli and Jordanian governments and presented to the United States as a fait accompli. But on the Israeli-Syrian and Lebanese negotiating tracks, there have been important missed opportunities since 1993. One example is the failed summit between President Clinton and the late Syrian president Hafez al-Asad, held in Geneva in March 2000. An agreement on this track would have had important strategic implications for the region as a whole and could have enhanced the prospects for a final status agreement between Israelis and Palestinians. Second, the Camp David summit that summer between President Clinton, Prime

Minister Barak, and Chairman Arafat deflated high expectations and set the scene for the tragic violence that followed, with hundreds of persons killed and thousands wounded, most of them Palestinians.

Third, in October 2000, for the first time since 1976 when they demonstrated over land confiscation issues, Israeli Arab citizens demonstrated once again within Israel, this time in solidarity with the Palestinians in the Occupied Territories during what is called the "Intifada al-Aqsa." This led to confrontations with the Israeli security forces, and thirteen Israeli Arabs were killed. That development has had a sobering effect on Israeli public opinion, since the threat to Israel was perceived to come both from within its borders and from outside. Subsequent attacks by Israeli Jews on Israeli Arabs have only exacerbated the problem. In general, the Israeli mood changed from relative optimism to pessimism and disillusionment over the prospects for either peace or security.

A fourth factor is the political symbolism of Hezbollah, seen throughout the Arab and Muslim world as a resistance movement that, in their eyes, has accomplished what Arab governments and armies could not—the evacuation of Israeli troops from occupied Arab territory; in this instance, from southern Lebanon in 2000. Hezbollah's perceived victories in 2000 and in the 2006 war in Lebanon have emboldened Palestinian groups, including Hamas, Palestinian Islamic Jihad, and even groups within Fatah such as Tanzim, who see violence and confrontation as a necessary path, or at least as a concomitant to negotiations.

Indeed, a major issue between Israelis and Palestinians is the question, "Who has the right to be violent?"

The Israelis assert the sovereign right of a state to protect its security and interests by the use of force, military or police, when deemed necessary. But the Palestinians, regarding themselves as an unwillingly occupied people, also claim the right to resort to violent means of resistance to the occupation.

THE ISRAELI-PALESTINIAN NEGOTIATIONS

The collapse of the Israeli-Palestinian negotiations after the Camp David summit in the summer of 2000, the tragic violence and killing that followed, the election of Ariel Sharon as Israel's prime minister and his policy of unilateral withdrawals, and the breakup of the Palestinian National Unity Government in June 2007, all necessitate new thinking about how the peace process should be pursued.

As the parties pursue the talks initiated at Annapolis in November 2007, they should learn from the successes and failures of talks and negotiations to date. One major guideline of the peace process should be the Latin proverb *Festina Lente* ("Make Haste Slowly"). This is not a formula for delay, indecision, or lack of leadership; rather, it implies that the parties should roll up their sleeves and engage actively and seriously in direct face-to-face negotiations with the strong support of the international community, especially the United States, to achieve *in a deliberate manner* what is obtainable at this point and prepare the way for the next stages toward a comprehensive settlement on final-status issues.

Agreement on Jerusalem could not be forced at Camp David without much more preparatory work and consultations in the Arab world. Further, former Israeli prime minister Barak's insistence on the "end of the conflict" without being able to come to closure on key final-status issues altered the very process at the heart of the Oslo agreement, which entailed a series of obtainable interim goals.

The political parties in Israel have to deal with the Palestinians as a separate and distinct national and political identity. As for the Palestinians, whether or not they unilaterally declare their status as a state, they will not be able to achieve their national requirements without a negotiated agreement with Israel. If there is to be peace in the Middle East, a viable and independent Palestinian state, living next to Israel in peace and security, will have to emerge through negotiations and not from unilateral actions by either side.

THE TWO-STATE SOLUTION AND A DEMOCRATIC JEWISH STATE

One of the most significant developments over the last five years has been the evolution in the thinking of some Likud leaders such as Ariel Sharon concerning a Palestinian state. Likud traditionally represents the concept of Eretz Yisrael, the biblical Land of Israel in Judea and Samaria. Likud leaders were the architects of the settlements policy to establish the Jewish footholds in this land. In a remarkable reassessment of the strategic stakes involved, Sharon, as prime minister, concluded that, given the demographic growth rates of the Arab population between the Jordan River and the Mediterranean Sea, Israeli Jews would be outnumbered by their Arab neighbors within a few decades, and Israel would not be able to exist as a "democratic *and* Jewish state." It could not remain democratic if it had to continue to occupy ever larger numbers of Palestinian Arabs, with all the measures that would imply. It would no longer be Jewish in the face of demographic realities both inside (the Israeli Arab/Palestinian population already constitutes 20 percent of Israel's population) and outside its borders in the Occupied Territories. Sharon and others determined that the separation of Israel from the Palestinian territories was the only way out—in effect, a two-state solution, either through a negotiated settlement or through unilateral actions and withdrawals to secure borders. When he determined that the prospects for negotiating with the Palestinian leadership were problematic, Sharon opted for the unilateral withdrawal from Gaza that he successfully concluded, only to be struck down by a cerebral stoke and coma before he could address the West Bank issue.

Sharon was focused on the Palestinian dimension. When I met with him in Jerusalem after I had left the U.S. government and briefed him on my discussions in Damascus with President Bashar al-Asad regarding the prospects for Israeli-Syrian negotiations, he listened politely, took notes as was his habit, and then stated simply that the risks of coming down from the Golan under current circumstances were too high. Nevertheless, Sharon's strategic decision—as a hardliner—to opt for a two-state solution with Palestine was a turning point that created opportunities for peace that the United States and the Arabs could build on.

On the Israeli-Palestinian front, it is critical to support and engage Palestinian president Mahmoud Abbas and the Palestinian Authority (PA) as the focal point of negotiations and move toward true conflict resolution.

Shortly before Hezbollah kidnapped Israeli soldiers and triggered the fighting on the Israeli-Lebanese border in the summer of 2006, the Israeli-Palestinian dialogue had reached the beginning of a way out of that crisis. An understanding was being brokered by Egypt whereby the Palestinians would commit to the safe release of the kidnapped Israeli corporal, Gilad Shalit, Qassam rocket attacks would stop, and a cease-fire would be declared and maintained. There were reliable reports that the Israelis were also prepared to release Palestinian prisoners to Abbas in return for the cease-fire.

THE POLITICAL DYNAMICS BETWEEN
FATAH AND HAMAS

After Hamas's electoral victory in the legislative elections in 2006, and before the crisis in Gaza when Hamas seized control of the strip and the dissolution in June 2007 of the National Unity Government between Fatah and Hamas, there was guarded hope that Hamas could be integrated into more responsible governance and a modification of its militant policies. The external wing of Hamas, led by Khaled Meshal in Damascus, has demonstrated its radical bent, while former Hamas Palestinian prime minister

Ismail Haniyeh and his colleagues inside the territories had to struggle with the requirements of governing and had to consider difficult political compromises. The collapse of the National Unity Government and the confrontations between Fatah and Hamas in Gaza have exacerbated the divisions within the Palestinian body politic.

U.S. policy should be sensitive to these political dynamics and, while fully supporting the Palestinian Authority, should also craft policies that would create the conditions to encourage Hamas to move in a more moderate direction, strengthening the positions of Fatah and Palestinian Authority president Mahmond Abbas. Only the Palestinians can make this accommodation from within their own ranks, but reconciliation will be an Arab mantra that cannot be ignored.

The Quartet—the United States, the European Union, Russia, and the United Nations—has laid out the requirements that Hamas recognize Israel's right to exist, give up terrorism, and respect all signed agreements. To facilitate movement in this direction Hamas should be required to do what other Arab governments have already done: accept fully the Arab peace initiative issued at the Arab League summit in Beirut in March 2002, which called for recognizing Israel in exchange for a comprehensive peace settlement based on UN Security Council Resolutions 242 and 338.

Hamas would be responding in this instance to an Arab initiative that Israel and the Quartet have accepted.

In addition, and to promote forward movement on the Palestinian track, the Quartet, with the United States in the lead, should encourage a clearly delineated multistage approach toward resolving the Palestinians' political, security, and economic issues.

THE BUSH ADMINISTRATION'S ROAD MAP

The political framework for Israeli-Palestinian peace negotiations is contained in the 2003 "Road Map," which was defined by the

Bush administration as "performance-based and goal-driven, with clear phases, timelines, target dates, and benchmarks aiming at progress through reciprocal steps by the two parties in the political, security, economic, humanitarian, and institution-building fields," under the auspices of the Quartet.

The destination of this map was to be a final and comprehensive settlement of the Israeli-Palestinian conflict by 2005, as presented in a speech by President Bush on June 24, 2002, and detailed previously in an April 30, 2002, statement from the Department of State: "A settlement, negotiated between the parties, will result in the emergence of an independent, democratic, and viable Palestinian state living side by side in peace and security with Israel and its other neighbors. The settlement will resolve the Israel-Palestinian conflict, and end the occupation that began in 1967, based on the foundations of the Madrid Conference, the principle of land for peace, UNSC Resolutions 242, 338, and agreements previously reached by the parties, and the initiative of Saudi Crown Prince Abdullah—endorsed by the Beirut Arab League Summit and referred to above in relation to Hamas—calling for acceptance of Israel as a neighbor living in peace and security, in the context of a comprehensive settlement. This initiative is a key element of international efforts to promote a comprehensive peace on all tracks, including the Syrian-Israeli and Lebanese-Israeli tracks."

PHASE I

Phase I of the Road Map aims at ending terror and violence, normalizing Palestinian life, and building Palestinian institutions. In this phase, the Palestinians are required to immediately undertake an unconditional cessation of violence according to specific steps accompanied by supportive measures undertaken by Israel. Palestinians and Israelis are to resume security cooperation to end violence, terrorism, and incitement through restructured and effective Palestinian security services. Palestinians are also to undertake comprehensive political reform in preparation for statehood, including drafting a Palestinian constitution and free, fair, and open elections upon the basis of those measures. Israel is to take all necessary steps to help normalize Palestinian life. Israel is to withdraw from Palestinian areas occupied from September 28, 2000, and the two sides are to restore the status quo that existed at that time, as security performance and cooperation progress. Israel is to immediately dismantle settlement outposts erected since March 2001 and freeze all settlement activity (including natural growth of settlements).

With regard to security, the challenge is to help stabilize the Palestinian territories, reform and reorganize the Palestinian security services, disarm and integrate individual armed groups into the new security force structure, and establish central control by the PA over the use of force. In both the Palestinian and the Lebanese contexts, the success of disarmament and integration of armed groups into a unified security force structure under the control of the state will ultimately be the barometer of the exercise of full state sovereignty. On the economic front, the international community must help promote reforms and avoid a humanitarian disaster in the Palestinian territories, particularly Gaza, by focusing on four key issues: the payment of monthly salaries to the PA's civil and police employees; the financing of health, education, and social programs for the population at large; covering the running costs of essential public institutions and municipal services; and the financing of infrastructure projects. Israel should also be encouraged, with due consideration for its legitimate security needs, to increase the number of Palestinian workers inside its economy and facilitate the movement of goods across its borders.

PHASE II

Phase II called for provisional Palestinian borders, to be established by 2003. This was rejected by the Palestinians and has been set aside in favor of moving directly to final-status issues.

PHASE III

Phase III objectives are consolidation of reform and stabilization of Palestinian institutions, sustained, effective Palestinian security performance, and Israeli-Palestinian negotiations aimed at a permanent status agreement.

After seven years of no serious and sustained engagement, the U.S. administration did bring the Israelis and Palestinians, as well as many Arab states, to a meeting in Annapolis in November 2007 to relaunch Israeli-Palestinian peace talks with the stated goal of trying to reach a final settlement by the end of 2008.

In a number of briefings and meetings I had with Secretary of State Condoleezza Rice, she explained that the U.S. approach succeeded in having the parties deal with the Phase I and Phase III aspects of the Road Map at the same time and that Phase II of the Road Map (provisional arrangements and borders) was not a focal point of the effort. I certainly welcomed this approach because I had always thought that "provisionalism" was a nonstarter.

In any case, a major effort by the U.S. president and his secretary of state will be required to reach the ambitious goal set down at Annapolis. The parties are going to have to make painful compromises. It is much easier for them to go to their domestic constituencies and say, "Look, this is not my preferred option, but the president of the United States is asking me to do this."

2002 STATEMENT OF PRINCIPLES

What is particularly important is that there be parallel movement forward on improving the situation on the ground in terms of the Phase I obligations of both the Israelis and the Palestinians, and that there be substantive engagement and movement on the final-status issues, including Jerusalem, the territorial issue of the border, the right of return and a just settlement of the Palestinian refugee problem, security arrangements, and access to water resources. As intractable as these issues may seem to be, they have been discussed extensively in previous negotiations and the general contours of a settlement are in sight.

The Statement of Principles signed on July 27, 2002, by Ami Ayalon, the former head of Shin Beth, Israel's internal security service, and Sari Nusseibeh, the president of Al-Quds University in Jerusalem and former PLO representative in Jerusalem, provides a framework that has been discussed and debated by the parties. Namely:

1. Two states for two peoples: Both sides will declare that Palestine is the only state of the Palestinian people and Israel is the only state of the Jewish people.
2. Borders: Permanent borders between the two states will be agreed upon on the basis of the June 4, 1967, lines, UN resolutions, and the Arab peace initiative (known as the Saudi initiative).
   - Border modifications will be based on an equitable and agreed-upon territorial exchange (1:1) in accordance with the vital needs of both sides, including security, territorial contiguity, and demographic considerations.
   - The Palestinian state will have a connection between its two geographical areas, the West Bank and the Gaza Strip.
   - After establishment of the agreed-upon borders, no Israeli settlers will remain in the Palestinian state.
3. Jerusalem: Jerusalem will be an open city, the capital of two states. Freedom of religion and full access to holy sites will be guaranteed to all.

- Arab neighborhoods in Jerusalem will come under Palestinian sovereignty, Jewish neighborhoods under Israeli sovereignty.
- Neither side will exercise sovereignty over the holy places. The state of Palestine will be designated guardian of al-Haram al-Sharif (The Temple Mount) for the benefit of Muslims. Israel will be the guardian of the Western Wall for the benefit of the Jewish people. The status quo on Christian holy sites will be maintained. No excavation will take place in or underneath the holy sites without mutual consent.

4. Right of return: Recognizing the suffering and the plight of the Palestinian refugees, the international community, Israel, and the Palestinian state will initiate and contribute to an international fund to compensate them.
   - Palestinian refugees will return only to the state of Palestine; Jews will return only to the state of Israel.
   - The international community will offer compensation toward bettering the lot of those refugees willing to remain in their present country of residence, or who wish to emigrate to third-party countries.

5. The Palestinian state will be demilitarized, and the international community will guarantee its security and independence.

6. End of conflict: Upon the full implementation of these principles, all claims on both sides and the Israeli-Palestinian conflict will end.

One can see here the general contours of an agreement that have emerged from years of Israeli and Palestinian engagement on these issues. Differences will have to be negotiated. What is needed is the political courage and will of all the parties to translate these general ideas into agreements.

THE ISRAELI, SYRIAN, AND LEBANESE NEGOTIATIONS

With the focus on the Israeli-Palestinian negotiations, the Israeli-Syrian and Lebanese negotiating tracks seem to have become the forgotten agenda of the Madrid Peace Conference initiated in 1991. In the short run, this situation may be tolerable. But as time goes on, failure to settle the issues at stake poses a threat to the peace and security of the region, as was dramatically demonstrated in the summer of 2006 in the military confrontation between Hezbollah and Israel in Lebanon, which threatened a wider regional conflict involving Syria.

SYRIA

Despite the somber outlook of recent years, there is a real opportunity to achieve a comprehensive settlement between Israel and Syria. This is suggested by the progress made in the past negotiations between the parties, by each side's perception that the other has impeccably implemented previous disengagement agreements, and by an analysis of their current and future interests. It is clear that achieving a settlement will require strong political will by the leadership in Israel, Syria, and the United States. It is crucial to the future of Middle East, U.S., and European interests to make such an effort.

On at least two occasions—August 1993 and November 1995—Israel and Syria came very close to an agreement, but the negotiations were not pursued to a successful conclusion. These negotiations have also led to a general expectation of the contours of an agreement, and these contours are well known. These negotiations have produced a series of "lessons"—not necessarily positive ones—about the experience. Each of the three parties (Israel, Syria, and the United States) is perceived by another to have failed to deliver what was expected at key points in the negotiations. Each party is seen by another to have lacked the requisite political will or determination.

Not surprisingly, the Israeli and Syrian narratives of the past negotiations differ. A good example is their views of the "Rabin Deposit." Israel asserts that, in 1993, Prime Minister Rabin made a *hypothetical and conditional* deposition that included the idea of exchanging Israeli withdrawal from the Golan for Syria's accepting Israel's requirements for security and normalization of relations in the context of peace. This formula included a five-year timetable and a phased implementation in which a heavy dose of normalization would be given by Syria early on, in return for a limited first phase of withdrawal. In the Israeli view, Rabin's expression of Israel's willingness to withdraw to the June 4, 1967, lines was *not* an absolute and unconditional commitment. Syria, however, interprets this pledge as *a firm Israeli commitment to full withdrawal* to the June 4, 1967, lines, which, the Syrians maintain, was made both through the U.S. interlocutor and directly by the Israelis.

While recognizing the essential role of the United States as the honest broker, Israelis and Syrians indicate that the United States made a number of mistakes during the negotiations and did not always play an effective role. In particular, both Israel and Syria referred to the lack of U.S. leadership and determination to pursue openings in the negotiations at key junctures (for example, August 1993, when Rabin made the aforementioned "deposit"; November 1995, when Shimon Peres was prime minister and talks went nowhere; and the March 2000 Geneva summit between Presidents Clinton and Hafez al-Asad, which ended abruptly). In 2008, in the absence of the Bush administration's playing this honest broker role, Israel and Syria turned to Turkey as an intermediary.

Back-channel talks through intermediaries between Israel and Syria during Prime Minister Netanyahu's mandate reportedly made some progress, but did not lead to any successful outcome and left each side suspicious of the other's intentions.

Nevertheless, much progress in the Israeli-Syrian negotiations was achieved from the time of the Madrid Peace Conference in 1991, and in subsequent negotiations on the key issues of land, peace, security, water, and the interrelationships of these factors.

THE RISKS OF CONTINUED STALEMATE

But while debate about the past is pertinent, the key challenge is how to get Israeli-Syrian negotiations restarted. The question is whether an Israeli government will be willing and able to come to an agreement with Syria based on full withdrawal. The other side of this equation is whether President Bashar al-Asad, given the experiences of the past negotiations, is willing to offer a Syrian counterpackage that will make an agreement politically feasible for his Israeli counterpart.

Most observers do not anticipate a war between Israel and Syria in the short run. But the danger will grow if no settlement is reached. For example, continued stalemate could lead to reactivating the front between a Syrian-backed Hezbollah and Israel on the Lebanon border, and, in the worst-case scenario, bring other Arab countries in the conflict. The dispute over the Sheba'a Farms area on the Lebanese-Syrian-Israeli border is a case in point. This is an approximately ten-square-mile area of verdant agricultural land, watered by abundant snowmelt and adjacent to Israel, Syria, and Lebanon, which was seized by Israel in the June 1967 Six-Day War. Though the borders have in fact been somewhat ambiguous, both Lebanon and Syria claim the land rightfully belongs to Lebanon, which was not a party to the war, and should therefore be returned to Lebanon. Israel has maintained that the area is part of the Golan Heights, which it seized from Syria in the war, and has refused to cede the land—and its vital water supply—to Lebanon. The United Nations has issued several resolutions disputing Israel's claim, and Hezbollah has used Israel's occupation of the Farms as a major justification for its continued attacks on Israel. Unsettled, the longstanding dispute remains a potential flashpoint.

In this stalemate, misunderstandings and suspicions will increase over time. The Israeli government will come under increasing pressure to spend the necessary resources to maintain its technological edge in the regional military balance with systems such as the Arrow tactical missile defense system and beyond. Despite serious economic constraints and the loss of its former Soviet patron, Syria will be tempted to proceed with the acquisition of military equipment to modernize its force structure and develop more weapons of mass destruction (it has long had a chemical and biological weapons program).

Given the delivery systems that Syria would use for these weapons (surface-to-surface missiles), such a situation would be destabilizing. Syria would fear that its weapons systems would be destroyed in an Israeli first strike and would have a strong incentive to "use them rather than lose them." The Israelis will reach the same conclusion and have a strong incentive to strike first, before these weapons could be used. This would be the classic spiral of mutual distrust, tension, and escalation that is discussed in much of the arms-race literature.

In sum, from a military point of view, there is a window of instability in the strategic relations between the two states. This situation can be exacerbated by the continuing violence on the ground, and especially by Hezbollah's actions on Israel's northern border.

THE PROSPECTS

The resumption of negotiations and the ultimate achievement of a Syrian-Israeli peace treaty requires strong political will by all sides. In this track, the legacy of past negotiations—both the understandings reached thus far and the lessons learned from past mistakes—can serve as a reference point for new negotiations. There seems to be sufficient common ground to provide a starting point. Ehud Barak, who attached much strategic significance to an Israeli-Syrian agreement, implied that Rabin's hypothetical formula for withdrawal to the June 4, 1967, lines could be put on the table with certain adjustments, including a band of territory, essentially an expanded roadway, along the northeastern coastline of the Sea of Galilee, which would provide the Israelis full access to the Galilee's waters.

The hastily arranged Geneva summit meeting in March 2000, between Clinton and the late Hafez al-Asad, was convened to convey Barak's ideas and rapidly ended in failure largely because Asad expected that the United States "understood his requirement" for a clear commitment from Barak on the Rabin formula, not just a presentation of Barak's proposal. President Clinton's negotiating team mismanaged this summit, with insufficient preparation and without bringing to the table a U.S. position or bridging proposal that addressed the key requirements of both sides—an American gesture that Asad would have expected at a summit meeting intended to come to some closure on key issues. Also, it would have been much more difficult for Asad to reject out of hand an American proposal put forward by the U.S. president. Some have argued that because of Asad's terminal illness he was not really interested in concluding a deal at Geneva, but was preoccupied with assuring the succession of his son, Bashar, to the presidency. There is serious reason to believe that the opposite is the case.

Hafez al-Asad came to Geneva with a strong contingent of political, security, and diplomatic advisors. He knew that, given his political ability to deliver Syria to the deal he signed with Israel, his son's succession would have been more assured than if he had died in the absence of an agreement, especially given his son's inexperience in politics and diplomacy. What Asad perceived he got at Geneva was basically Ehud Barak's position, which, in his eyes, an ambassador, special envoy, or secretary of state could have delivered to him in Damascus.

After his father's death, Syria's president Bashar al-Asad has reiterated his father's "strategic option for peace," based on the principle of land for peace and the return of all Syria's territory up to the June 4, 1967, borders. In an interview in the Saudi Pan Arab newspaper *al Sharq al Awsat* in February 2001, he stated, "What President Hafez Asad asked for is what I am asking for. I didn't omit or add anything. Syrian rights have not changed; and the Syrian street, to whom these rights are due, has not changed either. President Hafez Asad did not concede Syrian rights, and we in Syria did not, and will not, concede, now or in the future. . . . We tell everyone that these are our terms for peace. Whoever can meet them, we are prepared to continue the negotiations with them. We deal with facts, not expectations."

It is clear from Bashar al-Asad's remarks that the Syrians are determined to hang tough in their position and are signaling, characteristically, that the ball is in the Israeli court. I remember once telling Bashar's father that I was writing a book on the principles of Syrian diplomacy. Hafez al-Asad asked, "Do you have the time?" and I said it would be a very short book—just one page with one sentence: "The ball is in your court." He laughed and didn't deny the point. In any case and at the appropriate time, the United States could play a key role in both facilitating the resumption of negotiations and bringing them to a positive conclusion. For that role to be assumed, presidential leadership and commitment and backing of U.S. efforts in the field are crucial.

The basic foundations to any settlement are UN Resolutions 242 and 338. These resolutions entail the inadmissibility of the occupation of territory by war, advocate mutual recognition, respect for the sovereignty and the territorial integrity of all the states in the region, and the right of all states to live in peace within secure and recognized borders. The Syrians interpret these resolutions as requiring the withdrawal of Israeli armed forces from all the Syrian territories the Israelis occupied in 1967; that is, the Golan Heights. The Israelis require a clear definition of peace and normalization of relations, security arrangements, and access to water.

THE IRAQ STUDY GROUP ON THE SYRIAN ROLE

The 2006 "Baker-Hamilton" Iraq Study Group (ISG) report, discussed more fully in the following chapter, specified what actions Syria would have to take to achieve a viable peace agreement; namely, that negotiated peace should contain at least the following elements:

- Syria's full adherence to UN Security Council Resolution 1701 of August 2006, which provides the framework for Lebanon to regain sovereign control over its territory.
- Syria's full cooperation with the investigation by the United Nations commission on the assassination of Lebanese prime minister Rafik Hariri and the international tribunal approved by the United Nations Security Council.
- A verifiable cessation of Syrian aid to Hezbollah.
- A verifiable cessation of the use of Syrian territory for transshipment of Iranian weapons and aid to Hezbollah.
- Syria's using its influence with Hamas and Hezbollah for the release of the captured Israel Defense Forces soldiers.
- A verifiable cessation of Syrian efforts to undermine the democratically elected government of Lebanon.
- A verifiable cessation of arms shipments from or transiting through Syria for Hamas and other radical Palestinian groups.
- A Syrian commitment to help obtain from Hamas an acknowledgment of Israel's right to exist.
- Greater Syrian efforts to seal its border with Iraq.

In exchange for all of this and in the context of a final peace agreement, there should be an Israeli return of the Golan

Heights, with a U.S. security guarantee for Israel that could include an international force on the border, including U.S. troops if requested by both parties.

AN ISRAELI-SYRIAN PEACE

Progress on the Israeli-Syrian track should not be used as an excuse to forestall progress on the Israeli-Palestinian track. The reverse is also true. This principle should be explicit in U.S. policy. The approach of the Madrid Peace Conference in 1991 was that each bilateral track should proceed at its own pace and that, concomitantly, the multilateral track should proceed in a parallel manner on key issues of arms control and security, refugees, environment, economic development, and water. This overall comprehensive and structural approach was virtually abandoned subsequently.

The following ideas could be considered as means for restarting negotiations and raising the likelihood of their successful conclusion in a Syrian-Israeli peace treaty:

- To help the parties return to the table, the United States could present a series of questions to Israel and Syria regarding (a) their willingness to consider and build upon the legacy of past negotiations (of which the United States is custodian) and (b) specific aspects of their positions regarding the substantive issues under negotiations (that is, withdrawal, security arrangements, the nature of peace, water, and the interrelationship of these issues with one another).
- The purpose of these questions is to clarify the parties' positions to better determine the specific agenda and content of negotiations. These positions should be exchanged between the parties (directly or indirectly) to reduce mistrust and suspicion through policy transparency. Such questions may also be in the

form of a "what if" exercise. Such an approach was applied in the past and may have been instrumental in generating progress during 1993 and 1994.

- An alternative possibility is that if the differences between the parties have been sufficiently narrowed, the answers to these questions or clarifications may serve as the basis for the drafting by the United States of a Single Negotiating Text (SNT) that can serve as the foundation for negotiations. This SNT may be useful in that it can build on the legacy of past negotiations and incorporate new ideas and emphases by the parties. The parties will respond to the SNT by suggesting amendments, revisions, additions, and so forth. Using the SNT as the foundation of future negotiations may produce a more focused process.

- At some point during this period, separate but parallel negotiations on the Lebanese-Israeli track should be resumed and the parties should make a sustained effort to reach a comprehensive Syrian-Israeli, Lebanese-Israeli agreement.

- The United States should, as an honest broker, initiate a process of clarification of positions through "what if" questions on security arrangements through sustained talks between teams of military and security experts. These talks would include consideration of provisions for temporary security arrangements before final agreement. They could also include discussion of issues related to the Sea of Galilee.

- The United States should reiterate its willingness to guarantee, at the request of the parties, any security arrangements on the Golan that are agreed upon by all sides.

- The United States should coordinate efforts with other countries, in and outside of the region, which should use their influence with the parties to develop "carrots" that would provide additional incentives for negotiation and agreement.

- The United States should induce the Israeli and Syrian leaders to engage in public diplomacy, give press interviews, and issue public statements to help increase trust in both countries and facilitate the resumption of negotiations. Most important, both sides should avoid statements that hinder the prospect for resuming negotiations and reaching a settlement. Each side should make a significant statement to facilitate the restarting of negotiations. For example, Israel could state that, in principle, land for peace and security applies to the Golan and that if Israel's security and peace-related needs are met, it would be willing to make the necessary "painful" territorial concessions.

- In addition, Israel could acknowledge that the legacy of past negotiations is an acceptable basis for renewed negotiations, and that all options are open including full withdrawal for full security and peace. It could note, however, that the issues discussed in the past will need to be elaborated upon and clarified. Likewise, the Syrian leadership should reiterate to the Israeli people not only that Syria made the strategic choice for full peace with Israel, but that it recognizes the need for an agreement that would entail "full and normal relations" and that each side's security requirements need to be addressed fully within the agreement.

- An Israeli-Syrian settlement should be followed by a series of economic measures to aid Syria. As a prelude, economic talks involving the United States and the international community, including the Arab Gulf states, could be initiated in parallel to renewed Israeli-Syrian negotiations.

- To promote trust and reduce misperception, the parties should be encouraged to engage in informal and direct discussions and meetings. These informal discussions can serve as a useful supplement to formal negotiations—for example, to allow for a more complete exploration of "what if" questions.
- Finally, the United States should be prepared, at the appropriate time, to present positions and mediate issues at key junctures of the negotiation process itself.

LEBANON

Forward movement on the Israeli-Syrian track should lead to movement on the Israeli-Lebanese negotiating track. A key consideration of U.S. policy should be that any Israeli-Syrian peace agreement should not be made at the expense of Lebanon's political independence, sovereignty, and territorial integrity.

With the Israeli withdrawal from South Lebanon in 2000, a major issue has been resolved between the two countries. With the exception of the Sheba'a Farms area on the border, no territorial issues remain between Lebanon and Israel. One major issue connected to Israeli-Lebanese negotiations is a just and mutually agreeable relocation or resettlement of the Palestinian refugees. Lebanon insists that the four hundred thousand Palestinian refugees in Lebanon must be resettled elsewhere, lest their continued presence cause further internal political and confessional strife and instability in Lebanon, as witnessed in 2007 by the penetration of these camps by Al Qaeda groups such as Fatah al-Islam in the Naher el Bared camp in northern Lebanon.

In an article, "From Conflict Management to Conflict Resolution," that I wrote for the November/December 2006 issue of *Foreign Affairs*, I noted that the fighting in the Levant in the summer of 2006 presented a fundamental challenge for U.S. policy toward the Middle East—but also an opportunity to move from conflict management to conflict resolution. The United States should have seized that moment to transform the cease-fire in the Hezbollah-Israeli conflict into a step toward a comprehensive Arab-Israeli peace settlement. Doing so would have facilitated the marginalization of the forces of Islamic radicalism, driven a wedge between Iran and Syria, and enhanced the prospects for regional security and political, economic, and social progress.

The Hezbollah-Israeli confrontation has further proved what should already have been painfully clear to all: There is no viable military solution to the Arab-Israeli conflict. Even with its military superiority, Israel cannot achieve security by force alone or by unilateral withdrawal from occupied territories. Nor can Hezbollah, Hamas, Palestinian Islamic Jihad, and similar groups destroy Israel. Peace can come only from negotiated agreements that bind both sides.

Hezbollah may have ignited the spark that set off this confrontation, but it was not the root cause. The fighting was the combined result of the unresolved Arab-Israeli conflict and the struggle between the forces of moderation and those of extremism within the Muslim world—two issues that are linked by the radicals' exploitation of the Arab-Israeli conflict for their own political ends. U.S. policy in the region should thus focus both on trying to promote a peaceful settlement of the Arab-Israeli dispute and on helping Muslim moderates by facilitating political and economic reform across the Middle East.

THE 2006 HEZBOLLAH-ISRAELI WAR

The crisis on the Israeli-Lebanese border in the summer of 2006 erupted in an already tense environment. On June 25, Hamas kidnapped an Israeli soldier, which reignited fighting on the Israeli-Palestinian front. When Hezbollah captured two Israeli soldiers on July 12, it precipitated a strong Israeli military reaction, which, by his own admission, Hezbollah leader Hassan Nasrallah had not anticipated.

The Hezbollah-Israeli war lasted thirty-four days, with major Israeli incursions into Lebanon and the firing of some four thousand Hezbollah rockets. The fighting resulted in major casualties (approximately 855 Lebanese and 159 Israelis killed), as well as large displacements of people on both sides of the border. Lebanon sustained economic and infrastructure damage estimated at $3.9 billion, and the toll on Israel has been figured as running into the hundreds of millions.

When the hostilities began, the international community called for an immediate cease-fire, but the Bush administration held off, calling for a "sustainable" cease-fire instead. The Bush administration left the strong impression that it was giving Israeli prime minister Ehud Olmert's government time to inflict serious damage on Hezbollah's infrastructure and personnel. Meanwhile, the administration and Israel clearly identified Iran and Syria as the main state supporters of Hezbollah's actions, and the danger of a wider regional conflict was not dismissed.

Eventually, the international community stepped in to stabilize southern Lebanon and prevent the crisis from escalating further. The parameters for international action had been set by UN Security Council Resolution 1559, passed in 2004, which called for the withdrawal of Syrian troops from Lebanon and the disarmament of Hezbollah. Resolution 1701, passed on August 11, 2006, refers to the withdrawal of Israeli forces, the presence of a UN force, and the commitment of the government of Lebanon to extend its authority over its territory; it also takes note of proposals regarding the Sheba'a Farms area. In other words, it provides the necessary framework to support the Lebanese government's development and the implementation of Beirut's plan to regain sovereign control over the whole country.

Still, an outside stabilization program was urgently required to help this happen. Such a program would need to include an agreement on a lasting and comprehensive cease-fire, the return of both Israeli and Arab hostages and prisoners, and an international support package involving economic, humanitarian, and security assistance for Lebanon. It would also need to contain realistic plans for deploying the Lebanese army fully to the south of the country, disarming Hezbollah, and preventing illicit arms shipments to Lebanon. And it would need to include a solution to the disagreements regarding control and sovereignty over Sheba'a Farms. The successful implementation of such a stabilization program would not just help resolve current tensions; it could also provide the basis for moving forward on negotiations for an Israeli-Lebanese peace agreement in the context of a comprehensive settlement.

Syria, meanwhile, can be both a spoiler and a facilitator. The Asad regime could undermine security arrangements in southern Lebanon, hinder progress in Iraq, and continue to support Hezbollah, Palestinian Islamic Jihad, and radicals in Hamas. But it could also play a constructive role in the region—a possibility that has yet to be fully explored.

The main problems on Israel's northern front now are Hezbollah and the inability of the government of Lebanon to exert authority throughout the entire country. Since Syria facilitates Hezbollah's access to arms and money, any sustainable solution in southern Lebanon would require Syria to be on board. Given Syria's historically special relationship with Lebanon, Damascus would not countenance a separate deal between Beirut and Jerusalem, so the Israeli-Lebanese and the Israeli-Syrian negotiating tracks could proceed in a separate but parallel manner.

THE IRANIAN FACTOR

If Syria is Hezbollah's facilitator, Iran is its key ideological, political, and financial patron. Hezbollah is a grassroots Lebanese Shiite political party and militia. Nasrallah and the party decide and manage local political, social, and cultural issues on their own, including tactical decisions on paramilitary operations against Israel. But the group recognizes the absolute political and religious authority of Iran's supreme leader, Ayatollah Ali Khamenei, on doctrinal and strategic issues. Any sustainable agreement with Hezbollah in southern Lebanon, therefore, would also have to involve Iran.

Several different basic approaches to Arab-Israeli peace negotiations have been suggested by those involved over the years. The appeal of any one method depends greatly on the overall situation on the ground in the region and within each country, as well as the political situation of the international community, especially the United States. Three possible approaches are described below.

THE OUTSIDE HAND

As mentioned above, a comprehensive agreement along the lines of what was discussed at Camp David between Arafat, Barak, and Clinton, and at Geneva between Clinton and Hafez al-Asad, proved to be elusive at the time. According to the proponents of this approach, what is needed is for a strong outside hand—the United States—to exercise leadership and influence to induce the parties to come to a comprehensive agreement on the final-status issues. This implies that the United States would bring to the table, when necessary, positions and bridging proposals that the parties would be urged to consider and accept. For such an approach to be effective, however, both Israelis and Arabs must perceive the United States to be an "honest broker."

SECURITY NOW AND WAIT FOR A BETTER DAY

A second approach, favored by many in Israel, is grounded in the conviction that the Palestinians are not ready to make the necessary compromises and decisions on final-status issues, and therefore, the maximum agreements that can be achieved on security issues should be reached, preferably between the parties, but imposed unilaterally, if necessary, and that the parties should live in separation and wait for that day when perhaps changes in leadership and generational change would allow cloture on final-status issues.

Barak suggested that the forced separation measures the Israeli government put in place as a result of the recent violence could become permanent if "there is no partner for peace on the other side." He ordered planning for a permanent militarized border between Israel and the Palestinian territories, for a program substituting Filipino, Vietnamese, and other foreigners for Palestinian workers, and for disengaging Israel from the complex of utilities and other services shared with the Palestinians. Sharon went ahead with a bold unilateral withdrawal from Gaza. This unilateral separatist approach has proven to be a formula for continued strife and serious destabilization, as evidenced by the Hamas-Fatah confrontations in Gaza in June 2007 and the firing of Qassam rockets by Palestinians at targets in southern Israel. The Palestinians, while eager to establish their independent state, have a different idea of separation that does not have Israel controlling the borders, maintaining settlements, and leaving the Palestinians with only 40 percent of the land.

A PHASED AGREEMENT

Since the parties tried at Camp David to achieve a comprehensive agreement on final-status issues with the Palestinians and failed, some argue that consideration should be given to a lesser goal that will not include, at this stage, "an end to the conflict" — which Barak insisted on — and will not include agreement on the key final-status issues of the Palestinian refugees and Jerusalem. These two sensitive final-status issues can be put in separate but continuing negotiating tracks to explore compromise solutions. At the same time, agreements can be reached where possible on land, security, water, and economic relations. Some of the major settlements could be consolidated and these settlers could become more confident of their eventual status as part of Israel. In this context, it is important to note that unless isolated Israeli settlements are dismantled and major Israeli settlements are consolidated, there can be no viable territorial division.

For the Palestinians, it would be essential that any agreement remove Israeli control over their daily lives. This was the motivating force of the Intifada. Further, any separation must not be punitive. It must be negotiated and it must be in a territorial and legal context with the establishment of the Palestinian state. The Palestinians would also insist that all unilateral Israeli actions, such as land confiscation and new settlements, cease, lest the passage of time undermine legitimate Palestinian territorial and national rights. If settlements in the territories, other than those that could be consolidated in any future agreement, are not dismantled, there has to be at least a verifiable freeze on all settlement activity, including any in East Jerusalem.

Economic separation between Israelis and Palestinians would be a particularly heavy blow for the latter. One-third of the Palestinian GDP has depended on Palestinian labor working in Israel. In addition, Palestinian exports are highly dependent on Israeli markets. The Customs Union between Israel and the Palestinian Authority, under the terms of which Israel pays taxes on Palestinian goods, is an important source of funds for the Palestinians. In this respect, the creation of economic borders would be detrimental to the Palestinians especially. Security borders are another matter.

In any case, if such a phased agreement could be reached, and after Israel and an independent Palestinian state have coexisted side by side for a period of time, an effort can be made to bring the final-status issues of settlements, borders, Jerusalem, and the Palestinian refugees to closure.

Accordingly, and in the context of either a phased or a comprehensive agreement, economic arrangements should be pursued to foster Palestinian economic development, cooperation, and stability in areas where both sides have mutual interests, for example in the field of water and natural gas.

THE QUEST FOR ARAB-ISRAELI PEACE

In the overall context of the successes and failures in the quest for Arab-Israeli peace, and reflecting on the history of United States involvement in Arab-Israeli negotiations, a few "lessons learned" come to mind:

1. Do not act in haste, but act in a coherent and deliberate manner within a strategic policy framework and "political horizon."
2. Return to the basic and principled framework of the Madrid Peace Conference for direct, face-to-face negotiations between Israel and the Palestinians, Syria, and Lebanon, and reinvigorate the multilateral track.
3. Avoid short-term and politically expedient deadlines.
4. Do not lose sight of public opinion and the "street," both Arab and Israeli, and communicate publicly with both sides to give a realistic sense of direction.
5. Keep domestic constituencies informed of the administration's thinking on a timely basis, to help obtain the support of American public opinion.
6. Focus on what is doable and avoid a "bridge too far" where it is not feasible to narrow gaps in the positions of the parties.
7. Do not have summits when the groundwork has not been sufficiently prepared (as was the case in Geneva, March 2000, and Camp David, summer of 2000).
8. Keep separate channels of discussion and negotiation on final-status issues open and active.

9. Organize the U.S. negotiation team in a manner in which there is "adult supervision" by the secretary of state, and a full exchange of information and coordination within the national security team so that the secretary of state and the president are dealing from a full deck of cards.
10. Recognize that if the president of the United States is not politically committed in word and deed to the negotiations, the U.S. role as a valid interlocutor with the parties will be diminished and even undercut. Stating a vision is not a policy.

WAGING PEACE

The extremists in the Muslim world today define the conflict with Israel as an existential one, using terms similar to those prevalent in the region half a century ago. The moderates accept the possibility of a political settlement based on the principle of land for peace; for them, in other words, the issue is about Israel's borders, not its existence. UN Security Council Resolutions 242 and 338 (adopted in 1967 and 1973, respectively) embody this latter approach, and the United States should resume its traditional role of pressing for their implementation.

After the Yom Kippur War in 1973, President Richard Nixon and Secretary of State Henry Kissinger led the effort to obtain the disengagement agreements between Israel, Syria, and Egypt. In 1979, President Jimmy Carter brought Israeli prime minister Menachem Begin and Egyptian president Anwar al-Sadat together to sign the peace treaty between their two countries. In 1991, President George H. W. Bush and Secretary of State James A. Baker, III led the effort to bring Israel and all of its immediate Arab neighbors together for the first time in direct negotiations in Madrid. President Clinton presided over the signing of the Oslo Accords on the White House lawn in 1993, witnessed the signing of the 1994 peace treaty between Jordan and Israel, and made a major effort toward the end of his term in office that, while it did not lead to a signed agreement, helped to define the contours of an Israeli-Palestinian settlement. This track record proves that with strong presidential leadership, the United States can be an effective interlocutor between the Arabs and the Israelis.

President George W. Bush's vision of a comprehensive Arab-Israeli peace settlement, outlined in his June 2002 speech, including his explicit call for a two-state solution involving a Palestinian state living in peace and security next to the state of Israel, was a rhetorical breakthrough. Unfortunately, it was not pursued vigorously after he enunciated the policy. Nevertheless, the successful convening of the Annapolis meeting in November 2007 is a positive step forward that can be built upon along the lines of some of the ideas and suggestions outlined above. It could give the parties in the region the political space they need to make the tough decisions and compromises for a negotiated peace.

All the key issues in the Middle East—the Arab-Israeli conflict, Iraq, Iran, the need for regionwide political and economic reforms, extremism, and terrorism—are inextricably linked. Nothing short of a comprehensive strategy can solve the problems, marginalize the radicals, and promote the values and interests of the United States and the parties in the region. Washington has waged war in Afghanistan and Iraq. The question now is whether an American president can muster the political will to wage peace as well.

EIGHT

BAGHDAD

Do not try to do too much with your own hands. . . . It is
their war, and you are to help them, not to win it for them.
—T. E. LAWRENCE, 1917

The Bush administration's post-invasion policy in Iraq ignored a large body of advice from foreign policy and military professionals, with disastrous consequences.

Those who drove the policy had little understanding of the history, culture, politics, and complexity of Iraqi society or the region as a whole.

Zealous pursuit of ideological precepts not grounded in knowledge and coupled with arrogance trumped the warnings of those in the administration who knew better, but whose voices and expertise were ignored.

This was a war of choice, not of necessity. We should have contained and isolated Saddam Hussein's regime, as we did with that of Muammar Qaddafi in Libya. We had the whole world with us after 9/11. We could have led a comprehensive international sanctions effort against Saddam Hussein's regime.

As it turned out, there were no weapons of mass destruction. This war was about regime change from outside, with U.S. troops if necessary, coupled with the neoconservative drive for aggressive democracy promotion in the Middle East. It was a wrong-headed approach whose unintended consequences have cost us greatly in blood and treasure, exacerbated Sunni-Shia tensions in the region, allowed Al Qaeda to establish an important base of operations in Iraq, and diverted our focus on other urgent issues such as Afghanistan and Pakistan, the Arab-Israeli conflict, and our relations with Latin America, China, and Russia.

I made my first visit to Iraq in 1967, when I drove through the country on an exploratory trip to the region, tracing Abraham's itinerary from Ur to Canaan in reverse, starting from the Levant, where I was assigned to the American Embassy in Beirut. I knew that Iraqi history had included more than its share of violence and bloodshed, but I was nevertheless shocked when I drove into Tahrir (Liberation) Square in Baghdad and saw dead men hanging from the lamp posts around the square. They had been publicly executed, with the nature of their crimes written in Arabic on the white sheets that enveloped their bodies. This was a time of military coups and power struggles; in the following year, a military junta led by Major General Ahmed Hassan al-Bakr of the Baath Party and his second-in-command, Saddam Hussein, imposed authoritarian rule.

In 1979, Saddam took over and inflicted his brutal regime on Iraq. During my Foreign Service career both in Washington and in the field, Iraq and Saddam Hussein's policies loomed large in my various assignments, which included the Iran-Iraq War, Desert Storm, the so-called "Dual Containment" policy toward both Iraq and Iran, and Persian Gulf energy issues.

In 1990, when I was ambassador to Syria during the run-up to Desert Storm, I was explicitly informed that President George H. W. Bush and Secretary of State James A. Baker, III were thoroughly cognizant of the likely consequences of invading an Arab country such as Iraq and then occupying it. The United States, they made clear, was not a colonial power and had important relationships in the Arab world that could be jeopardized by such an action. Accordingly, the president wanted Arab military units to take the lead in entering Kuwait City, with strong support from the United States–led Coalition. That was why it was important to get Syria on board, along with Egypt and the other Arab members of the Desert Storm military Coalition. For the same reasons, Bush and Baker correctly decided not to pursue the war into Iraq and Baghdad after Coalition forces repelled Saddam Hussein's invasion of Kuwait. That decision helped preserve the Coalition alliances they had forged and facilitated their goal of advancing Arab-Israeli peace at the Madrid Peace Conference in 1991. President Bush and Secretary Baker took a great deal of flak for not "finishing off Saddam." History, in my view, has shown that they made the right decision.

DRAWING LINES IN THE SAND

After I left government in 1994, Iraq played an important part of my work as founding director of the James A. Baker III Institute for Public Policy at Rice University.

On August 25, 1995, I conveyed my views on Iraq in an oped piece I wrote for the *Washington Post.* I recounted the arbitrary drawing of the borders of many countries in the Middle East, in large part by the English and French colonialists in the Sykes-Picot Agreement (1916) and in other arrangements after World War I. According to one account, an American missionary advised Gertrude Bell, the well-known British Arabist who was working for the Crown on a unity scheme for the Mesopotamian provinces, "You are flying in the face of four millennia of history if you try to draw a line around Iraq and call it a political entity." I noted that the line the British drew on the ground after World

War I encompassed a diverse population of Kurds in the north, Sunnis largely in the center, and Shiites in the south—as well as minority Turkomans, Jewish, and Nestorian/Chaldean Christian groups. I pointed out that Iraq was still a diverse country ruled by a minority clan of Sunni Muslims from Saddam Hussein's hometown of Tikrit. The key question, then as now, is whether the forces of unity or separatism will prevail in the aftermath of regime change in Baghdad. The stakes are high because the dismemberment of Iraq would have serious geopolitical consequences in the Middle East. I averred that, given these potential consequences, the best way to maintain the unity and territorial integrity of Iraq is for a successor regime to provide the broadest political participation possible for the diverse ethnic and religious groups in Iraq, to enable them to share power and meet the political, economic, and social needs of their constituencies.

WINNING THE WAR, LOSING THE PEACE

Years later, I participated in two study groups that focused on U.S. policy toward Iraq. The first was a 2003 independent working group, cosponsored by the Council on Foreign Relations (CFR) and the Baker Institute. Leslie Gelb, president of the CFR, asked me to cochair that group, along with my close colleague and friend of many years, Ambassador Frank Wisner. That group's concise report, *Guiding Principles for U.S. Post-Conflict Policy in Iraq*, published a short two months before the U.S. military action in Iraq in 2003, made the following argument:

> Today's Iraq debate is understandably focused on the
> run-up to possible military action. However, the question
> of how the United States and the international commu-
> nity should manage post-conflict Iraq is even more con-
> sequential, as it will determine the long-term condition
> of Iraq and the entire Middle East. If Washington does

not clearly define its goals for Iraq and build support for them domestically and with its allies and partners, future difficulties are bound to quickly overshadow any initial military success. Put simply, the United States may lose the peace, even if it wins the war.

I served as senior policy advisor for the second group, the 2006 congressionally mandated bipartisan Iraq Study Group (ISG), cochaired by former secretary of state James A. Baker, III and former congressman Lee Hamilton.

These two reports provided cogent and achievable policy recommendations. Unfortunately, the officials driving the Bush administration's Iraq policy ignored the 2003 report, did not embrace the comprehensive thrust of the 2006 ISG report, and only belatedly embraced some of its recommendations. Both responses contributed to the failure to build a bipartisan consensus in our country regarding Iraq. I later learned that we were not alone in having our views set aside by the administration. Indeed, "The Future of Iraq Study," a classified interagency government policy paper prepared in 2002–3, laid out the issues the United States would face if it invaded Iraq and spelled out what the government needed to do to prepare itself for these challenges. In a more detailed and authoritative way, it laid out recommendations similar to those in our Baker Institute–CFR report. Senior civilian officials in the Department of Defense dismissed this report as well, because it did not conform to the course of action they were bent on following.

What were we saying to the administration in these two policy reports, both of which were made public?

GUIDING PRINCIPLES FOR U.S. POST-CONFLICT POLICY IN IRAQ

The basic purpose of the 2003 *Guiding Principles* report was to provide the Bush administration with a frame of reference for an occupation of Iraq, in the event that Saddam Hussein refused to comply with UN Security Council Resolution (UNSCR) 1441, which had passed unanimously on November 8, 2002, offering Iraq "a final opportunity to comply with its disarmament obligations." Such noncompliance would trigger U.S.-led military action. The report made clear, however, that if Saddam Hussein fully complied with UNSCR 1441 and dismantled Iraq's weapons of mass destruction (WMD) program, military action would not be necessary. As is well known, no WMD were found in Iraq after the invasion.

We urged the administration to take cognizance of our assessment and recommendations. The State Department apparently did so; the White House, National Security Council, and Department of Defense did not. In reading the following, much of which is taken verbatim from the report, note that we foresaw and spelled out many of the most important problems that seem to have taken the administration by surprise.

Establish Law and Order

A strong American presence will be needed to establish and maintain law and order. U.S. and coalition military units will need to pivot quickly from combat to peacekeeping operations in order to prevent post-conflict Iraq from descending into anarchy. Strong U.S. backing for an emergency government will be needed to fill the vacuum left by Saddam. Without an initial and broad-based commitment to law and order, the logic of score-settling and revenge-taking will reduce Iraq to chaos.

Preserve the Iraqi Army

Initial efforts must also focus on eliminating the Republican Guard, Special Republican Guard, intelligence services, and other key institutions of Saddam's regime, while preserving the Iraqi army (minus the uppermost leadership and any others guilty of serious crimes). The army remains one of the country's more respected institutions. How it is treated during the military campaign and after, including the removal of its top leadership, is one of the key pieces of a U.S. strategy. The army could serve as a guarantor of peace and stability if it is retrained in part for constabulary duty and internal security missions. Before reorganization and retraining of the military begins, it must be clear that the army will undertake the following tasks:

- Organize for the defense of Iraq and support the maintenance of law and order.
- Serve, rather than become, the principal instrument of governance.
- Be free of officers with high-level Baathist ties.
- Remove those officers guilty of major crimes or crimes against humanity.
- Determine advancement based on merit, not ethnic or sectarian differences.

Iraq Coordinator

A "U.S. Coordinator for Iraq" should have full White House backing, should be assigned a deputy to run the public diplomacy campaign, and should have responsibility for a post-conflict Iraq task force that draws its membership from all involved agencies.

The United States' Role

From the beginning, the United States and its allies should begin laying the groundwork for a short-term, international- and UN-supervised Iraqi administration that includes strong international participation, with an eye toward the earliest possible reintroduction of full indigenous Iraqi rule. The optimal strategy is for the United States to play a superintending role, one that maintains low visibility but is clearly committed to protecting law and order and creating a breathing space for a nascent Iraqi government to take shape. The U.S. role will be best played in the background, guiding progress and making sure that any peacekeeping force is effective and robust enough to do its job.

Humanitarian Assistance

Post-conflict conditions inside Iraq will be desperate, and the management of humanitarian relief operations will be an urgent priority for the U.S. military, as will repairs to major transportation links and lines of communication. U.S. forces will need to move quickly to provide for basic necessities, such as food, potable water, and health facilities for the Iraqi people.

The Danger of Imposed Solutions

The report also warned of the danger of imposed solutions, noting that the continued public discussion of a U.S. military government along the lines of postwar Japan or Germany is unhelpful. After conflict, Iraqis will be a liberated, not a defeated, people. While considerable U.S. involvement will be necessary in the post-conflict environment, such comparisons suggest a long-term U.S. occupation of Iraq that will neither advance U.S. interest nor garner outside support. Likewise, it will be important to resist the temptation, advanced in various quarters, to establish a provisional government in advance of hostilities or to impose a post-conflict government, especially one dominated by exiled Iraqi opposition leaders. Such a government would lack internal legitimacy and could further destabilize the situation inside the country. The external opposition has a significant role to play in determining Iraq's future, but it should be viewed as one important voice among many.

In approaching issues such as the status of the Kurds and

Shia, it will be essential not to repeat Saddam's attempt to organize Iraq along ethnic or religious lines, but rather to encourage territorial/provincial lines within a unified, federal framework. The U.S. goal should be to urge cooperation downward to regional, secular provinces, rather than on to ethnic enclaves.

The Lure of Iraqi Oil: Realities and Constraints

At a hearing before the Defense Subcommittee of the House Appropriations Committee on March 27, 2003, Paul Wolfowitz, the deputy secretary of defense, stated, "The oil revenues of that country could bring between $50 and $100 billion over the course of the next two or three years. Now, there are a lot of claims on that money, but . . . we are dealing with a country that can really finance its own reconstruction and relatively soon."

In light of such statements, our report observed that there was a great deal of wishful thinking about Iraqi oil, including a widespread belief that oil revenues would do much to defray war costs and the huge expense of rebuilding the Iraqi state and economy. Notwithstanding the value of Iraq's vast oil reserves, there are severe limits on them both as a source of funding for post-conflict reconstruction efforts and as the key driver of future economic development. Put simply, we did not anticipate a bonanza. We recommended that the U.S. approach regarding oil be guided by four principles:

- Iraqis will maintain control of their own oil sector.
- A significant portion of early proceeds will be spent on the rehabilitation of the oil industry.
- There should be a level playing field for all international players to participate in future repair, development, and exploration efforts.
- Any proceeds will be fairly shared by all of Iraq's citizens.

THE IRAQ STUDY GROUP—AN INSIDER'S VIEW

My role as senior advisor to the Baker-Hamilton Iraq Study Group gave me an opportunity to revisit, formally and in great detail, U.S. policy on Iraq. The ISG, mandated by Congress, was sponsored by four organizations: the United States Institute for Peace, the Baker Institute for Public Policy, the Center for Strategic International Studies, and the Center for the Study of the Presidency. The group's mission was not to look back and assess the pros and cons of the invasion and immediate occupation of Iraq, but to assess the situation there and in the surrounding region and to recommend a way forward for U.S. policy. The ISG was unique in its bipartisan nature and for the prominent Democrats and Republicans it included: Republicans James A. Baker, III (cochairman), Lawrence S. Eagleburger, Edwin Meese, III, Sandra Day O'Connor, and Alan K. Simpson, and Democrats Lee H. Hamilton (cochairman), Vernon E. Jordan, Jr., Leon E. Panetta, William J. Perry, and Charles S. Robb. At the group's first meeting, on June 14, 2006, Baker said, "What Lee Hamilton and I agreed on is that we will be forward looking; we don't want to engage in what happened or not in the past. We want to come to our conclusions via consensus, and do something that is helpful for the president, Congress, and the public. We want to take our exercise out of politics. We will not report earlier than December" (after the midterm elections). As one involved throughout the process, I can attest that the distinguished members of the group kept that pledge.

At the outset, President Bush publicly thanked the members of the ISG and said, "We look to them to give us a way forward in Iraq. We look to them to give us advice about the proper strategy and tactics to achieve success. We've got people with a lot of expertise, who have served in several administrations, and in the legislative and judicial branches of government, and thank them for their willingness to serve."

A MISSED OPPORTUNITY

Unfortunately, the Bush administration did not fully embrace the ISG report and its major policy recommendations at the outset, missing, in my opinion, a historic opportunity to move our Iraq and regional Middle East policy forward on a bipartisan and comprehensive basis. The ISG provided the administration with the only bipartisan consensus in the country on Iraq, at a time when the congressional elections had given the Democrats a majority in both houses. It provided the president and Congress a vehicle to find common ground on Iraq. It was a unique chance to bring the country together on the most important and contentious issue in our foreign policy. As the cochairs stated, "America's political leaders have a responsibility to seek a bipartisan consensus on issues of war and peace."

While many bits and pieces of the ISG report were adopted over time, its comprehensive policy thrust was not. The hope, explicitly expressed in the executive summary to the report, was that it be considered as fully as possible and that its recommendations "be implemented in a coordinated fashion. They should not be carried out in isolation," since "the dynamics in the Middle East region are as important to Iraq as events within Iraq." Unfortunately, with the 2008 presidential elections already in sight, the issue became bitterly partisan.

This is particularly disappointing in light of the Pew Research Center's findings in May 2007, some four months after the publication of the ISG's report, that the ISG's proposals remained "broadly popular" with the American public. "Of special note . . . with regard to the Baker-Hamilton proposals is the lack of partisan division. On no item do Republicans and Democrats take opposing views. Instead, the balance of opinion across party lines is remarkably even. This stands in stark contrast to virtually all other questions about the war in Iraq."

DANGER AND OPPORTUNITY
BAGHDAD 2006

In September 2006, I accompanied members of the ISG on a trip
to Baghdad that provided a firsthand assessment of the situation on
the ground and the opportunity to meet with a wide range of Iraqi
and United States civilian and military officials, Iraqi political and
religious leaders, heads of nongovernmental organizations, foreign diplomats, and representatives of international organizations
with a presence on the scene. There is no real substitute for direct contact of this nature. Our bipartisan group of former senior
members of past administrations and Congress included James
A. Baker, III, Lee Hamilton, Bill Perry, Bob Gates, Chuck Robb,
Ed Meese, and Leon Panetta. For security purposes, this mission
had been designated at the presidential level. As we approached
Kuwait City in a USG 737 aircraft, the Department of State security officer described the dangerous security situation in Baghdad
and outlined the precautions we had to take in our travel into the
city and even within the Green Zone, the most protected area
in Baghdad, which housed the massive U.S. military command
headquarters and the largest U.S. Embassy in the world.

On arrival in Kuwait airport, we boarded a C-130 military aircraft, a dark-gray cargo and transport plane. When we entered
the windowless, dark interior, we saw four long rows of a platoon
of American soldiers fully equipped in battle gear. They were returning to Iraq after some leave. We sat right next to them in heat
of 118 degrees Fahrenheit. I was struck by the contrast between
us much older former civilian policymakers and these young
men, in their late teens and early twenties, at the lethal edge of
the decisions made in Washington. I asked the corporal sitting
next to me in the bank of seats against the wall where his unit
was assigned. He said Mahmoudiya, located in the "Triangle of
Death." One could not help but have profound respect for their
service to our country and the sacrifice they were making.

As we were waiting to take off, for what seemed an eternity in that heat, the corporal gave me some envelopes to pass along to my colleagues. They contained plastic bags. He explained that the descent into Baghdad airport would be very steep and not great for one's stomach. Indeed, when we reached the airspace over Baghdad, the pilots went into a narrow, downward-spiraling path to avoid any enemy fire or rockets. It was a hell of a ride. Our security officer had showed us how to put on our flak jackets and helmets. It was quite a scene and I was glad to have the soldiers next to me help me put on this heavy gear. Upon deplaning, we boarded helicopters for the short trip to the Green Zone. The security detail told us not to be concerned by the release of flares to deflect possible incoming fire while flying over the Red Zone.

Flying in on the chopper gave us quite a bird's-eye view of Baghdad. Dry patches of land interspersed with palm trees and the fertile banks of the Tigris and Euphrates rivers' small houses, then the vast, spread-out neighborhoods of Baghdad, some quiet, some teeming with activity. The need for reconstruction was everywhere evident, but a few more affluent houses with gardens dotted the largely bleak landscape. Flying low over the houses as we approached the Green Zone, I couldn't help thinking that it would not be difficult for an Al Qaeda terrorist to secrete an RPG in one of those houses and fire on American helicopters. Luckily, we landed without incident and were taken to the palace compound in armored cars with a medic in the backseat.

The Green Zone is five square miles, protected by massive fortifications and walls. It is an amazing city within a city, housing not only the American presence but also many Iraqi government offices and other foreign embassies. A former Saddam Hussein palace and its immediate surroundings are the center of American activity both official and recreational. There are pools and bars that are frequented by the large American civilian and military community. It is an eerie and surreal contrast to the violence and killing that go on outside the walls daily. We were told that the one serious danger in the Green Zone was from indirect fire and mortar attacks. A European-sounding siren would signal an attack if there was warning. If we were not inside our trailer units, surrounded by sandbag barriers, when we heard such an alarm, we were to go immediately to the nearest bunker or hardened shelter.

In this ambience, after our arrival and after our meeting with General Casey and the chargé d'affaires, we changed into our business suits and went to meet with Prime Minister Nuri al-Maliki and President Jalal Talabani. The latter greeted me warmly after all these years, recalling our meetings in Washington in 1991 when we discussed the role of the Kurds in a post–Desert Storm and post-Saddam Iraq. Talabani, a leader of a major Kurdish party, was quite pleased with the status of the Kurds in the new Iraq, not without reason.

The following evening, after back-to-back meetings with Iraqi ministers, Embassy personnel, and Iraqi NGO representatives, Talabani invited us to a delicious Arab dinner at the presidential villa. We recounted old tales of those early and first senior-level meetings between American officials and members of the Patriotic Union of Kurdistan (PUK) and the Democratic Party of Kurdistan (DPK). Along with Foreign Minister Zebari, Deputy Prime Minister Barham Salih, and President Talabani, we raised our glasses in a toast to old and new times. I joked in Arabic that they had come a long way politically as ministers and as a president, while I had ended up as just an ambassador.

We followed a jam-packed schedule, meeting with Iraqi civilian and religious leaders, including Abd Al Aziz al Hakim, the leader of the Supreme Council for the Islamic Revolution in Iraq (SCIRI), who controls the Badr militia. The sectarian issue loomed large in all these discussions, and a central issue was whether Maliki's government would be capable of taking the hard decisions to control the militias, especially the Mahdi Army and the Badr Brigade. A Sunni opposition leader told us that, at the very beginning of the U.S. liberation/occupation of Iraq, we made a critical error in favoring religious and sectarian leaders instead of the secular, liberal Iraqi political and professional elite. One of Muqtada al-Sadr's representatives told me in private, "You created Sadr." I immediately had a strong sense that this government sorely needed to demonstrate its ability to move forward on the key issues—security, sharing of oil revenue, federalism, reconstruction, and reconciliation.

Outside the walls, the killing continued. On the last full day of our trip, there were four explosions around the edge of the Green Zone. Since they were the first our group had heard, we paid keen attention, but everyone else took them in stride. A young captain, a medic who worked in the emergency room on the base, told us the helicopters we heard in the dead of the night, shaking the mobile housing unit Bill Perry and I shared, are most often bringing American and Iraqi wounded to the ER to be operated on. He told of a young American soldier, brought in the night before, who had been severely wounded by an IED (improvised explosive device). Every effort was made to save him, but they couldn't. This was all so real that it was painful to absorb. Policy has consequences on the ground that are too often treated as mere statistics back home.

The discussions the study group had in Baghdad played an important part in the drafting of its report. The complexity of the challenges we faced in Iraq was reflected in the first two oft-quoted sentences of the report's executive summary: "The situation in Iraq is grave and deteriorating. There is no path that can guarantee success, but the prospects can be improved."

WHAT DIFFERENTIATES THE ISG REPORT

It is important to outline what differentiates the ISG report from past and current policy on Iraq. The report has three major elements: First, it asserted that the primary mission of the U.S. forces in Iraq should evolve to support the Iraqi army, which would take over primary responsibility for combat operations. The report stated that, by the first quarter of 2008, subject to unexpected developments in the security situation on the ground, all combat brigades not responsible for force protection could be out of Iraq. After that, U.S. combat forces in Iraq could be deployed only in units embedded with Iraqi forces, in rapid-reaction and special operations teams, and in training, equipping, advising, force protection, and search and rescue. The report recognized that the Iraqi government will need continued assistance from the United States, especially in the security field, but it also stated clearly that the United States must not make an open-ended commitment to keep large numbers of troops deployed in Iraq.

Second, the report recommended that the United States work closely with Iraq's leaders to support the achievement of milestones on three major issues: national reconciliation, security, and governance. In a key judgment, the report states:

> If the Iraqi government demonstrates political will and makes substantial progress toward the achievement of milestones on national reconciliation, security and governance, the United States should make clear its willingness to continue training, assistance, and support for Iraq's security forces and to continue political, military and economic support. If the Iraqi government does not make substantial progress toward the achievement of milestones on national reconciliation, security, and governance, the United States should reduce its political, military, or economic support for the Iraqi government.

The third major component of the report was the "New Diplomatic Offensive." It is evident that the policies and actions of Iraq's neighbors greatly affect its stability and prosperity. The report recommended that the United States launch this diplomatic initiative immediately, to build an international consensus for stability in Iraq and the region, and that this effort include all of Iraq's neighbors. It called for an Iraq International Support Group to be organized as an instrument of this initiative, consisting of Iraq's neighbors and key states inside and outside the region to reinforce security and national reconciliation inside Iraq. The report also recommended that, given the demonstrated ability of Iran and Syria to influence events within Iraq and their interest in avoiding long-term chaos in Iraq, which can negatively affect their own security interests, the United States should try to engage them constructively in a tough-minded diplomatic approach involving incentives and disincentives. Another important aspect of the New Diplomatic Offensive is the assessment and recommendation that the United States cannot achieve its goals in the Middle East unless it deals directly with the Arab-Israeli conflict and regional instability. Accordingly, it strongly recommended a renewed and sustained commitment by the United States to a comprehensive Arab-Israeli peace on all fronts: specifically, Lebanon, Syria, and President Bush's June 2002 commitment to a two-state solution for Israel and Palestine.

THE SYRIAN DIMENSION

As related in previous chapters, former secretary of state Baker and I deliberately spelled out in some detail in the ISG report what United States diplomacy with Syria would entail, because we knew there would be opposition to this approach and felt strongly that there was an opportunity to drive a wedge between Syria and Iran, and that this could be accomplished by engaging Syria on a broader agenda beyond Iraq, including Israeli-Syrian peace negotiations, Lebanon, terrorism, and Syria's relations with the United States and other countries in the region.

In our meeting with Syrian Foreign Minister Walid Mouallem in 2006, he was critical of the United States administration's "anti-Syrian" policies, but did come forward with specific measures that Syria was prepared to take to help secure the Iraqi-Syrian border, support the Iraqi government, and cooperate with the international commission investigating Lebanese prime minister Hariri's assassination. With regard to Arab-Israeli peace, he stated categorically that the Syrian government was ready to resume negotiations with Israel on the basis of the Madrid Peace Conference and the letters of assurances that the United States had given the involved parties at that time. To aid forward movement, he affirmed, Syria would use its influence over Hamas and Hezbollah.

Baker and I knew that these words would have to be translated into action by robust diplomacy, but it was clear that the opening was there.

THE IRANIAN DIMENSION

The ISG report recommended direct exchanges between the United States and Iran under the aegis of the New Diplomatic Offensive and the Iraq International Support Group. The ISG members fully appreciated the problematic nature of U.S.-Iranian relations, but recognized that both countries had cooperated successfully in Afghanistan in the overthrow of the Taliban regime after 9/11, had also engaged on Iraq in a limited manner, and were engaged on the contentious issue of Iran's nuclear programs in the context of the United Nations Security Council and its five permanent members (the United States, United Kingdom, France, Russia, China) plus Germany.

One key judgment of the ISG was that while Iran sees it as in its interest to have the United States bogged down in Iraq in the short term, Iran's interests would not be served in the long term by a failure of U.S. policy in Iraq that led to broad-based civil war and the territorial disintegration of the Iraqi state. It was important to note in the report that Iran's population is slightly over 50 percent Persian, but it has a large Azeri (Turkish-origin) minority that makes up 24 percent of the population, as well as Kurdish (7 percent) and Arab (3 percent) minorities. Accordingly, continued and growing sectarian strife in Iraq could spill over the border and spread similar tensions and instability in Iran. This would not be in Iran's national security interest. Therefore, there was the possibility of the United States and Iran engaging on stabilizing the situation in Iraq.

The ISG report recommended that Iran take several steps to improve the situation in Iraq:

- It should stem the flow of equipment, technology, and training to any group resorting to violence in Iraq.
- It should make clear its support for the territorial integrity of Iraq as a unified state and its respect for the sovereignty of Iraq and its government.
- It can use its influence, especially over Shia groups in Iraq, to encourage national reconciliation.
- It can also, in the right circumstances, help in the economic reconstruction of Iraq.

MEETING WITH THE IRANIANS

To explore the prospects for serious engagement with the Iranians, Baker and I contacted the Iranians on behalf of the ISG. Given the tense and limited relationship and communications between the two countries, we did not hold out much hope of eliciting any significant Iranian cooperation. As the ISG report stated:

> Our limited contacts with Iran's government lead us
> to believe that its leaders are likely to say initially that
> they will not participate with the United States in dip-
> lomatic efforts to support stability in Iraq. This is due
> to Iran's perception of the United States government's

attitude toward Iran's government, with particular
reference to the issue of regime change. Nevertheless,
Iran should be asked to assume its responsibility to participate in the Support Group as a neighboring country
of Iraq. An Iranian refusal to do so would demonstrate
to Iraq and the world Iran's rejectionist attitude and
approach, which could lead to its isolation. Further,
Iran's refusal to cooperate would diminish the prospects of engaging with the United States in the broader
dialogue it seeks.

We met with Ambassador Dr. Mohammad Javad Zarif, then the
permanent representative of the Islamic Republic of Iran to the
United Nations, in New York City on October 5, 2006. Baker
conveyed the view of the ISG that none of Iraq's neighbors had
an interest in a chaotic Iraq and a failed state. He asked that
the Iranians think about some of the things that might be done
separately or together with the government of Iraq, neighboring
countries, and other countries to bring stability to Iraq and to assist in its successful reconstruction. Did the Iranian government
believe there are bilateral or multilateral measures that could be
taken, and if so, what are they? Is there a possibility of United
States–Iranian cooperation in a multilateral context? Zarif made
it clear that he would have to convey these questions to Tehran
before he could provide authoritative responses regarding Iranian government positions. Still, he described the Iranian view
of failed efforts to establish a United States–Iranian dialogue,
which he claimed was exploited by third-party countries for their
own political ends. He said Iran had declared its readiness for a
dialogue in March 2003. He referred to an official announce-
ment by Iran's national security advisor that Iran was willing to
engage with the United States and that Iran's leader, the Ayatollah Khamenei, had been interviewed and approved of such talks.
Then, he recounted, Iran received the "buts" from the United
States—the nuclear issue, a new government being formed in

Iraq, and so forth—and the United States had put off the talks. Iran feels that the United States has an agenda and suspects it is regime change. Under these conditions, he concluded, a dialogue will lead nowhere.

Zarif also revealed serious Iranian misperceptions of United States policy in Iraq. For example, the Iranians had suspicions that the United States was not really supportive of Iraqi prime minister Maliki's government and was seeking to replace it. Abd Al Aziz al Hakim, the leader of the Islamic Supreme Council of Iraq (ISCI; formerly known as SCIRI, the organization removed "Revolutionary" from its name in May 2007), and others were reportedly telling the Iranians that the United States, Europeans, and Sunni Arabs all wanted the Maliki government to fail.

I assured Zarif that this was not true. In fact, when the ISG met with Hakim in Baghdad, Baker had specifically asked Hakim if he supported the current Iraqi government. Hakim and his colleague expressed surprise over the question. I commented that there is speculation that Hakim may have his own agenda, including the establishment of an autonomous Shiite region in the south. Zarif commented that if there is not the threat of separation in the south—that is, a "Shiistan"—it would be impossible to keep the Kurds from separating. Hakim, he said, believes this is what keeps Iraq together and concluded that he did not think there would be a separate Shiite entity in the south.

Baker made quite clear his view that the U.S. government wants the current government in Iraq to succeed—not fail. Zarif then raised other conspiracy theories. There were reports, he said, that certain U.S. officials were "in cahoots" with Sunnis and the insurgents, and that Saddam Hussein would be sent into exile to Qatar, the Sunni insurgency would end, and the Sunnis would then point their guns at the Shiites, not the U.S. presence.

Though he could make no commitment, Zarif claimed that the government in Tehran was interested in reaching a working relationship with the United States.

THE COSTS OF NOT TALKING TO
YOUR ADVERSARIES

I came away from the meeting with Zarif realizing, more than ever before, that the lack of official and sustained communication between the United States and Iran was not only facilitating misperceptions, certainly on the part of the Iranians as to United States policies, but it was also a serious impediment to our ability to influence Iranian behavior beyond sanctions and the implied threats of military action. The task is how to engage the Iranians in serious discussions that have the potential to identify whatever common ground may exist on specific issues and to resolve those issues in bilateral and multilateral forums, as appropriate. The Iranians have engaged with us on Iraq, but they do not want a dialogue on Iraq alone. They seek a broader agenda of discussions where the major issues, both bilateral and regional, are on the table. While the nuclear issue may best be discussed in the UN Security Council, as the ISG report recommends, serious and sustained engagement between the United States and Iran on other key issues (Iraq, Afghanistan, Arab-Israeli peace, terrorism, support for Hezbollah and Hamas, human rights, and bilateral relations) could facilitate progress on the nuclear issue.

I do not underestimate how difficult engagement with Iran on these issues would be. I have often commented to my colleagues in the State Department that, in dealing with the Iranians, you always have to keep one hand on your wallet. They are the craftiest negotiators in the Middle East and they should never be underestimated. But neither should we make Iran into more of a power than it is.

IRAN IN PERSPECTIVE

Without question, Iran is a regional power in the Gulf and Middle East, by virtue of its size, strategic location, rich history and culture, and oil and gas resources. But Iran is not the Soviet Union, which constituted a true strategic threat to the United States.

Iran can threaten its neighbors in the Gulf and the region, including Israel. But most of these countries have strong bilateral relations with the United States, and Iran knows that if it threatens or acts against them, it would be seriously risking the active opposition of the United States and other major powers. The concept of deterrence is real in this respect and could be extended from political and economic means to military measures. Also, Iran represents a political dichotomy. On the one hand, with the Iranian Revolution in 1979, Ayatollah Khomeini instituted the *velayat al-fiqh*, or rule of the Islamic Jurist, with the supreme power of the state in the hands of the religious leader and the clerics, creating a Shiite theocracy. On the other hand, Iran has a parliamentary system, with both legislative and presidential elections. It is a study in contrasts, with theocratic rule operating alongside a representative electoral system in which women and men can vote, albeit in a tightly controlled political system dictated by the ayatollahs.

We should also note that, despite the militant Islamic order established by Khomeini, Iranian political society is not a monolith, but has had moderate and liberal Muslim movements. As one example, New York University political scientist Farhad Kazemi has written about Mehdi Bazargan, who served briefly as prime minister after the fall of the shah and who "believed that Islam could accommodate modernity, accepting and gaining strength from acculturation with the West without losing its essential core." He envisaged an evolutionary and nonviolent path of progress. His supporters came from nationalist elements within the bazaar and among teachers, particularly those at pre-university levels.

We should not underestimate the level of tension in Iranian society, with a population whose median age is twenty-four, with unemployment at 12 percent, inflation at 15 percent, and 40 percent of the population below the poverty line. Even with its abundant oil and gas resources—Iran has the second-largest gas reserves and the third-largest oil reserves in the world—the government has to import large amounts of gasoline for local consumption because of the lack of refining capacity.

According to the Economist Intelligence Unit, Iran is unlikely to meet its target for oil production of 5.6 million barrels per day by 2010, up from its current production of 3.8 million barrels. President Ahmadinejad's populist economic policies have put further strains on the economy. The palpable need for political, economic, and social reforms is reflected in Iran's reform movement. According to Professor Kazemi:

> The regime has failed to deliver on the exalted twin
> goals of social justice and economic self-sufficiency. . . .
> The new Islamic elite soon amassed unprecedented
> wealth, failed to share it systematically with the under-
> class and tolerated an ever growing official and clerical
> corruption. . . . In the political sphere the problems are
> no less severe. A crisis of authority raises fundamental
> questions about the respective roles of religion and
> politics. . . . The near dictatorial concentration of power
> in the office of the supreme leader is a cause of great
> concern.

To complicate matters further, as was mentioned in the ISG report, Iran is not a homogeneous Persian state, with nearly half of its population divided among Turkish-origin Azeris, Kurds, Arabs, and more than a dozen other smaller ethnic groups. Iran is sensitive to what may happen along its borders in Iraq and Afghanistan, hoping to avoid any spillover effect of multiethnic or religious strife and separatist movements that could threaten its own territorial integrity. Given all these factors, Iran has strong reason not to antagonize the United States to the point of confrontation. Such a confrontation would be costly for both sides; for Iran, it would be devastating. This gives diplomacy a field of opportunity if it is conducted wisely.

As the world's preeminent power, the United States can certainly afford to take the first step in putting the Iranian regime to the test by offering a broad strategic dialogue on all the key issues. Our willingness to engage with Iran is not and in no way should be seen as a lack of United States resolve on the key issues that affect our national security interests and those of our friends, especially the issue of nuclear weapons. The United States–Iran relationship has been on a downward curve, and the situation in the region remains dangerous, even perilous. Both the interests of the United States and those of Iran are seriously implicated in the region's problems and conflicts.

While actively pursuing the nuclear issue in the multilateral forum, a first step in a dialogue could be an exchange of respective assessments regarding the key regional issues such as Iraq, Afghanistan, Arab-Israeli peace, Lebanon, Gulf security, and terrorism. The overall subset of these discussions would be the United States–Iranian bilateral relationship. Here we will have to make clear that, while we are not pursuing regime change, we would promote our positions on human rights, democracy, the role of civil society, and the rule of law as structural parts of the bilateral dialogue. In short, the stakes are high and we should not miss this opportunity to engage one of the most adversarial regimes we face in the region.

THE ROAD TO PEACE

As the George W. Bush administration prepared for war, Secretary of State Colin Powell and the Future of Iraq study team were bypassed. Powell informed the president that if we invaded Iraq we would be responsible for its future and all that that implied, famously warning Bush, "If you break it, you will own it." Powell was chairman of the Joint Chiefs of Staff in President George H. W. Bush's administration and was a chief architect of Desert Storm, where he applied what became known as the "Powell Doctrine." That approach consisted mainly of clearly defining the mission to be achieved; determining what force levels would be needed, with a view of "overmatching" the enemy with decisive force applied to a clear military objective; determining how the war should end; and determining what its political goals should be. Powell made a clear distinction between military and political objectives, stressing that it is important to have public support for any sustained military engagement. While our military forces executed the invasion of Iraq in a clearly successful and expeditious manner, the post-conflict situation was seriously miscalculated, especially by the civilian leadership at the Department of Defense, without real knowledge or understanding of the forces at play in Iraq and the region.

Army chief of staff Eric Shinseki, who had experience in Bosnia, where he had responsibility for managing a coalition of forty nations, was asked in fall 2002 for a plan for military action in Iraq. He calculated that, with Iraq having a population much larger than Bosnia's, some three hundred thousand troops would be required to accomplish the mission and secure the country following the invasion. Shinseki reasoned that we needed to match our capabilities to the multiplicity of tasks we faced in Iraq and thought it imperative to give combat commanders a range of options for accomplishing those tasks. His recommendations became a point of contention within the administration. He was publicly criticized by Deputy Secretary of Defense Paul Wolfowitz and went into retirement as a virtual outcast, having challenged the prevailing doctrine. But given the breakdown in law and order in the wake of our invasion of Iraq and the decisions made by the Coalition administrators in Iraq, it is clear that Shinseki was right from the very beginning.

The other key miscalculation the neoconservative forces in the administration made was that the Iraqis would welcome us as liberators, not occupiers; that because of Saddam Hussein's brutal repression of the Shiites, they would greet us with palm branches and rice. A democratic model would be created in Iraq, to serve as a paradigm for democratic regime change in the rest of the region, with positive implications for Israel. The road to Arab-Israeli peace, they argued, would go through Baghdad and Tehran. These policymakers understood little of the history and culture of the region. Their ideological precepts blinded them to the realities on the ground, extracting an exorbitant price within and outside the region.

WHAT BUSH IGNORED

It is instructive to see which key elements of the ISG report's recommendations the president embraced, and which he either ignored or rejected. ISG cochairs Baker and Hamilton addressed that question in a statement issued on January 11, 2007, a day after the president addressed the nation regarding Iraq.

First, they stated that they were pleased that the president had reviewed the ISG report carefully and seriously, and that some of its recommendations were reflected in the new approach the president had outlined, although others had not been adopted. They agreed with President Bush that "the situation in Iraq is unacceptable to the American people," the consequences of failure are severe, and "only the Iraqis can end the sectarian violence and secure their people." They underscored the president's statement that "the essential U.S. security mission" in Iraq is the training of Iraqi forces, and said they supported increasing the number of American advisors embedded in Iraqi army units, with the goal that the Iraq government would assume control of security in all provinces in Iraq by November 2007. They also noted that the ISG recommended many of the benchmarks President Bush outlined for Iraq, and they agreed with the president that the time had come for the Iraqi government to act.

At the same time, they expressed the hope that the president and his administration would further consider other recommendations of the ISG. They pointed out that the president had not suggested the possibility of a transition that could enable U.S. combat forces to begin to leave Iraq, and had not stated that political, military, or economic support for Iraq would be conditional upon the Iraqi government's ability to meet benchmarks. Within the region, the president did not assemble an international support group for Iraq, including all of Iraq's neighbors, nor mention measures the ISG suggested to reach a comprehensive Arab-Israeli settlement on all fronts, including Syria and Lebanon. (The president and Secretary of State Condoleezza Rice did launch Israeli-Palestinian talks at the Annapolis meeting in November 2007.)

With respect to the administration's plan to deploy a "surge" of troops in Iraq, the ISG had indicated that it could "support a short-term redeployment or surge of American combat forces to stabilize Baghdad," complemented by comprehensive political, economic, and diplomatic efforts. Questions, of course, remained about the nature of the surge. The cochairs noted that they were encouraged by the president's statement that "America's commitment is not open-ended" and by Secretary of Defense Robert Gates's statement that the addition of twenty-one thousand troops would be viewed as a temporary surge. They also emphasized the critical point that the violence in Baghdad will not end without a political solution—namely, national reconciliation.

PLAN B

Journalists and others regularly asked whether the members of the ISG considered a "Plan B" in case its recommendations for action were not accepted or proved ineffectual. There was no formal Plan B, but the ISG did acknowledge that if the milestones of national reconciliation, security, and governance failed, there could be the devolution of Iraq into three major regions.

Much attention has been given to the contrast between the ISG report and the proposal by U.S. senator Joseph Biden and President Emeritus of the Council on Foreign Relations Leslie Gelb calling for extensive devolution of power to the Iraqi regions as a priority. In a *Washington Post* op-ed piece, however, Biden and Gelb clarified their view:

> A federal Iraq is a united Iraq, but one in which power devolves to regional governments, with a limited central government responsible for common concerns such as protecting borders and distributing oil revenue. . . . Iraq's constitution already provides for a federal system. As for the regions forming along sectarian lines, the constitution leaves the choice to the people of its 18 provinces. . . . The Bush administration should be helping Iraqis make federalism work through an agreement over the fair distribution of oil revenue; the safe return of refugees; integrating militia members into local security forces; leveraging the shared interest of other countries in a stable Iraq; and refocusing capacity-building and aid on the provinces and regions—not scaring them off by equating federalism to partition, sectarianism and foreign bullying.

The ISG report, the Bush administration, and the Biden-Gelb plan all support federalism, which is part of the Iraqi constitution. The process for implementing a federal system exists. Not one of these three groups is against a federalist system of governance in Iraq with a central government in Baghdad exercising powers (such as oil-revenue sharing and border security) to maintain the territorial integrity and unity of Iraq. The administration itself scaled down the definition of its goals in Iraq as a country that can govern itself, defend itself, not be a threat to its own people and its neighbors, and not be a base for terrorism. This goal could be accomplished with varying degrees of central authority and regional governance. That said, advocating federalism or autonomy as a cover for the sectarian partition of Iraq would undermine the territorial integrity of the country. It would prove to be destabilizing not only for the Iraqi people themselves, but for the region as a whole.

AL-ANBAR PROVINCE

In a meeting with the top Sunni leaders of Al-Anbar Province at the Baker Institute for Public Policy in November 2007, I asked them how realistic they thought the recommendations of the ISG report were and how sustainable they thought the recent gains they had made in close cooperation with the U.S. military were in sidelining Al Qaeda and assuming more local control of the province. They made two major points. First, whatever the United States does in Iraq, it should not withdraw militarily until the Iraqi armed forces are reconstituted as a nonsectarian military organization. To do otherwise would be a formula for civil war. Second, the United States should not promote the division of Iraq along sectarian lines of Kurdish, Shiite, and Sunni entities. The only basis of a federal system in Iraq should be a geographical one and not a sectarian one; namely, that of the eighteen provinces.

THE WAY FORWARD

The basic thrust of the ISG report remains valid, and it indicates the direction the United States should take in Iraq and the region. Adjustments will need to be made, based on military, security, and political developments on the ground in Iraq and in the region. The "clear, hold, and build" strategy of the recent past and the surge and "population protection" approach under General Petraeus and Ambassador Ryan Crocker's leadership in

Iraq are all aimed at providing the Iraqis with the wherewithal to obtain security on the ground to protect the Iraqi people and create the political and economic space to achieve political and national reconciliation. That goal is essential for a sustainable and peaceful Iraq.

The primary recommendations of the ISG regarding the role of United States combat forces in Iraq and in the region, the milestones the Iraqi government must strive for and meet, be they top-down or bottom-up approaches, and a bold new diplomatic strategic approach to the Middle East region as a whole should be carried out to enhance the prospects of peace and stability in the Middle East and to allow our troops to start coming home.

NINE

THE GEOPOLITICS OF ENERGY

O ne of the major considerations in the struggle of ideas in the Muslim world is the geopolitical importance of the vast oil and gas reserves located in the broader Middle East. Destabilization in this region can lead to major global economic disruptions, at a time of limited excess oil capacity and growing energy demand, especially from the emerging global powers of China and India. An energy policy that responds to the urgency of the historical situation and looks ahead toward balancing supply and demand, with attention to the need for conservation and alternative sources of energy, is a compelling public policy challenge.

When I joined the Baker Institute in 1994, I knew that energy issues would be an important part of our institute's work. We were located in Houston, the energy capital of the world. Like many who were in public service in the 1970s, I understood the direct impact secure energy supplies have on daily life and prosperity in America and abroad. Moreover, energy supply and environmental issues go hand in hand and loom large among the major challenges of the twenty-first century.

THE THREAT FROM WITHIN

In this context, the Baker Institute began its energy research program in 1995 with a major inquiry into the Persian Gulf region. A study released in 1996 accurately found that oil markets were vulnerable to a major short-term supply disruption, and that "while the U.S. should be and is prepared to deter and defend against external aggression in the Gulf, we must also assess what the U.S. can and should do in the face of generational and regime change in the Gulf." The report warned that the threat to energy security might come from inside the Persian Gulf region, rather than from external factors, and that the United States and its allies needed to look beyond military issues and give greater attention to economic, political, social, and cultural change emerging in the countries of the Persian Gulf, with special consideration of the role of extremist Islamic groups. The study called on the United States to support governments of the Middle East in their efforts to promote political reform, privatization, and broader participation in the economic system, as ways of diminishing the manifestations of social injustice that facilitate the rise of extremism. It also recommended that the United States intensify its central role in advancing the Arab-Israeli peace process.

Over a decade later, the same issues loom large. President George W. Bush made democracy promotion a major tenet of his administration's approach to the Middle East. The long-term ramifications of this policy approach remain unclear, especially given the Iraq experience and the rekindling of sectarian divisions between major Sunni and Shia communities inside Iraq and throughout the Persian Gulf and the Indian subcontinent. The situation between Israel and the Palestinians remains fragile, adding significantly to existing pressures in the region.

As I have noted in earlier chapters, Israel's conflict with Hezbollah in Lebanon in the summer of 2006 highlighted the dangers of lingering conflict that could, if not properly addressed by effective diplomacy, expand to embroil a wider range of countries, including Syria and Iran, whose active support for such subnational groups as Hamas and Hezbollah continues to be a destabilizing factor. It is imperative that U.S. policy in the Middle East move from conflict management to conflict resolution.

IT'S NOT ONLY ABOUT OIL AND GAS

It is a popular belief in the United States (and in the Middle East, for that matter) that oil and energy interests drive U.S. policy in the region and that the U.S. military is engaged in the Middle East only because of the region's oil and gas resources. Without question, maintaining the free flow of oil and gas from the Persian Gulf to the world market represents a vital U.S. and global interest. This point has been made clear in official statements by senior officials in both Republican and Democratic administrations. But U.S. goals and interests in the Middle East go beyond the provision of oil and gas.

Even the decades-old relationship between the United States and oil power Saudi Arabia is about more than energy interests. Saudi Arabia and many other Middle Eastern allied countries were tapped in various political, diplomatic, military, and financial roles in support of the U.S. policy of containment against the Soviet Union and the communists, whom they accurately saw as politically and ideologically opposed to their regimes. Subsequently, Saudi officials, including Prince Saud al Faisal and Prince Bandar Bin Sultan, often reminded their U.S. contacts that, during the Cold War—and despite public perception that the wave of the future was with the revolutionary Arab regimes aligned with the Soviet Union, such as Egypt under Gamal Abdel Nasser and Syria under Hafez al-Asad—Saudi Arabia and other Arab Gulf countries maintained their close ties to the United States.

The Middle East has also been important to the U.S. strategic calculus because of its central geographical location and provision of land, sea, and air transit rights. During the Cold War, access to air space and basing operations in the Middle East was a critical part of sustaining U.S. military capability against the Soviet Union. More recently, U.S. relationships with various Gulf states continue to support U.S. military capabilities in the region.

In forging its Middle East policy, the United States is a strong supporter of Israel, plays a major role in the pursuit of Arab-Israeli peace, and responds to humanitarian and peacekeeping goals in places where oil is not at stake. Our past involvement, for example, in Lebanon—when we dispatched U.S. Marines to that country in 1958 and the 1980s during periods of civil strife—and U.S. military actions in Afghanistan to reverse the Soviet invasion of 1979 and to overthrow the Taliban regime and attack Al Qaeda after 9/11 were not driven by oil and gas interests.

The United States also has important economic, financial, commercial, and trade interests in the broader Middle East, which, while often connected with oil and gas, are distinct from these interests. Further, we have important educational and cultural ties to the region, such as the American University of Beirut and of Cairo, and branches of American universities in Education City in Qatar.

Still, one should not underestimate the role of energy interests in this region. Before the U.S. invasion of Iraq in 2003, participants in the Baker Institute's energy programs, including those from Japan, China, Europe, and South Korea, registered their concern that a military action against Saddam Hussein's regime could cause a major disruption in already volatile global oil and gas markets.

Unlike the situation in 1989, when the price of oil was still at moderate levels and the Organization of Petroleum Exporting Countries (OPEC) had spare capacity of over five million barrels a day, before the Iraq War began, the international community was facing the most difficult energy market it had seen in two decades. OPEC was operating at 99 percent of its total crude oil productive capacity versus 90 percent in 2001, and 80 percent just before Iraq's invasion of Kuwait in 1990. Spare production capacity inside OPEC was (and still is) limited to just a handful of countries, with the majority of capability focused in Saudi Arabia, some of whose spare volumes includes heavier, low-quality oil that cannot be used efficiently in Asian and European refining systems.

The Bush administration got some initial help to minimize the impact of the war on oil markets, because Saudi Arabia substantially increased its oil production just before the war and in the immediate aftermath of the invasion. As President George W. Bush began Operation Iraqi Freedom on March 19, 2003, King Fahd issued a public statement that "Saudi Arabia will not participate in any way in the war," and the kingdom tried to distance itself from the U.S.-led initiative. Still, Saudi Arabia quietly fulfilled its customary role as swing producer and actually increased its sales both to the United States and elsewhere in early 2003, before the war. In fact, in the first half of 2003, record high volumes of Saudi crude came to the United States as the kingdom replaced lost supplies resulting from cutbacks in Iraqi oil production due to the onset of Operation Iraqi Freedom. Reaching a record of 1.87 million barrels per day, Saudi Arabia continued to rank as the number-one supplier, providing more than 20.1 percent of the U.S. market share during the first six months of 2003.

As the war in Iraq dragged on and world demand for oil continued to rise, markets tightened further, and Saudi Arabia and OPEC became more aggressive in their supply and pricing policies, leading to a steady rise in oil prices over time. The razor-thin level of spare capacity, or excess capacity, is now more severe than was seen in past crises in 1973 and 1979, and is a significant factor in the escalation in the price of oil to over one hundred dollars a barrel. Our global energy situation represents a new and unique challenge, one not easily overcome. Many of the global economic trends apparent in markets today are quite reminiscent of 1973, when the U.S. dollar was weak, U.S. national debt high, and excess oil production capacity was limited in the face of rising world oil demand.

Given today's extreme shortage of spare capacity in OPEC, a sudden imbalance in the international supply picture, perhaps as the result of an accident or major disruption, will generate larger and more rapid price responses now than those seen in the past. This situation is a problem all importers share, whatever the success of their national oil companies or the level of their equity oil holdings. In the globalized, commodity-based world of oil, no single consuming country can insulate itself fully from a global oil price shock, regardless of its relative degree of self-sufficiency.

In the past, the industrialized West counted on the countries of the Persian Gulf to make the sizable investments needed to maintain enough surplus capacity to form a cushion against disruptions elsewhere in the world. And major investments by international oil companies in the Organisation for Economic Cooperation and Development (OECD) constituted a large share of increases in oil supply over the last thirty years—as much as 40 percent of new supply. Looking forward, however, experts question whether the Persian Gulf countries (and OPEC in general) will invest adequate amounts to meet the rise in oil demand in the United States, China, and emerging economies in Asia and elsewhere.

The challenge of meeting this growing demand for oil will be daunting in the years ahead. Consumption is expected to rise by more than 20 million barrels per day by 2030; the investment required to provide this petroleum could run to $2 trillion or more. The question of who will be responsible for making these massive investments to fuel the future world economy is critical and evolving. Unlike past decades when private, publicly traded oil companies played a major role in the worldwide oil exploration business, national oil companies (NOCs) will be responsible for a lion's share of the increase in oil output and investment in the next twenty years.

Today, NOCs hold nearly 80 percent of global reserves of oil; they also dominate the world's oil production. Of the top twenty oil producers worldwide, fourteen are NOCs or newly privatized NOCs. The international oil majors such as Exxon, BP, and Shell, which stood as the world's largest oil producers throughout the twentieth century, have been relegated to second-tier status. NOCs are increasing their importance in the twenty-first century, and understanding their emerging policies and priorities is critical to understanding the future of the energy industry. This change will represent a major shift for international energy markets—one that deserves our careful attention.

The growing importance of NOCs to the global supply-demand balance raises questions about their emerging policies, objectives, and priorities. It also raises questions about the role governments play in the day-to-day management of their NOCs. National oil companies have important responsibilities in their home nations. They aid in redistributing national wealth from domestic energy resources and they play a strong role in the pursuit of national energy security and domestic industrial and economic development. In some cases, NOCs are a tool of foreign policy. But all these objectives, while extremely important to national goals, can have a huge impact on an NOC's ability to expand its oil and gas production.

Many observers are concerned about the ability of NOCs to meet growing global demand for hydrocarbons. To be honest, the skeptics have a point. I have already touched on the staggering investment that will be required over the course of the next twenty-five years. OPEC production, which represents a large share of NOC output, is lower today than it was in 1979. Moreover, there are serious questions about the capability of NOCs to use their resources efficiently, risking underproduction and higher prices. Bloated workforces, expensive consumer fuel subsidies, and debilitating political interference remain features of a number of major NOCs; all reduce their ability to return the maximum production per investment dollar.

There are highly effective NOCs, but they vary widely in their efficiency and, on average, are only about 60 percent as efficient as their international oil company (IOC) brethren. So, unless NOCs as a group increase their efficiency, world energy markets may be headed for a rocky future.

CHINA AND INDIA—HUNGRY FOR ENERGY

Some Asian countries, most notably China and India, have responded to the emerging energy security challenges posed by greater NOC dominance of world markets by seeking bilateral energy relationships with large oil-exporting countries. By doing so, Asian powers ignore the instructive, historical experiences of the West in managing oil crises and energy security. Hard lessons have been learned in the West about the ineffectiveness of strategic bilateral relationships with key oil-exporting countries to safeguard energy supply.

Not only are China's and India's levels of equity oil ownership—the rights to oil produced by a given oil company—relatively small compared to their growing import needs, but mere ownership of reserves does not alter the impact of a global change in oil prices. By hoarding oil for one's own use, equity owners would miss the chance to sell at the higher price, which would effectively cost them the same as if they bought oil on the open market. Moreover, many host oil-producing countries might be tempted during a major market failure to take a larger share of rents from foreign investors, leaving less (or perhaps no) economic advantage to owning oil abroad. Equity oil itself can also be disrupted, forcing equity oil owners to scramble into spot markets in the same manner as those who didn't invest to obtain equity oil. Bilateral sales agreements are even less effective—as history has shown—because suppliers are likely to sell their oil to the highest bidder during a period of market crisis or a supply emergency.

UNITED STATES ENERGY POLICY

Some are speculating that the United States itself will need to create a national oil company to compete for scarce resources. This seems unlikely, or at least a bad idea. As a recent Baker Institute study on the role of the national oil company in international energy markets demonstrates, the privately held American corporations that currently look for oil worldwide are more efficient and productive than any new government-run entity likely to be created by the U.S. government. The question of the future competitiveness of American companies and their continued access to resources is best answered by U.S. government initiatives in areas where Washington already has jurisdiction and experience:

- Promoting and enforcing bilateral and multilateral trade and investment treaties such as WTO, NAFTA, the Energy Charter and others.
- Utilizing foreign aid in oil-rich places where social and economic development assistance is badly needed.
- Enhancing the profile of important international institutions such as the World Bank and the Asian Development Bank in fostering transparency and governance in oil-producing regions.
- Most important, fostering a comprehensive domestic national energy policy that would enhance our energy security and increase U.S. credibility on the world scene.

It has been the policy of the United States for many years to promote the diversification of oil supplies around the globe. This policy was successful in the 1980s and 1990s, with new production areas opening in West Africa and Central Asia, and with unconventional oil and gas production in North America. But the rate of gain in non-OPEC oil production has been flagging recently despite very high oil prices, reflecting the geological limitations and the political and bureaucratic barriers to investment in such attractive areas as Russia, the Caspian Basin, and Mexico.

We are seeing greater resource nationalism among major oil exporters, thwarting collaboration between IOCs and NOCs. We are also seeing greater discontent and violence in oil-producing communities. To the extent that local populations feel, as did the indigenous peoples of Bolivia or the citizens of the Niger Delta, that they will not share in the economic benefits of oil and gas development but will be left with environmental and other social burdens, they may deny their support for such development, creating license-to-operate issues for potential oil and gas investors and potentially worsening the shortage of global energy supply.

This situation is forcing policymakers in the United States, Europe, South Korea, China, and Japan to consider new options to ensure energy security for their citizens.

ENERGY VERSUS GEOPOLITICS

The tenuous situation of international oil markets sits atop the growing risk of political instability in the Middle East related in previous chapters of this book. Political and economic reform in the Middle East faces formidable challenges. A huge gap exists between the agenda of the "Islamic radical jihadists" and the existing "electoral autocracies." The region as a whole faces severe social and economic problems as governments are challenged to put policies in place that could provide the resources, jobs, and adequate services for growing and restive younger populations. The delicate compromise that now represents the status quo ante among the middle class, reformists, Islamists, and ruling regimes in many countries in the Middle East, if upended, could usher in prolonged instability and social and political unrest.

Saudi Arabia faces particularly grave challenges. The Saudi security budget was estimated to total more than $8 billion in

2004, and the kingdom has stepped up its attacks on internal domestic terrorist cells, making real headway in eliminating domestic branches of Al Qaeda. However, Saudi Al Qaeda has planned
several major attacks on Saudi energy infrastructure over the last
several years. So far, Saudi internal security forces have thwarted
those plans, but few believe Al Qaeda will give up its efforts, and
terrorism remains a significant threat to oil facilities in the region. Between 2002 and 2004, Saudi Arabia spent an estimated
$1.2 billion to increase security at all of its energy facilities. It is
estimated that between twenty-five thousand and thirty thousand
troops currently protect the kingdom's oil infrastructure.

In 1995, Osama Bin Laden wrote a letter to the late King
Fahd of Saudi Arabia, enumerating his grievances against the
governments of Saudi Arabia and the United States. One of his
complaints was the servitude of Saudi oil policy to U.S. interests
and the loss of oil revenue the kingdom had suffered as a result
of these policies. Bin Laden called Saudi cooperation with the
United States, which has kept oil prices low, "the greatest theft
in human history." He argued that since the real price of oil was
held artificially low, the Muslim world has lost $36 trillion over a
quarter century, or thirty thousand dollars for each of the world's
1.2 billion Muslims.

Despite grievances related to oil, Bin Laden and other Islamic
radicals initially believed energy facilities in the Muslim world
should be spared, since they constituted the wealth of a future
Islamic state. But by December 2004, Bin Laden had a change
of mind and called on the faithful to attack oil facilities as part
of the jihad against the West. Al Qaeda unsuccessfully tried to
attack the major crude-oil-processing facilities at Abqaiq in February 2006. In a message claiming responsibility for the attack,
Al Qaeda of the Arabian Peninsula said the attack was part of the
war against "Christians and Jews to stop their pillage of Muslim
riches." Al Qaeda's political and physical attacks are only one
factor in the kingdom's internal debate about the appropriate
level for oil prices. Still, whatever the disagreements within royal

circles about the optimum strategies, Saudi Arabia continues to increase its oil production capacity to enhance its global role as the key world swing oil producer.

As global economic growth has continued, key OPEC producers Venezuela and Iraq have seen their oil production capacity decline. Domestic political factors have stalled Kuwaiti and Iranian investment. Saudi Arabia has stepped up its upstream capacity investment. Saudi Aramco's development budget for 2007, originally pegged at $2.4 billion, was raised to $4 billion, reflecting both rising costs and an urgency to achieve targeted expansion goals regardless of cost. Saudi upstream spending reflects recognition that oil markets face four potential flashpoints in the OPEC supply chain—Iran, Iraq, Nigeria, and Venezuela. Saudi Arabia's policy is aimed at making sure the kingdom can influence crude oil prices and markets at any time and under any contingency, maintaining its geopolitical importance. The kingdom is also adding refining capacity at home and abroad to make sure it has outlets for its "extra heavy" grade of crude oil.

Saudi Arabia has publicly stated that one goal is to have enough spare capacity to offset a disruption of all Iranian exports. Further, the kingdom has made clear that it can gear its oil policy to respond to geopolitical challenges. Iran's role in Iraq and elsewhere in the region has great bearing on the stability of the Middle East and, by extension, on energy security. An expanded proxy war in Iraq—fanned by the actions of its neighbors—could create a political and humanitarian crisis of even greater proportions and would be detrimental to the region as a whole. An expansion in violence in Iraq and beyond would greatly damage the stability of the oil market.

A POTENTIAL IRANIAN THREAT

Saudi Arabia has expressed concerns about such a scenario from the highest political levels. The kingdom is deeply worried about the crisis in Iraq, the possibility of deepening violence in Iraq, and the fate of the Sunni Arab community there. The Saudi government has a strong interest in national reconciliation in Iraq and in the peaceful coexistence of Sunni and Shia Arab populations. Saudi Arabia itself has a large Shia population, which resides in the oil-producing areas of the kingdom's eastern province and constitutes the majority of Saudi Aramco's workforce. Because of its regional leadership role, its position as the guardian of the holy sites of Medina and Mecca, its close ties to Iraq and Lebanon, and its large Shia population, Saudi Arabia has a strategic interest in reining in Tehran.

Hints that Saudi Arabia might back Sunni fighters inside Iraq to protect its interests against Iranian-backed militias are a warning of possible negative scenarios that could emerge if stability cannot be achieved in Iraq through political means.

For its part, Iran has put its Gulf neighbors on notice that it could be more aggressive, with Hussain Shariatmadari, an advisor to Iranian supreme leader Ali Khamenei and managing editor of the Iranian daily *Kayhan*, claiming in 2007 that Shia populations in Bahrain demand the reunification of "this province of Iran to its motherland." While this statement was modified by other Iranian leaders' comments, it had its political impact on the Arab Gulf countries. So far, the Gulf Cooperation Council has responded to Iranian threats by increasing spending on military defense. Some Saudi analysts have suggested that Saudi monarch King Abdullah may decide to strangle funding of Iranian-backed militias—which Saudis see as a force destructive to national unity in both Lebanon and Iraq—through oil policy. If the kingdom boosted oil production and oil prices fell 25 to 50 percent, the kingdom would still be able to finance its current spending, but lower oil revenues would have a devastating effect on Iran, which is facing economic difficulties. Iran is facing a budget deficit of over $15 billion per quarter. Commentators point to Saudi Arabia's reluctance to cut production in December 2006, when oil prices were sliding toward fifty dollars, as a signal to Tehran that there would be consequences if it didn't show more cooperative policies in Iraq and in negotiations about its nuclear aspirations. In any case, the delicate dance between Iran and the Gulf States will continue, with efforts made to adopt cooperative policies while each side remains wary of the other. This situation is reflected in an old Persian mosaic we have in our home: two princes are seated, offering fruit as a symbol of peace with one hand, while keeping their other hand on their respective swords.

The possibility of expanded conflict in the Middle East remains a major risk factor for energy markets. Today's persistently tight crude oil markets and prices that have risen above one hundred dollars a barrel highlight the vulnerability of the global economy to conditions in that region.

Beyond the political challenges facing the Persian Gulf, the region must also address the issue of proliferation of weapons of mass destruction. In considering how to deal with Iran on its nuclear policy, it cannot be forgotten that Tehran has geographical leverage on the international flow of oil and gas via the Strait of Hormuz, and Iran's pursuit of nuclear capability must be seen in this light. Iranian threats to use the oil weapon in response to U.S. initiatives to block Iran's nuclear ambitions sent oil prices up by several dollars a barrel in the autumn of 2006 and remain a feature driving price volatility today.

Maintaining the free flow of oil through the Strait of Hormuz is of vital strategic importance to the world economy and to the United States and its Asian allies. There have been several challenges to the freedom of navigation in the Strait of Hormuz and adjacent territories over the last several decades. The most prolonged threat to navigation in the Persian Gulf in recent years arose during the eight-year war between Iraq and Iran. The United States responded to this challenge of attacks on Persian Gulf shipping by organizing a fleet of frigates, destroyers, and minesweepers in the region to combat the threat against shipping. U.S. Navy vessels have been called into service to repel attacks by terrorist suicide bombers on both of Iraq's offshore oil-shipping terminals, and shippers from the Persian Gulf region are again asking the U.S. military to provide naval escorts. The delicacy of such operations hit home with the brief crisis surrounding the capture of fifteen British sailors by Iran in 2007. Gulf Arab leaders remain concerned about the possibility of an Iranian attack on oil facilities in the Gulf, either directly or through the sponsorship of terrorism.

Maintaining the free flow of oil to world markets is not just a critical national concern to the United States but also a global one. Conflict resolution and international cooperation will be key to confronting the strategic challenges of our future energy needs. There needs to be much broader discussion at the governmental level of the global challenges we face in the energy arena and the best means to achieve energy security. If countries feel more confident about the ability of international energy markets to supply their economies, they will feel less inclined to hedge their bets, for example, by using NOCs to build alliances with unsavory regimes. And if producers feel secure in their access to important consumer markets abroad and confident that their stake in the global system will bring a better life for their citizens, they should be disinclined to use their energy resources as a lever to bully a neighboring state or wealthier trading partner.

GLOBAL CLIMATE CHANGE

The challenge of meeting the world's future energy needs goes beyond the debate about the future of the Middle East. Global climate change has also raised profound questions about our energy usage. Consuming countries—the United States first among them—can and should do more. President George W. Bush's State of the Union proposal to raise fuel efficiency standards of U.S. automobiles and to try to curb the growing appetite for gasoline in our country is a long-overdue step in the right direction.

We all recognize the gravity of the United States' "addiction to oil." Clearly, we need a better and more comprehensive energy strategy in this country.

The International Monetary Fund recently noted that U.S. gasoline consumption, as a share of gross domestic product, is nearly five times that of other major industrialized countries. Gasoline accounts for close to 45 percent of U.S. oil consumption and 70 percent of the expected increase in oil demand in the coming decades. Fuel efficiency in America is 25 percent lower than that in the European Union and 50 percent lower than that in Japan. To quote *New York Times* columnist Thomas Friedman, "No wonder the world doubts our seriousness on energy issues."

It has been thirty years since the Arab oil embargo spurred a quadrupling of the price of oil. The embargo inspired the industrialized West to undertake dramatic and important actions to prevent oil blackmail from recurring. Interest soared in the 1970s in science and energy policy, and we saw the birth of important energy technology research programs at our national labs and universities. But, in part because of the diversification spurred by the 1970s response to sudden oil insecurity, oil demand fell in the 1980s and with it, the price of oil. Unthinkably, complacency set in. We cut science research budgets, dropped promising initiatives, and got back into large cars. Sadly, now thirty years after the 1973 oil crisis, we are being forced back into introspection concerning the lack of progress where energy supply and use are concerned.

Beginning in 2003, the Baker Institute began a new venture with Rice University's science faculty to explore more fully how scientific developments, including breakthroughs in the nanotechnology field, might contribute solutions to the global energy problem. The rate of growth in energy demand worldwide runs the risk of outpacing affordable, clean supplies unless we can muster not only conservation and evolutionary improvements to existing technologies, but also revolutionary new breakthroughs in the energy field.

Promoting this kind of research in alternative energy sources and new conservation technologies and design should be a top national priority. While hydrocarbons, including oil and gas, will remain the backbone of global energy consumption for at least several decades to come, renewable resources can and should represent an increasing share of energy production. Scientific innovation has a key role to play.

A FUTURE BASED ON PARTNERSHIP

Enhanced energy regional export networks, joint research and technology transfer in usage efficiency, and joint emergency preparedness could be among the end results of cooperation on energy policy among large consuming nations in the West and Asia. Our focus needs to be on building bridges for global cooperation for dealing with energy issues collaboratively and avoiding potentially dangerous bilateral rivalry for supply that could lead to conflict and market failure. My main point is that it is in the vital interest of importing and exporting countries alike that our energy future be based on partnership, not conflict. We cannot allow the Middle East, already home to tragic violence, to become the scene of great-power confrontation over energy.

Cooperative international research and development must also be a major vehicle in promoting effective energy policy and laying the groundwork for technology breakthroughs in clean, distributed energy sources that can benefit rural populations in the developing world. Such research should be aimed at revolutionizing advances in solar-derived fuel, wind, clean coal, hydrogen, fuel cells and batteries, and a new electrical energy grid that can tie all these power sources together. Such a research effort, led by the industrialized world, would yield benefits for all peoples, both in reducing energy poverty and in promoting global environmental protection.

A global approach to the challenging energy issues we face is compelling for the peace and prosperity of all countries. For the United States to lead such an effort, it must muster the political will to have an effective energy policy at home. An effective and broad-based American effort to reduce oil use by adopting more efficient transportation technologies and shifting to nonoil fuels would be very effective in contributing to a more positive global energy future.

A greater political effort to create a more comprehensive domestic energy policy and a greater effort overseas to assure energy supply and security would serve national and international interests and enhance the credibility of the United States at home and abroad.

TEN

PUBLIC DIPLOMACY —
THE VOICE OF AMERICA

Jean-David Levitte, the former ambassador of France to the United States and now French president Nicolas Sarkozy's national security advisor, told the *New Yorker*'s Adam Gopnik, "When Sarkozy met with [Secretary of State] Condoleezza Rice, she said, 'What can I do for you?' And he said, bluntly, 'Improve your image in the world. It's difficult when the country that is the most powerful, the most successful — that is, of necessity, the leader of our side — is one of the most unpopular countries in the world. It presents overwhelming problems for you and overwhelming problems for your allies. So do everything you can do to improve the way you are perceived — that's what you can do for me.'" With guarded optimism, he added, "I think it's entirely possible; the reservoir of good will has been drained somewhat, but it is far from dry."

In fact, Secretary Rice was acutely aware of the need for effective public diplomacy — the promotion of the national interest by, first, listening and understanding, and then informing, engaging, and influencing people around the world. She also knew that I regarded public diplomacy as a major instrument that had been allowed to grow rusty with disuse. In 2003, at the request of then secretary of state Colin Powell, I agreed to chair a congressionally mandated bipartisan advisory group for public diplomacy for the Arab and Muslim world. Colin Powell and I had worked together during the Reagan and Bush administrations and, given our close personal and professional relationship, I agreed immediately to take on this task and try to be as helpful as I could.

The impetus for that effort had come from members of Congress who were frustrated that our public diplomacy strategy and operations had been woefully inadequate ever since the dismantling of the United States Information Agency in 1999. In the wake of the events of 9/11 and the wars in Afghanistan and Iraq, they sought recommendations for reorganizing the public diplomacy functions in government, to help the United States meet the national security and foreign policy challenges we were facing, especially in the Arab and Muslim world.

I recruited members for the group, both Democrats and Republicans, from the private sector, academia, and former public officials. We met regularly between July and September 2003 and contacted numerous experts and practitioners in the United States, Europe, and the Arab and Muslim world, from Africa and the Middle East to Pakistan and Indonesia. On October 1, 2003, we published our findings in a report we called *Changing Minds, Winning Peace—A New Strategic Direction for U.S. Public Diplomacy in the Arab and Muslim World.* Much of this chapter draws on that report.

In 2005, shortly after President Bush appointed her to head the State Department, Secretary Rice asked me to prepare a strategic game plan for U.S. public diplomacy, based on the advisory group's report. I then worked closely with her and Karen Hughes, the undersecretary of state for public affairs, and her deputy, Dina Powell. They made significant organizational changes and increased the resources devoted to public diplomacy along the lines of the advisory group's recommendations. As I stressed in the strategic game plan, however, the overall task of conveying America's policies and values abroad in a much more effective manner remains a major challenge.

In the 2002 National Security Strategy of the United States of America, a periodic report prepared by the executive branch, President George W. Bush recognized the importance of adapting public diplomacy to meet the post-9/11 challenge: "Just as our diplomatic institutions must adapt so that we can reach out to others," he wrote, "we also need a different and more comprehensive approach to public information efforts that can help people around the world learn about and understand America. The war on terrorism is not a clash of civilizations. It does, however, reveal the clash inside a civilization, a battle for the future of the Muslim world. This is a struggle of ideas and this is an area where America must excel."

This central statement of the strategic objective for the public diplomacy of the United States in relation to the Arab and Muslim world should guide our policy. Unfortunately, in the actual conduct of our policy, the struggle of ideas between the forces of moderation and extremism within the Muslim world has been subsumed under the so-called Global War on Terror. It should be the other way around. Indeed, the war on terrorism is a lethal subset of this greater struggle, with direct consequences for the national security interests of the United States, as the attacks of 9/11 made clear. The strategic objective should be to marginalize the extremists, be they religious or secular, and to support and sustain the moderates in the individual countries of the Muslim world. This will require a broad strategy, of which public diplomacy is an important instrument.

REINVENTING THE UNITED STATES INFORMATION AGENCY

It was an error to dismantle the USIA in 1999, under the mistaken assumption that, with the end of the Cold War, our ideological struggles were over and we no longer needed an organization distinct from the State Department to focus on the struggle of ideas. September 11 put an end to that misperception.

The integration of the USIA into the State Department was also meant to bring public diplomacy closer than ever to policy-making, but that aim fell short. First, the institutional culture of much of the Department of State persisted in its view of public diplomacy as a secondary function and career path. Second, the clarity of coordination and communication that characterized the relationship between USIA's strategic center in Washington and its operational posts in the field has yet to be duplicated fully within the new structures that the Clinton and Bush administrations put in place.

Efforts to combine the Department of State's traditional focus on policy representation, analysis, and reporting with USIA's primary focus on public outreach and programs have made some progress in recent years. For example, the president's letter of instruction to chiefs of mission has been revised to emphasize the critical importance of public diplomacy to national security and to highlight the expectation that chiefs of mission, our ambassadors, will personally participate in public diplomacy and ensure that the members of their staffs do likewise. The secretary of state has reinforced this step by reiterating that message in formal communications to U.S.-based employees through the department's assistant secretaries. The work requirements for every department employee serving abroad have been amended to include appropriate participation in public diplomacy, and each employee is to be held accountable for this participation in the performance evaluation process.

Within USIA, clear two-way channels of communication and coordination linked senior agency management with field practitioners through the geographical area officers. These channels provided the means for developing and communicating strategic guidance, developing country-specific programs, allocating human and financial resources at home and abroad, following trends in foreign public opinion, reporting program results, and holding practitioners accountable for their performance.

With the integration of USIA into the State Department, these channels lost their clarity. The previous direct link between senior USIA management and public affairs officers through the area offices became indirect, with the undersecretary for public diplomacy and public affairs and the geographic assistant secretaries often providing separate guidance, and the chiefs of mission or their deputies undertaking the performance evaluation of public affairs officers. To remedy this, we recommended in both the advisory report and the strategic game plan that the role of the undersecretary be strengthened in recognition of the incumbent's ultimate accountability for the effectiveness of the department's public diplomacy programs. Much has subsequently been done to implement this recommendation.

THE FOREIGN LANGUAGE GAP

For public diplomacy to play its crucial role in meeting the strategic challenge the United States faces in the Arab and Muslim world, there must be significant increases in funding, and additional professional staff must be recruited and dedicated to the issues of the Arab and Muslim world. The professional level of fluency in local languages and knowledge and understanding of Arab and Muslim societies must be dramatically enhanced. The key languages are Arabic, Farsi-Persian (Iranian), Dari-Persian (Afghan), Turkish, Urdu, and Bahasa Indonesian.

We need to review Foreign Service language and regional training, as well as the pattern of assignments, to assure that regional expertise and language fluency are sustained throughout a Foreign Service officer's career.

The struggle of ideas is generational, and we simply must prepare for the long term by training our people in the languages and culture of the countries of the region. When I was assigned to the United States Embassy in Moscow, I was struck by how many Soviet diplomats were truly fluent in English and could handle whatever linguistic situation they found themselves in. This was the result of a determined effort by the Soviet state to ensure that they had the human resources to face their major foreign policy and national security challenge—the United States. The challenge we face today in the Muslim world is a major one, and we must be certain that our Foreign Service, military, and intelligence personnel have the necessary linguistic tools to deal with it effectively.

The Department of State has focused on these language requirements and has made progress. It is not, however, sufficient to the task. The number of language officers who are fluent in the languages of their region should be much higher. Moreover, many officers are not trained for public diplomacy, and funds to train them are inadequate. As a result, only a handful of our Arabic speakers are sufficiently fluent and skillful to be able to debate and present our policies effectively on Arabic radio and television.

When I presented the advisory group's report to the Congress and the public in 2003, I purposely asked if the audience knew how many Foreign Service officers could be called on to discuss and debate a current hot issue in Arabic on Al Jazeera, the major Arabic satellite TV station. After a rhetorical pause, I would hold up my right hand and indicate only five were up to the task! As of 2003, only 54 out of 279 State Department personnel tested at the 3/3 or higher fluency level, indicating ability to speak and read Arabic well enough to handle basic professional requirements.

The situation with other languages in the Muslim world is equally bad, if not worse.

KEEPING UP WITH AND AHEAD OF AL JAZEERA

I became a passionate advocate of a proposal in our advisory group report that called for an "Arab and Muslim Countries Communications Unit." This was modeled, in part, on the highly effective Islamic Media Unit established by the Foreign and Commonwealth Office of the United Kingdom after the attacks of 9/11. We urged the State Department to establish this unit under the direction of the undersecretary for public diplomacy. Specifically, the new State Department unit, working with embassies abroad, would determine, in real time, the content of broadcasts and press reports from the region, with a view toward achieving accurate and effective presentations of U.S. policies, decisions, and initiatives, as well as quick reaction to views, opinions, and perceptions appearing in the press and media in the Arab and Muslim countries. It would coordinate, on a daily basis, the U.S. government's media outreach (print, television, radio, and internet) to Arab and Muslim nations and provide "rapid response," both in disseminating timely messages and in reacting to inaccuracies and distortions in the foreign media.

This unit, which would work closely with the Office of Global Communications in the White House, would be staffed by public diplomacy officers with regional knowledge and fluent professional language competence, covering the Arab, African, South Asian, Central Asian, and Southeast Asian Muslim countries. These officers would draw on the resources of the geographical bureaus and interact with them to share information.

The unit would produce substantive content (talking points, op-ed pieces, scripts) to meet these requirements and suggest and schedule media appearances by U.S. government officials in the United States and abroad. The long-term goal would be to provide content and context that will improve attitudes toward the United States in the Arab and Muslim world. This model could be used for establishing such units for other geographical regions.

To my delight and great satisfaction, this proposal was adopted fully by Undersecretary of State Karen Hughes and the State Department, and the unit was established in record time. It is functioning quite effectively today. When I visited the facility for the first time I was heartened to see young Foreign Service language officers monitoring the Middle Eastern TV satellite programs and writing their analyses. One officer of Arab-American origin was monitoring the internet and blogs in Arabic, which provided another dimension and insights into opinions and thinking in the region.

I felt that this was a good beginning.

THE INSTRUMENTS OF PUBLIC DIPLOMACY

The following major instruments of public diplomacy need to be moved to a new level of effectiveness.

Education and Exchange Programs

Americans and, for the most part, peoples of the Arab and Muslim world agree on the vital importance of education, but the United States has not taken sufficient advantage of this important shared value. To the contrary, key programs, such as funding scholarships for future Arab and Muslim leaders, have been cut to the bone. Many who have studied here did so on scholarships funded by USAID. But USAID scholarships have been drastically reduced, from 20,000 in 1980 to only 900 in 2003. Between 1995 and 2001 alone, academic and cultural exchanges (such as the Fulbright programs) dropped from 45,000 to 29,000 a year. After 9/11 the number of students visiting our country dropped for a number of reasons—increased security measures, misperceptions about whether students were welcome, cost factors. The State Department announced in 2007 that the corner is being turned and the number of international students coming to America is once again increasing. According to the State Department's Open Doors 2007 report, 582,984 international students studied in the United States during the 2006–7 school year, roughly equal to the previous record. These efforts to welcome more foreign students to the United States must be strongly encouraged. The Open Doors report also shows a record number of Americans studying abroad—nearly 224,000 American students during the 2005–6 school year, an 8.5 percent increase from the previous year. This two-way student traffic is a good sign.

We need to expand, where appropriate, academic and cultural exchange programs and international visitors programs, especially in areas such as journalism and media studies, which can have a direct impact on how the United States and its policies are viewed in the Muslim world. We must strike a proper balance between post-9/11 security requirements and policies and procedures regarding student visas to stem the decline in the number of foreign students studying in this country. The Department of State's Education and Cultural Affairs Bureau and the International Military Education and Training programs need to devote more resources to the Arab and Muslim world. Major increases are needed to help Arabs and Muslims gain access to American education; the greatest long-term impact would come from scholarships to needy students from throughout the broader Middle East, especially those from poorer countries. We need also to create new ways to link American educational institutions with those in the Arab and Muslim countries. This could include channeling increased support to American educational institutions in the Middle East, such as the American University of Beirut, the American University of Cairo, the Lebanese-American University, and Robert College in Istanbul. American financial assistance—both public and private—should also be directed to Arab and Muslim universities that build or expand American Studies centers and public policy centers that would promote critical thinking on key issues and broaden economic, social, and political opportunities for the region.

English Language Teaching

United States public diplomacy has always included the teaching of English in one form or another. Employing native and non-native teachers, texts, and classroom interaction on a daily basis, education-based diplomacy enjoys great credibility, respect, and access to broad audiences. Little else is as effective at conveying information and shaping attitudes. In the case of English, the potential scope of this influence is enormous. Accordingly, we should 1) increase the small number of English Language Officers in the field and enlarge the size of their negligible budgets; 2) expand the English Language Specialist Program, which sends American professors abroad; and 3) expand the English Language Fellows Program, which places American teachers in local host institutions each year on a ten-month grant to teach, train teachers, and develop curricula.

American Corners

In an age in which terrorism and security concerns have moved United States facilities into fortresslike perimeters in our consular and diplomatic establishments, our ability to reach out to local audiences in foreign countries has diminished. The American Corners concept, which establishes a venue in urban centers that is detached from an Embassy, provides an effective alternative to the classic cultural centers and libraries. They provide a multifunctional programming platform to tell America's story, especially to the young, through books, periodicals, the internet, music, film, and other means. The Corners also serve as cost-effective meeting places for American events.

American Corners should be expanded in the Arab and Muslim world. They can be launched with outlays of only thirty thousand dollars to forty thousand dollars. Materials in the Corners should be expanded far beyond current offerings, and resources should be provided to increase translations into local languages. American Corners can be home to the "American Knowledge Library," an advisory group proposal to offer essential readings about the United States, both in English and in translation. I would personally insist that a translation of *The Federalist Papers* be a standard item in every one of these libraries.

Speakers Programs

The United States Speaker and Specialist Program is one of the most direct manifestations of smart public diplomacy. It should be expanded by a substantial increase in funding, with the caveat that it find and furnish speakers who can help improve attitudes toward the United States and that methods be developed to measure the effectiveness of individual speakers and the program as a whole.

Center for United States–Arab/Muslim Studies and Dialogue

A Center for U.S.-Arab/Muslim Studies and Dialogue should be established in this country, with U.S. government support. This would be a public policy think tank to study ways of strengthening understanding and relations between the United States and the countries of the Arab and Muslim world. It could be modeled along the lines of the Dante Fascell North-South Center at the University of Miami, which studies Western hemispheric issues, and the East-West Center at the University of Hawaii, which promotes better relations between the United States and the countries of the Asia-Pacific region. The U.S. government funds these centers. Amazingly, the government funds no such center for promoting understanding between the U.S. and the Arab and Muslim world.

Interfaith and Intercultural Dialogue

Practitioners of public diplomacy should encourage interfaith and intercultural dialogue between Muslims, Christians, Jews, and those of other faiths through American NGOs and educational and religious institutions, as appropriate.

Technology and Communications

Information and communications technologies are essential to public diplomacy. This is especially the case since Islamic radicals successfully use the internet to propagate their views and to recruit militants to their cause. Accordingly, senior U.S. officials involved in public diplomacy should establish clear-cut incentives, not just bureaucratic requirements, to use the vast and growing array of information technology networks, platforms, and applications more effectively. Substantially more public diplomacy resources must be set aside for the translation of internet-linked information and news on U.S. government websites in Arabic, Farsi, Turkish, Urdu, Bahasa Indonesia, and other key regional languages.

Private Sector Role, Including NGOs

United States policymakers should encourage the role of the American private sector in contributing to the strategic goals and direction of our public diplomacy. We should support local NGOs in Arab and Muslim society as such organizations develop independent of extremist groups and ideas. These local groups and initiatives could provide the building blocks for a new middle class that could be the basis of a democratic cadre and an indigenous force for economic and political reforms.

Government-Sponsored International Media

For the United States to be successful in the struggle of ideas in the Arab and Muslim world, it must develop an effective press and media strategy. We are not there. First, we must understand the environment we are dealing with in that region. The basic, hard reality is that most of the countries of the Arab and Muslim world are led by authoritarian regimes, with the result that state institutions, the media, and other key sectors of society work closely together. A public diplomacy campaign developed for media in the free world is totally different from a campaign developed for press and media in an authoritarian setting. This needs to be recognized, even when dealing with state-controlled "private media." Also, policymakers should be aware that in most Arab countries, such as Saudi Arabia and Egypt, it is illegal to do survey research. Thus, it is impossible to measure audiences in the same way as we do in the United States. This is an impediment to the development of the media and can be changed only by substantive political processes.

The United States has been spending more than $600 million a year on government-sponsored international broadcasting—about the same amount it spends on all the public diplomacy programs in the State Department combined. Broadcasting has played an effective and distinguished role in U.S. public diplomacy. The Voice of America (VOA) was launched in 1942 to disseminate information about American policies and interests globally by radio. Radio Free Europe and Radio Liberty served as "surrogate" radio stations for Eastern Europeans and Russians behind the Iron Curtain and are generally credited with helping to win the Cold War. The fall of communism changed the role of broadcasting profoundly. In 1999 (the same year the USIA was dismantled), Congress passed legislation to bring all government-sponsored international broadcasting services under the authority of the Broadcasting Board of Governors, which describes itself as an "independent, autonomous agency." The board comprises the secretary of state and eight private citizens, most of whom have been drawn from media businesses.

How valuable is government-sponsored international broadcasting in the Arab and Muslim world? With much of the potential broadcast audience harboring strongly critical perceptions and views of United States policies and, unlike the citizens of the former Iron Curtain countries, receiving abundant information from other electronic media, we had to admit in our advisory group report that we did not know. But the information that is available indicates that a serious review of our radio and television broadcasting is sorely needed, and that we will need substantive and operational changes to meet the challenge we face in this part of the world.

The residents of Arab and Muslim countries harbor deep skepticism toward any state-sponsored press and media, having experienced decades of authoritarian control of these institutions by their rulers. Consequently, any United States–sponsored TV or radio station would have a high credibility problem at the outset.

The Broadcasting Board of Governors operates Radio Farda, which broadcasts in Farsi-Persian (Iranian), and Radio Sawa, which broadcasts in Arabic. In 2004, the BBG launched an Arabic satellite station called Al-Hurra ("The Free One"). Their performance record to date is mixed, to say the least. Measured by the U.S. public diplomacy criteria of "listen, understand, inform, engage, and influence," the results are disappointing, despite millions of dollars allocated to these radio and television stations. All three operations suffer from a lack of creative, professional, substantive management and should be subject to regular objective and professional internal reviews of programming and other aspects of the operations. Particular attention should focus on the personnel recruitment policies of these stations. For better or worse, one of the reasons for the success of Al Jazeera in the region is the careful and politically deliberate mix of Arab speakers from all over the Arab world. The chief editor of one of the most important daily newspapers in the Arab world, *al Sharq al Awsat* (*The Middle East*), wrote regarding Al-Hurra, "We were expecting high-quality American television like CBS *60 Minutes,* or ABC *Nightline* or NBC *Meet the Press,* instead we were treated to second-rate civil war Lebanese television."

Al-Hurra faces a further problem in that it competes in a field already saturated with Arabic news networks. Approximately 170 satellite TV channels now ply the crowded Middle Eastern airwaves; however, with the exception of the two best-known, Al Jazeera and Al Arabiya, and some forty other stations owned by the Gulf States and their surrogates, the rest of the stations are financially poor. They rely on talk shows and other staples of cheap TV. The most common format on these stations is one person preaching. In many instances, to fill the time, stations carry live communal prayer services accompanied by religious speeches that are by their nature xenophobic, excluding non-Muslims. Sometimes, they rerun Al Jazeera and Al Arabiya material or Egyptian soap operas. They want to have a variety of TV channels, but they cannot afford the cost of producing good TV. The advisory group therefore strongly recommended creating a private foundation for public diplomacy that produces high-quality programs to be provided free of charge to Arab TV channels, especially for new independent organizations. If we offer these TV channels quality programs, we can easily shape their message, especially in less affluent Arab countries.

The strategy of Radio Sawa, launched in 2002 to replace Voice of America's Arabic service, is to attract a large, youthful audience through popular music, and then to inform the audience about U.S. policies, values, and interests during interruptions for news and features. The effort has achieved success in reaching out to a large audience by this mix of Arabic and Western music; however, Radio Sawa needs an objective and role beyond simply building a large audience. The BBG's "Sawa Strategy" does not mention changing minds or improving attitudes toward the United States as objectives. Instead, the BBG says Radio Sawa aims to "cover U.S. policies and actions in full," which it patently does not do, and to "engage the audience with dynamic, interactive features," at which it is more successful, but to what end? It should aspire to change attitudes of Arab listeners toward the United States along the lines of our public diplomacy strategic goals. Radio Sawa has yet to prove that its current strategy can accomplish this goal, especially at a time when it faces significant and increasing competition from broadcasters who understand the region and can respond to events and policy issues quickly.

Given the important role that television and radio play in the Muslim countries, U.S.-sponsored international broadcasting, with the exception of the news function itself, should be brought under the strategic direction of the public diplomacy policies and goals of the United States government as defined by the president, the secretary of state, and the undersecretary for public diplomacy.

In addition, it would likely be far more effective to create a tax-exempt foundation for public diplomacy, supported by both private and public funds, that would acquire and produce high-quality American programs to be provided free of charge to TV channels in the Arab and Muslim countries. This organization would also make grants to individual producers and to independent, indigenous media channels, with the aim of creating and disseminating quality programming in the region. Such a foundation would complement the outreach of the U.S.-sponsored international broadcasting operations. Also, it would not be perceived as another government-controlled — in this case, the U.S. government — information station. This, in my mind, is the most effective option for the United States to pursue.

America's Image

According to many recent polls, hostility toward and negative opinions of America have reached shocking levels. A 2005–6 Pew poll concluded that "the bottom has fallen out of Arab and Muslim support for the United States." This is why public diplomacy must be given the highest priority. What is required, as we stated in the advisory group report, is not merely tactical adaptation, but strategic and radical transformation of our public diplomacy strategy and operations. Often, we are simply not present to explain the context and content of our national values and policies.

In Morocco, members of our advisory group were told, "If you do not define yourself in this part of the world, the extremists will define you." And, indeed, they do define us — as negative actors in the Arab-Israeli context, as ruthless occupiers in Iraq, and as bigots toward Muslims, including American Muslims. These characterizations of the United States have free play in the region because there are few, if any, spokespersons in the region to take up our side of the story and because we have deprived ourselves of the means to respond effectively.

I asked one of the members of the group who traveled to Morocco, "What was the worst nightmare you saw?" She said it was in the *bidonvilles* (slums) of Casablanca, where each dwelling had no running water or sanitation facilities, but had a satellite dish capturing the affluent lifestyle of the West and the daily broadcasts and anti-American biases of the Arab satellite TV stations—a dangerous study in contrasts that exemplifies the problems we face.

If we are to win the war against extremism, we must couple our policies with effective public diplomacy. Effective public diplomacy will require strategic direction from the president on down. When the president says, "This is an area where America must excel," his words should be translated into action. In *Changing Minds, Winning Peace*, we stated that "America has not excelled in the struggle of ideas in the Arab and Muslim world and those attitudes toward the United States have gone from bad to worse. Hostility toward the United States has reached shocking levels." We face an uphill battle, but I am convinced we can still achieve our objectives if we are able to muster the necessary political will and take the necessary steps.

The enhanced definition of public diplomacy needs to be underscored: "First to listen and understand, and then inform, engage, and influence foreign audiences." This is the modus operandi of public diplomacy. It should be a key objective of a United States administration to get this done effectively, with clarity of purpose and vision.

Further, the strategic direction of public diplomacy must encompass our policies and values. The vast majority of people in the Arab and Muslim world identify with our basic values such as life, liberty, equality before the law, equality of opportunity, political participation, and human rights. They also respect American economic, educational, scientific, and cultural achievements. Where differences exist, they are over specific policies. In the

Arab world, and in most Muslim countries, *perceptions* of the United States are currently formed through three major prisms: 1) the Arab-Israeli conflict and the issue of Palestine; 2) Iraq; and 3) the broad issues of political and economic governance. Simply put, they see us as biased toward Israel, as occupiers in Iraq, and as hypocritical to our values in our support of autocratic regimes and our reaction to elections when the results are not what we wished for, as in Hamas's electoral success in 2006. We often hear the complaint that "it's the policy, stupid. Not public diplomacy." But the reality is that, if our policy determines, say, 80 percent of how people perceive us, for better or worse, that still leaves a significant 20 percent, which constitutes the substance and manner of how we communicate with and inform foreign audiences of our policies and values.

As part of our universal support for democracy, the United States often bolsters regimes in the Arab and Muslim world that are inimical to our values but that, in the shorter term, may advance some of our policies. Many Arabs and Muslims believe such support indicates that we are determined to deny them freedom and political representation. This belief often reflects our own fear that democracy's first beneficiaries in the Arab and Muslim world will be extremists, especially Islamic radicals. We have been caught in a deep contradiction—one from which our official policies and our public diplomacy can extricate us. Public diplomacy provides a way to explain our broader values and longer-term goals for political, economic, and social reforms that would respond to the basic needs of the people in the region and help to marginalize the Islamic radicals and other extremists.

REASSERTING UNITED STATES POLICY GOALS

We can and should, positively and clearly, lay out the larger strategic framework for United States policy goals in the region. These would include the following:

- Peaceful settlement of the Arab-Israeli conflict, Kashmir, and the Western Sahara.
- Peace, security, and democratic and economic development in Afghanistan and Iraq.
- Stability and democratic evolution in Pakistan.
- Combating terrorism.
- Regional security cooperation.
- Global energy security.
- Managing and preventing the proliferation of nuclear and other weapons of mass destruction.
- Free, open, representative, and tolerant political systems leading to democracy.
- Economic growth through private market economies, free trade, and investment.
- Educational systems that prepare students to participate constructively in civil society and the global marketplace.
- A free press, with public and private media that educate, inform, and entertain.
- Full participation of women and minorities in society.
- Human rights.

These elements constitute a policy and values framework for the strategic direction of public diplomacy in the region. We must articulate these goals to the Arab and Muslim world more clearly and candidly than we have, tailoring our approach to specific audiences in different countries and regions of the Muslim world. And we must underscore the common ground between our values and policies and theirs. This is a formula for effective United States public diplomacy, and it can be implemented.

ELEVEN

The Strategic Challenge in the Arc of Crisis

In 1993, President Bill Clinton hosted King Hussein of Jordan at the White House. In addition to Middle East issues, they discussed the Bosnian crisis. As I accompanied the president back from a farewell ceremony for the king on the South Lawn, he remarked to me that the Europeans, instead of viewing the creation of a multiethnic Bosnian entity in the heart of Europe as an opportunity to build "a multiconfessional bridge to the Muslim world," were looking at Bosnia more as an Islamic threat within the continent. He thought they were missing a historic opportunity. I asked the president if he wanted us to send him some policy recommendations to follow up on this excellent insight. He said yes and we sent the recommendations. Unfortunately, as events evolved, the opportunity was largely missed. The need for bridges, however, is greater than ever.

While accepting Islam as one of the world's great religions, with its mainstream message of tolerance and recognition of the "People of the Book" (Jews, Christians, and Muslims), U.S. policy must strongly differentiate in word and deed between this mainstream of Islam, on the one hand, and Muslim individuals, groups, and regimes that work against U.S. interests by their advocacy of terrorism, violence, and repression and their quest for authoritarian rule, on the other.

Because of their historical role, several key countries will have an important influence on the direction the struggle of ideas within the Muslim world will take. They should be considered as potential bridges, for good or ill, for the future of Islam in the broader Middle East, Central Asia, South Asia, and beyond, with a hope that they can serve as positive forces for moderate Islam beyond their borders. Prominent among these are Turkey, with its secular model of Islamic society and potential outreach to the Turkic-speaking countries of Central Asia; Egypt, site of an important debate between moderate and radical Islamic thinkers and the home of Islam's greatest university, Al Azhar; and Saudi Arabia, with its petroleum resources and its role as custodian of Islam's holiest sites, Mecca and Medina. Also crucial are Malaysia and Indonesia, the world's most populous Muslim state and the site of an important Islamic revivalist movement.

There are some positive signs. At the conclusion of a conference of Arab interior ministers in Tunis in January 1995, Saudi minister of interior Prince Naif Bin Abdul Azziz emphasized the necessity of collective Arab action to fight terrorism and counteract the tendency to link terrorism and extremism to Islam. "Islam," he said, "is a religion of peace, love, and security," adding that "it is wrong to use Islam to serve political purposes. Instead of bending Islam to serve group or individual desires, all Muslim persons, organizations, societies, or governments should serve Islam and highlight its honorable face."

We in the United States will need to proceed realistically, without any grand illusions. In individual countries, we will find religious figures expressing a diversity of views, from moderate to radical, and each country has to deal with internal problems involving Islamist political movements and groups.

Shortly after the demise of the Soviet Union, the conventional wisdom foresaw a contest between Turkey and Iran, another "Great Game" to win the "hearts and minds" of the Muslims of Central Asia. In fact, neither country has been able to exert a defining influence over the region, given the complexity of local, nationalist, cultural, religious, and economic factors. Even Iran, enabled by the war in Iraq and the overthrow of Saddam Hussein in 2003 to expand its influence with Shiite political and religious groups in Iraq, will be limited in its geographical and political reach in the Arab world by these same factors.

European governments have demonstrated, despite historical knowledge of and direct experience in the Middle East, a kind of myopia when dealing with Islam in their own societies. The pressing economic and security requirements of large immigrant Muslim populations in their countries, while obviously important in their domestic political calculations, have dominated their decision-making, hindering a focus on the need for a more comprehensive approach. I believe that one important difference between the American and the European experiences concerning immigrant populations is that the American model is based on assimilation and the European one more on equality before the law, but with social differentiation that leads to ghetto mentalities and even violence, as seen in recent years in the urban riots by Muslim youths in France.

PROMOTING DEMOCRACY

Powerful as it is, the United States is limited in its ability to shape developments in this region. The military action undertaken in 2003 to overthrow Saddam Hussein is a case study of the difficulties involved in trying to promote democracy by force. The burdens of the occupation of Iraq have been huge in terms of blood and treasure. Rather than resort to military force to promote democracy, a better path for the United States is to pursue a consistent policy of urging and working actively with governments and representative groups and parties in the Arab and Muslim world to reach out to their societies to broaden participatory government, build institutions, civil society, and free-market economies as expeditiously as their circumstances permit. This is a generational challenge. There are no "cakewalks." While promoting representative government, the rule of law, human rights, and market economies as the most effective approach to diminish the social injustice that helps give rise to extremism and terrorism, we must be sensitive to the complexities involved.

In some parts of the world, the modernization process of the West is viewed with suspicion, even hostility, especially by antimodernist Islamic extremists who view it as alien to their culture and their beliefs. The imposition of secular ideas can lead to resistance, as we see to this day even in modern Turkey, with its strong secular tradition established by Kemal Ataturk in the 1920s. This antimodernist sentiment is particularly common among those individuals, groups, parties, social classes, and organizations that are not sharing in the modernization process and that see themselves largely as dispossessed victims. This is a breeding ground of extremism and terrorism.

Islamic radical jihadists exploit these situations in efforts to seize political power in Muslim countries and to establish a totalitarian system of Islamic rule and law. Any effort to launch and foster modernization programs must take care to ensure that the fruits of political participation, market reforms, and economic and social development are shared by the largest possible number of a country's people.

As Americans, we can be proud of the principles on which our country is founded. They have withstood many severe challenges over more than two centuries. Because we know they work, we are therefore committed to continuing to improve our experiment in democracy and to encourage greater openness and responsiveness of political systems throughout the world. But we should not try to impose an American model on others. Each country must work out, in keeping with its own traditions, history, and circumstances, how and at what pace to broaden political participation.

There needs to be real political dialogue between governments and the people, parties, and institutions they represent, coupled with viable economic policies that benefit large sectors of the populations involved and foster the creation of jobs and the growth of middle classes. The United States should tailor its approach to each country in a differentiated manner.

PARACHUTING THE JEFFERSONIAN MODEL OF DEMOCRACY ONTO THE SANDS OF ARABIA

We need to display much more cultural sensitivity to the societies we are dealing with than we have in the past and not embark on misplaced visionary policies that lump foreign countries and societies together in a worldview grounded only in our imagination. Specifically, we should live up to and expound our values and our adherence to the principle of democracy, but not try to force Western models on societies that are traditionalist in nature and have their own forms of "consultation." A Jeffersonian model of democracy cannot be parachuted onto the sands of Arabia.

In the 1990s I proposed that we urge the Saudis to begin expanding their appointed and limited "Consultative Assembly" (Majlis as-Shura) by making it more representative of the broader population and working toward making it elective. King Abdallah, then the crown prince, now is moving in this direction, albeit with great caution, given ultraconservative Salafist and Wahhabi opposition to electoral reforms. The Saudi rulers are at least discussing elections of representatives to the Majlis as-Shura, but it seems to be a bridge too far at this point. The current compromise provides for local elections for half the members of the municipal-level assemblies, but not for higher-level bodies. Without trying to force its will, the United States can encourage this movement toward representative government, but it cannot demand it.

In the economic realm, the evident failings of the communist and state-socialist models within and outside the Muslim countries have made the merits of private enterprise and free-market economies increasingly evident, with governments playing the necessary role of providing social safety nets, especially for the poor. The United States and its international partners, such as the G8 nations, must adopt a more assertive role in encouraging the governments of this region to initiate and sustain market reforms and anticorruption campaigns, especially in those countries that are still hamstrung by archaic and inefficient statist systems. But again, it is important in this effort to tailor our approach to the particular political, economic, cultural, and religious context in each country. For example, the economic situation in countries such as Syria and Algeria, with their inheritance of socialist state economic models, contrasts sharply with the dynamic forward lurch of the Arab Gulf states as they create new financial, investment, trade, and business centers. They will evolve in different ways and at different paces. Common to most of these societies, however, is the plague of systemic corruption and large discrepancies in income and wealth, both of which contain the seeds of political and social instability.

THE ROAD TO PEACE

During the run-up to the war in Iraq, some neoconservatives argued that the road to Arab-Israeli peace was not through Jerusalem but through Baghdad and Tehran, and that overthrow of these regimes would lead to a wave of democratization in the Middle East that would then facilitate Arab-Israeli peacemaking. This view has been discredited by events.

U.S. policymakers must realize that the Arab-Israeli conflict, and especially the issue of Palestine, remains the core political issue in the Middle East, with strong implications throughout the Muslim world. Resolving this conflict will do much to help stabilize the region, defuse anti-Western sentiment among Muslims, and undercut the influence and the spoiler potential of the Islamic radical jihadists, especially in the Levant. This conflict has been an important factor in forming Arab and Muslim attitudes toward the United States and the West. It has exacerbated the humiliation of many Arabs who are already burdened with the frustrations of the deficits of political participation, economic opportunities, education, and human rights.

We have seen how the brutal secular dictator of Iraq, Saddam Hussein, cynically wrapped himself in the cloak of Islam during the first Gulf War in 1991 and attacked Israel and its Western supporters. And we have watched the ayatollahs of the Islamist regime in Iran translate their strident stance against Israel and the West into active support of the violence and terrorism of such groups as Hezbollah, Hamas, and Palestinian Islamic Jihad.

In this context, it is crucial for the United States to engage fully and accelerate its efforts to advance Arab-Israeli peace. Peace negotiations seem always to be in a race with terrorism that erodes Israeli support of peace talks, but diplomacy should not permit the terrorists to trump peace efforts. The president and the secretary of state of the United States have key roles to play and should use their status and influence as valid interlocutors between Israel and its Arab neighbors. For peace to have a chance, it is essential that our highest-level leaders be directly involved in an active and sustained manner in bringing key aspects of the negotiations to closure.

The road to peace in this region lies not through Baghdad and Tehran, but through Jerusalem, Beirut, and Damascus.

We must move from conflict management to conflict resolution. Many of the contours of final-settlement issues on the Israeli-Palestinian, Israeli-Syrian, and Lebanese negotiating tracks have been discussed and advanced by the parties. What is needed now is the political will and courage to bring these negotiations to their conclusion. A comprehensive Arab-Israeli peace settlement on all fronts between Israel and the Palestinians, Syria, and Lebanon is possible, despite all the setbacks of recent years. The road to peace is clear. All we lack is the resolve to make the journey.

RELIGION, CULTURE, AND POLICY

One of the most important lapses in policy formulation, especially after the Cold War era of Realpolitik, is the underestimated role of culture and religion in both domestic and foreign affairs. We must enhance our political, economic, and security policies with an understanding of religious and cultural factors in statecraft. This means reorganizing and redirecting our national security establishment to obtain the necessary expertise in foreign languages, regional area studies, culture, and religion. We have lost much of our "human intelligence" capacity and need a coherent restructuring of our foreign affairs and intelligence organizations to fill the gap.

We should foster, wherever appropriate, dialogue among different religious groups. It is clear that enhanced exchanges among Christians, Jews, Muslims, and Hindus can help identify areas of possible common ground. I am not a proponent of dialogue for the mere sake of dialogue, but it will be even more difficult to fill the gap of knowledge of "the Other" without a great deal of talk.

Much of our diplomacy in recent years has suffered from the ignoring of Martin Buber's "I-Thou" discourse. The knowledge of "the Other" is essential in the conduct of successful diplomacy. Exchange and dialogue could at least facilitate understanding and the search for common ground. In the best of circumstances, it can help promote peace and understanding in the Middle East. For example, the discussions that preceded the establishment of diplomatic ties between the Vatican and Israel were an important step toward enhancing religious dialogue between Christianity and Judaism. Such a dialogue between Jews and Muslims is sorely lacking.

While the pernicious influence and destructive actions of Islamic radical jihadists capture the headlines, the views and aspirations of mainstream Muslim groups need to be highlighted and empowered. Political space must be created for them to voice their views. In 1995, two of the Arab world's leading religious authorities, Sheikh Ibn Baz of Saudi Arabia and Sheikh Mohammad Sayid Tantawi of Egypt, stated in religious edicts (called *fatwas*) that Arab rulers have the right, according to the Qur'an, to seek peace with Jews. These statements produced a counterreaction from other sheikhs who claimed that, according to the same text in the Qur'an, peace with Jews was not possible under prevailing circumstances. This debate will doubtless continue, but an important taboo was broken.

Within Israel itself, the role of religion and the religious parties is highly relevant to Arab-Israeli peace. I personally witnessed Prime Minister Rabin's efforts in the early 1990s to have the ultraorthodox Shas Party join his government coalition. This could have had an important impact on the Israeli-Syrian negotiations. Rabbi Ovedia Youssef, Shas's religious leader, preaches the sanctity of life over the sanctity of land. Getting Shas into Rabin's government coalition would have strengthened Rabin's hand in any peace agreement with Syria that included the return of the Golan Heights, providing religious support for the position that peace is more important than property.

In the Balkans, a dialogue among Eastern Orthodox Christians, Roman Catholics, and Muslims could help serve the cause of peace. The Organization of the Islamic Conference and the Muslim World League could expand their educational programs and efforts to help resolve inter-Arab disputes by reaching out to other religious groups and organizations to promote interfaith dialogue. In the South Asian context, efforts to promote dialogue between Hindus and Muslims should be fostered. In 2008, Tony

Blair, the former prime minister of Britain, launched a global interfaith initiative aimed at both dialogue and action to address global issue.

BRIDGES, NOT WALLS

People of faith have made important contributions in conflict situations when other approaches have failed, as in the following examples.

- The Moral Re-Armament Movement's efforts to promote reconciliation between France and Germany after World War II.
- Efforts on the part of the Clergyman's Emergency Committee for Vietnam, Clergy and Laymen Concerned about Vietnam, the Catholic Peace Fellowship, the National Council of Churches, and the Synagogue Council of America in opposing the Vietnam War, calling for a halt to bombing, and asking for a greater role for the United Nations.
- Protests by mainline Protestant and Jewish groups that mobilized American opposition to apartheid in South Africa.
- The role of Moravians in effecting conciliation between the Sandinista government and the Miskito Indians of eastern Nicaragua in the 1980s.
- The Catholic Church in the Philippines during the 1986 revolution.
- The role of the East German churches in promoting peaceful change in the years building up to the collapse of the former Soviet Union.
- The unassuming yet persistent work of Quakers in defusing civil war in Nigeria.

- The positive contribution made by various religious actors in the transition of Southern Rhodesia to Zimbabwe.

So, while religious differences have been and remain a cause or pretext for conflict and wars, the work and actions of religious groups and individuals can also help foster the peaceful settlement of conflicts. Instead of building walls, we need to build bridges. Indeed, the challenge before us at a time of ethnic, religious, and political strife is to determine how we can maintain and develop our own values and, at the same time, coexist and interact with other value systems and cultures that will continue on their own paths. The anthropologist Clifford Geertz contends, "You can't assert yourself in the world as if nobody else was there. Because this is not a clash of ideas. There are people attached to these ideas. If you want to live without violence, you have to realize that other people are as real as you are."

THE NEED FOR COHERENCE

There is obvious and compelling need for a coherent policy approach to address the strategic challenge of the struggle of ideas in the Arab and Muslim world. I hope the personal narratives, analysis, and policy proposals contained in these pages can help enhance the prospects for preventive diplomacy, peaceful conflict resolution, representative democratic institutions, economic and social reforms, and human rights. By acting creatively and intelligently and in the context of our values and interests, the United States can effectively promote its own national security interests at this historic crossroads by pursuing policies that can help to marginalize the forces of extremism and enhance the forces of moderation in this vitally important region of the world.

ACKNOWLEDGMENTS

This book could not have been written without the scholarly help of my collaborator, William Martin. Bill is the Harry and Hazel Chavanne Emeritus Professor of Sociology and Chavanne Senior Fellow for Religion and Public Policy at the James A. Baker III Institute for Public Policy at Rice University. Bill is a noted writer in his field and biographer of Billy Graham. His outstanding job in translating my "diplomatese" into plain English helped me immeasurably in the preparation of the manuscript according to the exacting guidelines set down by the publisher, Simon & Schuster. Despite the pressure of deadlines, we did not take any sabbatical to write the book, and spent many early and late hours, weekends, and vacation time to get the job done. We managed to maintain our sense of humor and even to gain a mutual friendship that I greatly value.

Lisa Queen, my literary agent, deserves special thanks and credit. From the onset she believed that I had something important to convey and skillfully persevered to assure that this book would be written and published. She encouraged me throughout the effort of my first foray into the world of writing a book and getting it published. I respect her professionalism, admire her tenacity, and enjoy her optimism.

I am particularly appreciative of the insights and expertise of Simon & Schuster's Vice President and Senior Editor, Mitchell Ivers, whose wise counsel, superb editing skills, and suggestions improved the text and made it more accessible to the reader. He truly does "champion his authors" and was instrumental in seeing this book through to publication.

Since this book is, in part, a narrative of my life in and out of public service, many people had an important role in what I have done, achieved, and failed to achieve. They are, of course, too many to mention by name. My mother and father gave me the strength to survive hardship. My wife, Françoise, and our children Gregory and Francesca have been a true inspiration in my life and were at my side at home and abroad on my journey in service to our country. Françoise has been my wisest and most loyal advisor throughout my career, both in and out of government service. She and our children encouraged me to tell this story and kept me focused on the task. They were my sharpest critics in the writing of this book and enhanced both its accuracy and substance. In many ways this book is also dedicated to them and the families of our government's civilian and military branches who serve abroad and represent our nation, often in dangerous places and situations, without due recognition.

I was fortunate in the Foreign Service to have early mentors such as Ambassador Philip Habib, who encouraged me to join the Foreign Service and act with professionalism; Undersecretary of State George W. Ball, who taught me the value of voicing dissenting policy views despite the risks; and Undersecretary of State Joseph Sisco, who taught me how to achieve constructive results in the maze of Washington bureaucracy; Ambassador Richard Murphy, who gave me key opportunities to serve in important State Department and overseas assignments; and Colin Powell, whom I had the honor and pleasure of serving with during the

Reagan and Bush 41 administrations and with whom I have kept a close relationship. While I was in government, I had the privilege of working with several secretaries of state, including Henry Kissinger, George Shultz, and James A. Baker, III. Each one of them had an influence on my development as a career diplomat and I learned much from their example. This was particularly the case with Secretary Baker, with whom I developed a solid working relationship while I was ambassador to Syria and assistant secretary of state for Near Eastern Affairs. His confidence in me, his stewardship of United States foreign policy at the end of the Cold War, and the work we were able to accomplish during the administration of George H. W. Bush were high points in my career. That professional and personal relationship extended beyond government service when he asked Françoise and me to come to Houston in 1994 to establish a public policy institute in his name at Rice University. The institute has now become an important policy forum and was ranked in 2008 among the top thirty think tanks in the United States. I wish to express my deep gratitude to the Baker Institute's fellows and staff for their loyal support and work over the years, which aided me in the writing of this book.

Last but not least, I would like to pay tribute to my Foreign Service colleagues who serve our country with courage and distinction at home and abroad.

NOTES

9   "Where roads end, the Taliban begins." Former U.S. military commander in Afghanistan, Lt. Gen. Karl Eikenberry; oft-quoted, with slight variations. See, for example, http://www.usatoday.com/news/world/2007-06-19-afghan-road_N.htm; http://www.themonthly.com.au/tm/node/478.

11   "The U.S. as a Nation . . . has not gone to war." Lieutenant General Peter W. Chiarelli, U.S. Army, with Major Stephen M. Smith, U.S. Army, "Learning From Our Modern Wars: The Imperatives of Preparing for a Dangerous Future," *Military Review* (September–October 2007), p. 4.

18   "not with a bang but a whimper." T. S. Eliot, "The Hollow Men," 1925.

19   Samuel P. Huntington, "The Clash of Civilizations?" *Foreign Affairs*, Summer 1993, p. 22. http://www.foreignaffairs.org/19930601faessay5188/samuel-p-huntington/the-clash-of-civilizations.html.

32   Aslan, citing Harvey Cox. Reza Aslan, *No God but God* (New York: Random House, 2005), pp. 261–66, quoting Harvey Cox.

39 Tanzimat guarantees and abolition of religion as a criterion for full citizenship. A. Hourani, *Arabic Thought in the Liberal Age, 1798–1839*, 2nd ed. (Cambridge: Cambridge University Press, 1983), p. 46; Abdulmecit I, in Halil Inalçik, "The Nature of Traditional Society," in Robert E. Ward and D. A. Rustow [eds.], *Political Modernization in Japan and Turkey* (Princeton: Princeton University Press, 1964), pp. 57–58, quoted in Antony Black, *The History of Islamic Political Thought* (New York; Routledge, 2001), p. 281.

40 Shaikh Ali abd al-Raziq, op. cit, p. 318.

44 Islam willing "to destroy all states." Sayeed Abu Ala Maududi, *Jihad in Islam* (Beirut, Lebanon: The Holy Koran Publishing House, 2006), p. 9. www.muhammadanism.org/terrorism/jihah_in_islam/jihad_in_islam.pdf. Text of an address delivered by Maududi on April 13, 1939.

46 Vartan Gregorian, *Islam, A Mosaic, Not A Monolith* (Washington: Brookings Institution Press, 2003).

47 John L. Esposito and Dalia Mogahed, *Who Speaks for Islam? What a Billion Muslims Really Think* (New York: Gallup Press, 2008), p. 48.

50 Dialogue with Hamas's unavoidable. Shlomo Ben-Ami, "From Radical Jihad to the Politics of Compromise," http://www.haaretz.com/hasen/spages/850714.html.

50 Muslim Brotherhood prepared to talk to Americans. Muhammad Akef, quoted in James Traub, "Islamic Democrats?," *New York Times Magazine*, April 29, 2007, http://www.nytimes.com/2007/04/29/magazine/29Brotherhood.t.html?_r=1&oref=slogin&pagewanted=print.

51 Muslim Brotherhood: "We do not want a country like Iran." Magdy Ashour quoted by Traub, ibid.

57 "My older son came home from school." Badria al-Bisher, *Al Riyadh* newspaper (Saudi Arabia), February 24, 2005.

59 Ghannouchi letter, personal correspondence with the author.

62 "Soft and hard power." For elaboration of these terms, see Joseph S. Nye, Jr., "The Decline of America's Soft Power," *Foreign Affairs* (May/June 2004).

71 Musa Al Sadr, "I removed him from the dust of the ages." Reported in *Al Irfan*, 54 (September, 1966), 408, quoted in Fouad Ajami, *The Vanished Imam: Musa al Sadr and the Shia of Lebanon* (Ithaca: Cornell University Press, 1992), p. 85. I am indebted to Professor Ajami for a number of insights from this important book.

71 Sadr, no difference between black and white turbans. op. cit., p. 133.

71 "What sort of ice cream?" Ibid.

72 Sadr, "Religions sought to liberate men." op. cit., pp. 134f.

74 Fadlallah, "all means of self-defense are legitimate," et al. Muhammad Hussein Fadlallah, *Al Islam wa Mantaq al Quwwa (Islam and the Logic of Force)*, 3rd ed. (Beirut, 1985), quoted in Ajami, op. cit., pp. 215–17.

82 The Sphinx of Damascus. Moshe Ma'oz, *The Sphinx of Damascus* (New York: Grove Press, 1st American edition, 1988).

96 James Baker's meeting with Asad. See Secretary Baker's version of this meeting in James A. Baker, III, *The Politics of Diplomacy* (New York: G. P. Putnam, 1995), pp. 454–59.

112 Sadat in Jerusalem. For the text of Sadat's speech before the Knesset, see http://www.ibiblio.org/sullivan/docs/Knessetspeech .html.

118 Rabin: "Whatever was done in private . . ." For an authoritative Israeli account of Rabin's thinking and positions on the Israeli-Syrian negotiations, see Itamar Rabinovich, *The Brink of Peace—The Israeli-Syrian Negotiations* (Princeton: Princeton University Press, 1998). Rabinovich was Israel's ambassador to the United States from 1992 to 1996 and was also the chief negotiator with Syria.

136 Rabin: "Total nonsense!" Author's personal notes. For reference to this speech, see Clyde Haberman, "Peace Pact With Syria Needed to Prevent War, Rabin Says," *New York Times*, June 25, 1994; http://query.nytimes.com/gst/fullpage.html?res =9C02E7DB1F3DF936A15755C0A962958260&sec=&spon =&pagewanted=all.

137   Rabin's UNESCO Peace Prize speech, Paris, July 6, 1994. Israel
        Ministry of Foreign Affairs website, http://www.mfa.gov.il/MFA/
        Archive/Speeches/ADDRESS%20BY%20PM%20RABIN%20
        AT%20AWARDING%20OF%20UNESCO%20PEACE%20PR

157   The Bush Administration Road Map. U.S. Department of
        State Press Statement, April 20, 2003, http://www.state.gov/r/
        pa/prs/ps/2003/20062.htm June 24, 2002 speech. For the text
        of President Bush's speech of June 24, 2002, see http://www
        .whitehouse.gov/news/releases/2004/05/20040524-10.html.

161   Israel-Palestine 2002 "Statement of Principles." http://domino
        .un.org/UNISPAL.NSF/d80185e9f0c69a7b85256cbf005afeac/
        1273b3972da8e47185256dd00055a0cf!OpenDocument.

163   Israel and Syria have come close to an agreement. See Baker Insti-
        tute Policy Report No. 8, "The Prospects for the Israeli-Syrian Ne-
        gotiations," August 1998, http://bakerinstitute.org/publications.

168   Bashar al-Asad: "We deal with facts." Interview in the Saudi
        Pan Arab newspaper *al Sharq al Awsat* in February 2001.

178   "A Phased Agreement." See Baker Institute Working Paper
        "Regional Aspects of a Comprehensive Arab-Israeli Peace Set-
        tlement: Next Steps to Preserve and Promote the Peace Pro-
        cess" July 1996, James A. Baker, III Institute for Public Policy,
        Rice University, http://bakerinstitute.org/publications.

181   Madrid Peace Conference. Secretary of State James A. Baker's
        role in constructing the Madrid Peace Conference provides the
        model for diplomacy in translating a vision of peace into practical
        steps and compromises each side was encouraged to make. Baker
        spelled out this modus operandi in a conversation with Spanish
        prime minister Felipe Gonzalez in October 1991 before the
        opening of the conference, illustrating what is needed in United
        States diplomacy to translate policy into action in the Arab-Israeli
        context. "Never will there be peace in the Middle East," Secre-
        tary Baker said, "unless the parties talk directly to one another. For
        twenty-four years they argued over how to talk to one another. Asad
        says an international conference. Shamir says direct negotiations.
        We set out to overcome that forty-three-year-old hurdle and to get

them to agree to talks. We did that by marrying two positions: The Arabs get a conference and the Israelis get direct negotiations. But the conference is not what Asad would have liked because it doesn't take decisions. The ground rules are clear or the Israelis wouldn't come. The bilaterals are not all the Israelis want. What they really want is clear acknowledgment of the right to exist and their goal is true reconciliation evidenced by peace treaties. The Arabs are not willing to commit to that fully. Each detail of the conference will be symbolically important—for example, the speaking order, heads of delegation, no flags, representation on the joint Jordanian-Palestinian delegation, an issue of extreme sensitivity. In negotiating this agreement we have one cardinal principle—we are not going to change any United States principle regarding United States policy toward the Middle East during this process." Author's personal notes of the meeting, October 19, 1991, Madrid.

183   Lawrence, "Do not try to do too much with your own hands." T. E. Lawrence, "Twenty Seven Articles," *Arab Bulletin*, August 20, 1917, Article 15. See, among other locations, http://net.lib.byu.edu/~rdh7/wwi/1917/27arts.html.

185   Bush and Baker take flak for not "finishing off Saddam." See James A. Baker, III, *The Politics of Diplomacy*, pp. 436–38.

187   *Guiding Principles for U.S. Post-Conflict Policy in Iraq*, Report of an Independent Working Group Cosponsored by the Council on Foreign Relations and the James A. Baker III Institute for Public Policy at Rice University, Edward P. Djerejian and Frank G. Wisner, Co-Chairs; Rachel Bronson and Andrew S. Weiss, Project Co-Directors, 2003.

193   ISG recommendations should be considered fully. *The Iraq Study Group Report*, James A. Baker, III, and Lee H. Hamilton, Co-Chairs. (New York: Vintage Books, 2006), p. xviii.

193   Pew survey re ISG Report. *Baker-Hamilton Redux*, Pew Research Center Publications, May 29, 2007.

205   Mehdi Bazargan. Farhad Kazemi, "The Precarious Revolution: Unchanging Institutions and the Fate of Reform in Iran,"

Journal of International Affairs, Columbia University School of International & Public Affairs, Fall 2003, pp. 81–95.

206 Kazemi, "The regime has failed." Op. cit., p. 93

211 Biden-Gelb op-ed. Joseph R. Biden, Jr., and Leslie H. Gelb, "Federalism, Not Partition," *Washington Post*, Wednesday, October 3, 2007; A23. http://www.washingtonpost.com/wp-dyn/content/article/2007/10/02/AR2007100201824.html.

218 King Fahd, "Saudi Arabia will not participate," http://www.fas.org/sgp/crs/mideast/RL33533.pdf.

220 "The Changing Role of National Oil Companies in International Energy Markets" April 2007, James A. Baker III Institute for Public Policy, Rice University, principal author Amy Myers Jaffe, Baker Institute Wallace S. Wilson Fellow for Energy Studies.

232 Jean-David Levitte, "Improve your image," Adam Gopnik, "Letter From France, The Human Bomb," *New Yorker* (August 27, 2007), p. 45.

233 *Changing Minds, Winning Peace* (Washington, D.C.: Advisory Group on Public Diplomacy for the Arab and Muslim World, 2003).

252 Saudi Minister Azziz, "Islam is a religion of peace." Quoted in Ute Reissner and Justus Leicht, "What is the Path to Genuine Democracy in Turkey," World Socialist Web Site, http://www.wsws.org/articles/1999/oct1999/turk-o06.shtml.

260 Peacemaking efforts of religious groups. See William Martin, "With God on Their Side: Religion and American Foreign Policy," in Hugh Heclo and Wilfred M. McClay, *Religion Returns to the Public Square: Faith and Public Policy in America* (Washington, D.C.: The Johns Hopkins University Press/Woodrow Wilson Center, 2003), pp. 327–39, drawing on Douglas Johnson and Cynthia Sampson, eds., *Religion: The Missing Dimension of Statecraft* (New York: Oxford University Press, 1994).

261 Clifford Geertz: "Other people are as real as you are." Quoted in David Berreby, "Unabsolute Truths; Clifford Geertz," *New York Times Magazine*, April 9, 1995, http://query.nytimes.com/gst/fullpage.html?res=990CE2DC1E38F93AA35757C0A963958260&sec=&spon=&pagewanted=4.

INDEX

38–39; and pluralism, 31–32; and political parties, 53–55; promotion of, 9, 22–23, 31, 215, 253–55; and public diplomacy, 249; and reason, 37–38; and reassertion of U.S. policy goals, 250; and secularism/secularization, 31–32; and Sharia, 35–37; strengthening advance of, 17; and Sunni-Shia divide, 35–37; and tradition and modernity, 47–51; and trends in Middle East, 130; unintended consequences of, 31; universal applicability of, 107–8; and Wahhabism and militancy, 41–46; and what went wrong with U.S. foreign policy, 17. *See also specific person or nation*

Democratic Front for the Liberation of Palestine, 135–36

Deri, Aryeh, 129–30

Desert Storm (1991): and Arab-Israeli relations, 89, 185; buildup to, xvii; and Bush (George H.W.) administration, 92–95; Ghannouchi views about, 60; and Madrid Peace Conference, 185; and oil, 26, 218; Powell as chief architect of, 208; and Saddam Hussein, 257; and Soviet-Iraq relations, 101; support for, xvii, 11; and Syria, 88, 91, 92–95, 106, 145, 150, 185. *See also specific nation*

dialogue: and arc of crisis, 258; benefits of, 52–53;

importance of, 4–5, 18, 52–53, 58–62; Israel-U.S. strategic, 131–32; Muslim Brotherhood–U.S., 50–51; and promoting democracy, 255

Djerejian, Edward: appointed assistant secretary of state for Near Eastern Affairs, 96; Armenian background of, 126; family background of, 84–86; mentors of, 92; professional career of, xi, xii–xvi, 2, 19, 265; retirement from Foreign Service of, 132; threats against, 106

Djerejian, Francesca, 106, 109, 110, 113, 264

Djerejian, Françoise, xviii, 86, 100, 103, 104, 105, 109, 110, 125, 132, 264, 265

Djerejian, Gregory, 109, 113, 264

draft, military, 12

drug trafficking, 8, 81

Druze, 64–65, 68, 69, 83, 91

Eagleburger, Lawrence S., 192

economy: and Arab-Israeli relations, 179, 182, 257; and Asad (Bashar al-) and Djerejian meeting, 145; and Baker Institute's Syria-U.S. dialogue, 141, 144; and energy, 56; and Islam and democracy, 40, 56, 62; and Israeli-Palestinian relations, 179, 180; and Israeli-U.S. relations, 114; and Lebanon-Israel relations, 175; and need for coherent U.S. Middle East policy, xvii; and promoting democracy, 254; and

Iraq *(cont.)*
    reassertion of U.S. policy
    goals, 250; reconstruction of,
    197, 201; refugees from, 142,
    147, 148–49, 211; and regime
    change, 184, 209; sanctions
    against, 183; and Saudi
    Arabia, 226;
    sectarianism/diversity in, 36,
    142, 184, 186, 190–91, 196–97,
    200–201, 203, 209, 211, 212,
    215, 226, 253; security in,
    198, 209, 210, 213; and
    Soviet Union, 101; Sunni
    domination of, 186; support
    for war in, 11; "surge" in,
    210, 212–13; and Sykes-Picot
    agreement, 91; and Syria, 106,
    141–42, 145, 146–47, 148, 176,
    185, 199–200, 210; and Syria-
    U.S. relations, 145; and
    terrorism, 211; and UN, 188;
    unintended consequences of
    U.S. in, 31; U.S. goal in,
    10; U.S. invasion of, 7, 11,
    150, 217, 218; U.S.
    occupation of, 27, 190, 249,
    253–54; U.S. role in, xvii, 189–
    90, 198, 199, 209, 213; and
    U.S. as winning the war and
    losing the peace, 186–87;
    U.S. withdrawal from, 210,
    212, 213; way forward for,
    212–13; weapons of mass
    destruction in, 184, 188.
    See also Desert Storm;
    Hussein, Saddam; Iraq Study
    Group, Baker-Hamilton
Iraq International Support
    Group, 198–99, 200, 202, 210
Iraq Study Group (ISG), Baker-
    Hamilton: and Al-Anbar

province, 212; and Baker-
Djerejian trip to Baghdad, 11,
194–97; and Bush (George W.)
administration, 187, 192, 193,
209–10, 211; Congressional
mandate for, 192;
differentiation between past
and current policy and, 197–
99; Djerejian role in, xvi;
findings of, 192–204, 213;
and Golan Heights, 169–70;
and Hezbollah, 169; and Iran,
200–203, 204, 206; and
Lebanon, 169; and mission in
going to war, 10; Plan B of,
210–12; and Syria, 149–50,
169–70, 199–200

Islam: Americans' views about,
2–3, 21, 251–52; and
conflicting trends in Middle
Eat, 130; and democracy, 30–
62; differentiated dialogue
concerning, 58–62; difficult
choices concerning, 51–53;
diversity within, 9–10, 21,
35–37, 130, 252; future of,
252; history of, 21, 33–34,
35–46, 252; and jobs and
education, 55–58; medieval,
33–34; and modernity, 23, 39–
41, 47–51; as next "ism"
confronting U.S., 19, 21; and
Ottoman reforms, 38–39;
political parties in, 53–55;
as political vehicle, 53; and
reason, 37–38; reform in, 21;
revival of, 252; role of
religion in, 30; spread of,
33; universal character of, 41–
42; U.S. policy toward, 252;
and Wahhabism, 41–46
Islamic Media Unit, 238

Index

9 781439 114124